D0192221

100 SCIENCE LESSONS

YEAR 4
Scottish Primary 5

Published by Scholastic Ltd,
Villiers House,
Clarendon Avenue,
Leamington Spa,
Warwickshire CV32 5PR

© **Scholastic Ltd 2001**
Text © 2001 Kendra McMahon

4567890 34567890

Series Consultant
Peter Riley

Author
Kendra McMahon

Editor
Janet Swarbrick

Assistant Editor
David Sandford

Series Designers
David Hurley
Joy Monkhouse

Designers
Paul Cheshire
David Hurley
Anna Oliwa

Cover photography
Martyn Chillmaid

Illustrations
Debbie Clark

British Library Cataloguing-in-Publication Data
A catalogue record for this book is available from the British Library.

ISBN 0-439-01805-6

The right of Kendra McMahon to be identified as the Author of this work has been asserted by her in accordance with the Copyright, Designs and Patents Act 1988.

All rights reserved. This book is sold subject to the condition that it shall not, by way of trade or otherwise, be lent, hired out or otherwise circulated without the publisher's prior consent in any form of binding or cover other than that in which it is published and without a similar condition, including this condition, being imposed upon the subsequent purchaser.

No part of this publication may be reproduced, stored in a retrieval system, or transmitted, in any form or by any means, electronic, mechanical, photocopying, recording or otherwise, without the prior permission of the publisher. This book remains copyright, although permission is granted to copy those pages indicated as photocopiable for classroom distribution and use only in the school which has purchased the book, or by the teacher who has purchased the book, and in accordance with the CLA licensing agreement. Photocopying permission is given for purchasers only and not for borrowers of books from any lending service.

Teachers should consult their own school policies and guidelines concerning practical work and participation of children in scientific experiments. You should only select activities which you feel can be carried out safely and confidently in the classroom.

Acknowledgements
The National Curriculum for England 2000
© The Queen's Printer and Controller of HMSO. Reproduced under the terms of HMSO Guidance Note 8.
The National Curriculum for Wales 2000
© The Queen's Printer and Controller of HMSO. Reproduced under the terms of HMSO Guidance Note 10.

Contents

Introduction

100 Science Lessons is a series of year-specific teachers' resource books that provide a wealth of lesson plans and photocopiable resources for delivering a whole year of science teaching, including differentiation and assessment.

The series follows the QCA *Science Scheme of Work* in the sequencing of topics. However, instead of having six or seven units as in the QCA scheme, the book for each year contains eight units. These units are the familiar topics: 1. Ourselves, 2. Animals & plants, 3. The environment, 4. Materials, 5. Electricity, 6. Forces & motion, 7. Light & sound, 8. Earth & beyond. They appear in the same order in every book, but have sub-titles which describe the emphasis of the work in that year. For example, in this book Unit 1 is Ourselves: How I move. By having eight units, this resource builds on the QCA scheme to accommodate the demands of the curricula for Wales, Scotland and Northern Ireland. It also creates opportunities to visit each topic in every year: after visiting a topic in synchrony with the QCA scheme, you can make a further visit the following year for extension or consolidation of the previous year's work. The Series topic map on page 208 shows how the topics are mapped out through the whole series.

Each unit is divided into a number of lessons, ending with an assessment lesson. The organisation chart at the start of each unit shows the objectives and outcomes of each lesson, and gives a quick overview of the lesson content (Main activity, Group activities, Plenary). The statements of the national curricula for England, Wales, Scotland and Northern Ireland (given in the grids on pages 196–207) provide the basis for the lesson objectives used throughout the book.

ORGANISATION (9 LESSONS)

	OBJECTIVES	MAIN ACTIVITY	GROUP ACTIVITIES	PLENARY	OUTCOMES
LESSON 1	● To elicit children's existing ideas about the body.		Drawing what children think is inside our bodies into an outline of a body.	Discussion of children's ideas of the functions of different parts of the body.	● Teacher has understanding of the children's existing ideas. ● Children have more awareness of their own ideas and are motivated to learn more.
LESSON 2	● To know that the skeleton is made from bones. ● To understand that we have lots of joined bones to give a greater range of movement. ● To make observations.	Comparing the movements of joints of dolls with our own joints.	Observing how different parts of our bodies move and noting this on a drawing of a skeleton. Mirroring each other's movements.	Identifying ribs, skull and spine. Discussing why joints are needed.	● Can recognise that the skeleton is made up of lots of different bones. ● Can recognise and name the skull, ribs and spine. ● Can understand why the skeleton is made of lots of different bones.

LESSON PLANS

Each lesson plan is divided into four parts: Introduction, Main teaching activity, Group activities and Plenary. In many of the lessons, the introduction is supported by background information and a vocabulary list that will help in delivering the lesson and support assessment of the work. The lesson introduction sets the context for the work. The Main teaching activity features direct whole-class or group teaching, and may include instructions on how to perform a demonstration or an experiment in order to stimulate the children's interest and increase their motivation. There are then usually two Group activities to follow up this teaching. (In those lessons where whole-class investigation takes place, there may only be a single group activity related to this, and occasionally a 'circus' of group work is suggested.) Advice on differentiation and formative assessment linked to this work is provided. Finally, there are details of a concluding plenary session.

About 60% of the lesson plans in this book, including those for the assessment lessons, are presented in full detail. Many of these are followed by outlines for closely related lessons on the same topics or concepts, using the same background information. To avoid repetition and allow you to focus on the essentials of the lesson, these plans are presented as grids for you to develop. They contain the major features of the detailed lesson plans, allowing you to plan for progression and assessment.

Detailed lesson plans

The lessons in this book have been designed to encourage and develop the children's investigative skills. Children at this stage are expected to carry out a fair test with help, and they should be able to recognise when a test is not fair. In this year, they need to develop their independence in skills of making predictions, planning a fair test, choosing appropriate resources, collecting data and drawing conclusions. A particular focus for this year is developing independence in using tables and graphs. Even lessons that focus on knowledge and understanding are approached in an investigative way through questioning, in order to make the new ideas meaningful and to develop the children's thinking skills.

Objectives

The objectives of the lessons are derived from the statements in all the UK science curriculum documents. They are stated in a way that helps to focus each lesson plan and give a unique theme to each unit. At least one objective for each lesson is derived from the statements related to content knowledge. In addition, there may be one or more objectives relating to scientific enquiry; but you may choose to replace these with others to meet your needs and the skills you wish the children to develop. The relationship of the curriculum statements to the coverage of each unit's lessons is given in the grids on pages 196–207.

Wherever relevant, the focus and content of each unit coincides with that of the matching unit in the QCA *Science Scheme of Work*. However, we have not distinguished in the lesson objectives which content is specific to any one curriculum, and have left it to your professional judgement to identify those activities that are best suited to the age and ability of your class, and to the minimum requirements spelled out in your local curriculum guidance. If you wish to check whether a particular activity cross-references directly to your curriculum, please refer to pages 196–207.

Resources and Preparation

The Resources section provides a list of everything you will need to deliver the lesson, including any of the photocopiables presented in this book. Preparation describes anything that needs to be done in advance of the lesson, such as arranging a time convenient to other classes for your class to do a survey. As part of the preparation for all practical work, you should consult your school's policies concerning the use of plants and animals in the classroom, so that you can select activities for which you are confident to take responsibility. The book *Be Safe!* published by The Association for Science Education, is a useful addition to the staffroom bookshelf.

Background

The Background section provides relevant facts and explanations of concepts to support the lesson. In some cases, the information provided may go beyond what the children need to learn at Year 4/Primary 5; but you may need this further knowledge in order to avoid reinforcing any misconceptions the children may have.

Vocabulary

Each fully detailed lesson plan has an associated vocabulary list containing words that should be used by the children in discussing and presenting their work, and in their writing. The words relate both to scientific enquiry and to knowledge and understanding. You may wish to use these lists as the basis for a word bank that is displayed on the classroom wall and added to as new words are introduced.

It is important that children develop their science vocabulary in order to describe their findings and observations and to explain their ideas. Whenever a specialist word is used, it should be accompanied by a definition, as some children in the class may take time to understand and differentiate the meanings of words such as 'loud' and 'high pitched'. The use of specialist vocabulary, for example 'predator', should be developed alongside the children's understanding of the concepts.

Introduction
The lesson introductions contain ideas to get each lesson started, to 'set the scene', and help the children relate it to previous lessons. You may also wish to make links with other lessons in your schemes of work, including curriculum areas other than science.

Main teaching activity
This section presents a direct, whole-class teaching session to follow the introduction. This will help you to deliver the content knowledge outlined in the lesson objectives to the children before they start their group work. It may include guidance on discussion, or on performing one or more demonstrations or class investigations to help the children understand the work ahead. These parts of the lesson are interactive, and suggestions are given for questions to engage and challenge the children's thinking.

The relative proportions of the lesson given to the Introduction, Main teaching activity and Group activities vary. If you are reminding the children of the previous work and getting them on to their own investigations, the group work may dominate the lesson time; if you are introducing a new topic or concept, you might wish to spend all or most of the lesson engaged in whole-class teaching.

Group activities
The Group activities are very flexible. Some may be best suited to individual work, while others may be suitable for work in pairs or larger groupings. In the detailed lesson plans, there are usually two Group activities provided for each lesson. You may wish to use one after the other; use both together, to reduce demand on resources and your attention; or, where one is a practical activity, use the other for children who complete their practical work successfully and quickly. Some of the Group activities are supported by a photocopiable sheet.

The Group activities may include some reading and writing. These activities are also aimed at strengthening the children's science literacy, and supporting their English literacy skills. They may involve writing labels and captions, developing scientific vocabulary, writing about or recording investigations, presenting data, explaining what they have observed, or using appropriate secondary sources. The children's mathematical skills are also developed through number and data-handling work in the context of science investigations.

Differentiation
For each of the lessons, where appropriate, there are suggestions for differentiated work to meet the different needs of children in the class. For example, strategies may be suggested to support recording for children who are lower attainers in writing. Differentiated Group activities are designed so that all the children who perform these tasks can make a contribution to the Plenary session. The activities are suitable for all abilities, with children contributing at their own level.

Assessment
Each unit begins with some means of finding out children's existing ideas in order to inform the teaching of the rest of the unit. Each lesson includes advice on how to assess the children's success in the activities against the lesson objectives. This may include questions to ask or observations to make to help you build up a picture of the children's developing ideas and tailor the planning of future lessons to the particular needs of the class. A separate summative assessment lesson is provided at the end of each unit of work, but it is expected that the ongoing assessments will also inform the summative assessments made.

Plenary

This is a very important part of the lesson. It is important not to let it get squeezed out by mistiming other activities in the lesson. Suggestions are given for drawing the various strands of the lesson together in this session. If an investigation has been tried, the work of different groups can be compared and evaluated. The scene may be set for another lesson, or the lesson objectives and outcomes may be reviewed and key learning points highlighted.

Homework

On occasions, small tasks may be suggested for the children to do at home. Tasks such as observing stars cannot easily be done in school time, while other lessons may offer opportunities for follow-up work, for example using the provided photocopiables at home, or to research a broader knowledge of the topic under discussion.

Outcomes

These are statements related to the objectives; they describe what most children should have achieved through the lesson.

Links to other units or lessons

The lesson may be linked to other lessons in the same unit to provide progression or reinforce the work done, or it may be linked to other units or lessons elsewhere in the book. You may like to consider these links in planning your scheme of work – for example, linking work on insulation and conductivity in Lessons 4–6 of Unit 4: Warm liquids, cool solids, with the use of the terms 'insulator' and 'conductor' in Lesson 4 of Unit 5: Switches and conduction.

Links to other curriculum areas

These are included where appropriate. They may include links to subjects closely related to science, such as technology or maths, or to content and skills in subjects such as history or geography.

Lesson plan grids

These short lesson plans, in the form of a grid, offer further activity ideas to broaden the topic coverage. As the example below shows, they have the same basic structure as the detailed lesson plans. They lack the Introduction, Background and Vocabulary sections, but these are supported by the previous and related detailed lesson plans. Notes suggesting a Main activity and with ideas for Group activities are provided for you to develop. Generally there are no photocopiables linked to these lesson plans.

LESSON 8

Objectives	● To know that when muscles work hard in exercise they also affect the body in other ways. ● To relate their work in science to PE.
Resources	A PE lesson.
Main activity	Ask the children what they will be using to help them move. (The skeleton and the muscles.) During the lesson, and as the children are cooling down, ask them to describe how they are feeling. (Tired, hot, out of breath and can feel the heart beating fast.)
Differentiation	Target questions to involve those children who are enthusiastic about sport and less so about science!
Assessment	Are the children able to describe the changes to their bodies? Can they make connections between their science work and the PE lesson?
Plenary	Back in class, ask the children: *When your muscles had to work hard to move you quickly, how did that make you feel? Does this link to anything else we have been learning?* (The heart and lungs are working hard, too.)
Outcomes	● Can describe how their body feels after exercise. ● Can relate their science work to PE.

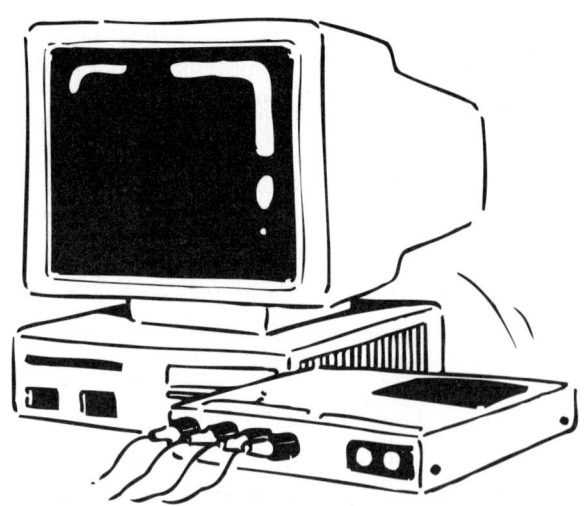

RESOURCES
Photocopiable sheets

These are an integral part of many of the lessons and are found at the end of the relevant unit, marked with the 'photocopiable' symbol:
They may provide resources, quizzes, instructions for practical work, information, written assignments, means of recording by writing or drawing, activities and so on.

Classroom equipment and space

A wide range of resources are needed for the lessons in this book. However, every attempt has been made to restrict the list to resources that will be readily available to primary schools. You may wish to borrow some items (such as a data-logger) from the science department of your local secondary school, though these would be a very useful permanent addition to your science resources.

Each lesson plan includes a resources list. When you have planned which lessons you wish to use, you could make up your own resources list for the term's or year's work. Encourage your colleagues to do the same for other years, so that you can compare lists, identify times when there may be a high demand for particular resources and make adjustments as necessary. Educational resource companies such as TTS (Technological Teaching Systems: Unit 7, Monk Road, Alfreton, Derbyshire, DE55 7RL; tel 01773 830255) can supply items such as switches for use in simple circuits that can be disassembled (see Unit 5, Lesson 6) or bags of assorted springs (see Unit 6, Lesson 1).

ICT

Many of the lessons in this book can be enhanced by the use of ICT. As new products are entering the market all the time, few are specified in this book. However you may like to plan your ICT work under these headings:

Information retrieval

Children should be encouraged to start to find information from secondary sources, including CD-ROMs and the Internet. Where this is the case, it is important that the children have a focus for their enquiries, that the materials offered are at an appropriate level, and that the task of information retrieval is sufficiently challenging. It is important to guard against children simply retrieving pages of information in answer to a question without using skills in comprehension or analysis. For example, a question such as 'What can you find out about the Solar System?' may produce a booklet of colourful pictures of the planets and text straight from a source which has demanded little intellectual activity. Prior to an information retrieval exercise, it is a good idea to examine the CD-ROM or selected website and set questions to test comprehension and analysis so that the children must interact with the material in some way as they prepare their answers.

Interactive programs are available for the youngest children in the school, and some (such as those on the skeleton, food, habitats and experimental technique) are useful to reinforce skills with older children.

Data-logging

Data-logging equipment could be introduced in Year 4/Primary 5 to record the change of temperature, light or sound over a given length of time, providing an instant record of the changes and a graphical representation. Higher attaining children should be encouraged to use this equipment themselves with support, but for lower attaining children the data-logger can provide a clear visual record of an environmental change without introducing anomalies due to the children's lower level of recording and graphing skills.

Presentations

Children should be taught to use a wide variety of methods to present their results and conclusions. This may include personal presentations or their beginning to use multimedia applications.

Some children may be able to design and produce booklets of their work using their own written material, graphs, charts, photographs and information retrieved from other sources using desktop publishing.

A visual record of an investigation may be made by taking photographs (with a conventional or digital camera) or recording an activity with a video camera, and storing the information on the computer for use in a presentation. Visual records should be annotated to provide a complete record, not just a picture of the children's experiences.

As well as using displays and written records, presentations may be made using video sequences that have been recorded during an investigation with a digital or video camera.

ASSESSMENT

The assessments in this book indicate the likely progress of children in Year 4/Primary 5. The statements relate specifically to work in this book, and are arranged in groups to reflect different levels. In this year's work, it is expected that most children will achieve National Curriculum Level 3/Scottish Level C; but some may not progress so well and achieve only Level 2/Scottish Level B, while others may progress further in some aspects to achieve Level 4/Scottish Level C/D.

It is important to determine what the children already know and understand before embarking on each unit. If appropriate, look at the previous books in the series, find the corresponding unit and check with your colleagues what work has been covered. Use the first lessons of each unit to talk to the children about what they know, and use the results to plan differentiated activities and provide materials as you teach the unit.

The last lesson in every unit focuses on summative assessment. This assessment samples the content of the unit, focusing on its key theme(s); its results should be used in conjunction with other assessments you have made during the teaching of the unit. The lesson comprises one or two activities which may take the form of photocopiable sheets, a 'question and answer' session, or practical activities with suggested assessment questions for you to use while you are observing the children. These activities may include a mark scheme, but this is not related directly to curriculum levels of attainment. These tasks are intended to provide you with a guide to assessing how the children are progressing relative to an average expectation of Level 3 attainment/Level C in Scotland by the end of Year 4/Primary 5.

A sample of the children's work from the lessons in this book, kept in a general portfolio, will be very useful in supporting your teacher assessment judgements.

SUPPORT FOR PLANNING

Developing your scheme of work

This book is planned to support the QCA *Science Scheme of Work* and the statements of the UK national curricula. In planning your school scheme of work, you may wish to look at the units in this book or throughout the series along with those of the QCA scheme. You may also wish to address the objectives in your curriculum planning more directly to those of the curriculum documents. The grids on pages 196–207 show how the statements of the national curricula for science enquiry and knowledge and understanding for England, Wales, Scotland and Northern Ireland provide the basis for the lesson objectives used throughout the eight units in this book. In the tables, each statement is cross-referenced to one or more lessons to help with curriculum planning.

Planning progression

The Series topic map on page 208 shows the focus of each of the units in the books in this series, to help you work out your plan of progression. By looking at the charts of curriculum coverage and the organisation chart for each unit, you can plan for progression through the year and from one year to the next, covering the whole of the work needed for Reception and Key Stages 1–2/Primary 1–7.

You may choose to use all or most of the lessons from the units in this book in their entirety, or make a selection to provide a 'backbone' for your own curriculum planning and supplement it with lessons you have already found successful from other sources. The pages in this book are perforated and hole-punched, so you can separate them and put them in a planning file with other favourite activities and worksheets.

TEACHING SCIENCE IN YEAR 4/PRIMARY 5

The units in this book introduce children to the work in the national curricula and build on the work done in Year 3/Primary 4. It is expected that most children will attain NC Level 3/Scottish Level C as they work through this book, though some may still be working towards Level 2/Level B, and some may attain Level 4/Level C/D in some areas.

An underlying theme of this book is the application of science knowledge to our everyday world. As the children are maturing, this approach allows them to consider the ways in which science can alter our everyday life. This should help them see that it is important to know about science (to become scientifically literate) and to form opinions that, in future, can help in the sensible development of their world.

This book builds on earlier work to develop children's independence in planning and carrying out their own investigations. There is a particular focus on developing an understanding of how variables can be controlled to make tests fair and on the use of tables and graphs, but a broader interpretation of scientific enquiry is also encouraged, with the use of focused observation and surveys.

A brief description of the unit contents follows, to show more specifically how the themes are developed.

● **Unit 1: Ourselves** focuses on 'How I move', including an understanding of the functions of the skeleton in humans and how it works with muscles to produce movement. The position of the main organs of the body is also introduced in the context of the skeleton's protective role.

● **Unit 2: Animals & plants** focuses on 'Different sorts of skeletons'. In this unit, which builds on Unit 1, children find out about the different kinds of skeletons animals have, and the importance of these, particularly the existence of a backbone, in assigning animals to groups. They also learn to use a simple key to identify animals.

● **Unit 3: The environment** focuses on 'Habitats and food chains'. It looks at the habitats of plants and animals, and begins to develop children's understanding of the relationship between the physical environment and the kinds of living things that can survive there. It introduces ideas about food webs, including relevant vocabulary, such as 'prey' and 'predator'. Through this unit, the children are asked to consider how to study animals and plants without damaging them.

● **Unit 4: Materials** focuses on 'Warm liquids, cool solids', exploring the properties of solids and liquids. This includes investigating solids that dissolve in water, and the thermal insulation properties of materials. The children then apply their knowledge of the different properties of materials to sort different mixtures.

● **Unit 5: Electricity** focuses on 'Switches and conduction', including introducing ideas about the generation of electricity. Children explore materials that do and do not conduct electricity, and how these can be used in making switches. They also start to explore more complex circuits, investigating changing the numbers of batteries and bulbs in a circuit.

● **Unit 6: Forces & motion** focuses on 'Friction'. In this unit the children investigate friction between surfaces and the effect it has on movement. They explore water resistance and air resistance and consider the importance of streamlining.

● **Unit 7: Light & sound** focuses on 'Travelling and reflecting'. The children learn about how light and sound travel. They explore the different effects when light and sound are reflected. The relationship between the size of a vibrating object and the pitch and volume of the sound it makes is investigated.

● **Unit 8: Earth & beyond** focuses on 'The Sun and stars'. In this unit, the children observe the Sun's apparent movement across the sky and relate this to the shadows and the temperature at different times of the day and the year. Children are introduced to some common constellations.

ow I mov

ORGANISATION (9 LESSONS)

	OBJECTIVES	MAIN ACTIVITY	GROUP ACTIVITIES	PLENARY	OUTCOMES
LESSON 1	● To elicit children's existing ideas about the body.		Drawing what children think is inside our bodies into an outline of a body.	Discussion of children's ideas of the functions of different parts of the body	● Teacher has understanding of the children's existing ideas. ● Children have more awareness of their own ideas and are motivated to learn more.
LESSON 2	● To know that the skeleton is made from bones. ● To understand that we have lots of joined bones to give a greater range of movement. ● To make observations.	Comparing the movements of joints of dolls with our own joints.	Observing how different parts of our bodies move and noting this on a drawing of a skeleton. Mirroring each other's movements.	Identify ribs, skull and spine. Discussing why joints are needed.	● Can recognise that the skeleton is made up of lots of different bones. ● Can recognise and name the skull, ribs and spine. ● Can understand why the skeleton is made of lots of different bones. ● Can make observations.
LESSON 3	● To know that the skeleton grows from birth to adulthood. ● To plan a survey (on bone growth). ● To consider what sources of information they will use to answer questions.	Discuss how children's arms grow as they get older.	Planning a survey of children's forearm length in different age groups. Practising measuring the length of forearms.	Finalise planning for the survey.	● Can state that the skeleton grows from birth to adulthood. ● Has participated in the planning of the survey. ● Can consider the information that needs to be collected to answer a question.
LESSON 4	● To know that the skeleton grows from birth to adulthood. ● To carry out a survey of bone growth. ● To interpret the data from the survey.	Organisation of survey of forearm length.	Carry out the survey by visiting other classes and measuring children's forearms.	Collating the data in the form of a graph and discussion of patterns in it.	● Can carry out a survey in collaboration with others. ● Can use the data from the survey to develop their ideas about bone growth.
LESSON 5	● To know that a skeleton supports the body. ● To explore ideas by making models.	Making model joints with straws and pipe cleaners.		Discuss how the skeleton supports the soft body parts.	● Can recognise that a skeleton provides support. ● Can use model making to explore ideas.
LESSON 6	● To know that the skeleton supports and protects organs in the human body. ● To locate and name some of the organs of the body. ● To use secondary sources of information to answer questions.	Positioning and naming the main organs of the body.	Answering questions about the body by using information books and presenting this information as a diagram.	Groups present their findings to the class.	● Can name and locate some of the organs of the body. ● Can describe how the skeleton protects some of the internal organs.
LESSON 7	● To know that the action of muscles helps the body to move. ● To observe their own bodies closely.	Demonstration and model of how muscles work in pairs.	Observing how muscles harden and soften as limbs move. Making models of how muscles work.	Discuss how muscles help us to move.	● Can explain that we need both skeleton and muscles to move. ● Can explain that muscles pull on the bones to move our limbs. ● Can observe themselves in a focused way.
LESSON 8	● To know that when muscles work hard in exercise they also affect the body in other ways. ● To relate science work to PE.	Observing changes in their bodies during a PE lesson.		Linking understanding of muscles to activity in PE.	● Can describe how their body feels after exercise. ● Can relate their science work to PE.

	OBJECTIVES		ACTIVITY 1	ACTIVITY 2
ASSESSMENT 9	● To assess the children's knowledge and understanding of the skeletal system. ● To assess the children's ability to interpret survey data.		Can the children explain that the skeleton has a role in protecting organs and in movement?	Can the children interpret the table of data provided?

LESSON 1

OBJECTIVE

● To elicit children's existing ideas about the body.

RESOURCES

Group activity: Thick felt-tipped pens, pencils, large sheets of paper such as wallpaper.

PREPARATION

Put the resources out ready for each group.

Vocabulary

body, human, ourselves

BACKGROUND

Children will hold their own ideas about what is inside their bodies. For example, some may be aware that we have bones, but imagine them as separate items without the joints. They may be aware of the existence of some internal organs, but may not know what they look like. A common example is to represent the heart as 'heart-shaped'. Children are likely to have little awareness of the digestive system as a whole and often represent it as a sack that food goes into. An awareness of the ideas held by different children can inform differentiation, and this activity will also give you an insight into the levels of understanding across the class so that planning can be adjusted accordingly.

INTRODUCTION

Explain that you are beginning a science topic on 'Ourselves' and that you want to find out what ideas the children already have about their bodies.

MAIN TEACHING ACTIVITY

In this lesson, the focus is on finding out the children's existing ideas about their bodies, before introducing new ones.

GROUP ACTIVITY

The children work in groups of three or four. Ask one of the children in each group to lie on a large sheet of paper while the others draw around his or her outline. Then, ask the children to draw inside the outline what they think they would find inside their bodies.

Circulate, asking children questions about what they have drawn, for example: *What can you tell me about that part there? Do you think these are connected? What do you think this does?*

DIFFERENTIATION

Spend extra time observing individuals who are likely to be high or low attainers in this unit to ascertain their contribution to the group. Ask questions such as: *Could you tell me your ideas about this part of the body?*

ASSESSMENT

When analysing the drawings the groups have produced and considering their responses to your questions, look out for ideas they hold that are not in line with scientific ideas (see Introduction). Note any children who will need particular support or extension.

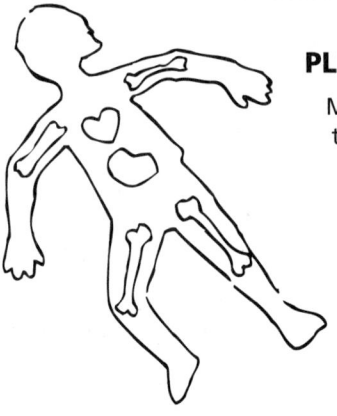

PLENARY

Make a temporary display of the pictures and discuss the ideas shown on them with the class. Bearing in mind that the focus of this unit is on our muscles and bones and how they move and grow, ask questions such as: *How does this part help us?*

OUTCOMES

● Teacher has understanding of the children's existing ideas.
● Children have more awareness of their own ideas and are motivated to learn more.

LESSON 2

OBJECTIVES

● To know that the skeleton is made from bones.
● To understand that we have lots of joined bones to give a greater range of movement.
● To make observations.

RESOURCES

Main teaching activity: A collection of male and female dolls (or ask the children to bring in their own); a model of the skeleton (card or realistic); large labels for the skull, ribs and spine; Blu-Tack.
Group activities: 1. Copy of photocopiable page 23 for each child, pencils, secondary sources such as books and CD-ROMs showing pictures of the human skeleton, a full-length mirror.

PREPARATION

Share the dolls between each group, or ask the children to use their own. Have the resources for the Main teaching activity to hand.

Vocabulary

bone, joint, rib, skeleton, skull, spine

BACKGROUND

The human skeleton is made up of about 206 bones (some people have more bones in their hands and feet than others). Bones are living tissue – they are supplied with blood vessels and can grow and repair themselves. Children often think of bones as dead, because that is their common experience of bones.

Another idea held by some children is that bones are not joined, but separate from each other – this may have been evident in the drawings in the initial assessment. Some of the joins are fixed, other joints allow movement in certain directions.

INTRODUCTION

Begin with the children seated in groups, with one or more dolls per group. Explain that you want them to look at how the parts of the dolls move, compare them with how humans move and then talk to the class about it. Give them ten minutes to explore the movement of the dolls and themselves. They will need to stand up and move around to compare their movements and those of the dolls.

MAIN TEACHING ACTIVITY

Ask some children to explain and show how their dolls move and how they move. Ask them: *Do we move in the same way? In what ways are our movements the same? In what ways are they different?* Discuss with the children how some of the dolls have rigid knees and elbows, whereas ours bend, and that we can move our shoulders and hips in a wide range of movements, but dolls often can't.

Ask the children: *What have we got inside our bodies that helps us to move?* (Bones and muscles.) Show the children the skeleton and explain that where the bones meet there are 'joints' – places where the bones join but can still move. We have more joints than the dolls and so more of our parts can move. Ask the children to look at their hands and identify different joints. Look back at the skeleton and pick out all the small bones that make up the hand. Ask: *Which directions can we move our fingers and thumbs in? Which directions can't we move them in?*

Show the children the ribs on the model. Ask them to feel their own torsos and see if they can feel their own ribs. Stick the label for the ribs on the model with Blu-Tack. Do the same with the skull. Look at the spine on the model. Ask: *Is it all made of one bone?* (No, it's made of lots of small bones.) *Can you suggest a reason for that?* (So that the back can bend.) Put the label for the spine on the model. Explain that each of the bones has a name, but that you want the children to concentrate on the names you have labelled.

GROUP ACTIVITIES

1. Give each child a copy of photocopiable page 23. Ask the children to label the skull, spine and ribs on the drawing of the skeleton. Then ask them to annotate different joints with a comment about how they move by exploring their own bodies. Have secondary sources available for the children to read and look at.
2. Ask the children to work in pairs, taking it in turns to 'mirror' the movements of their partner. Challenge them to find a movement for every joint in their body. Ask: *Can you work out how many joints you are moving now?*

DIFFERENTIATION

Extend higher attainers by asking them to find out the names of some other bones and label them on their sheet. Some children with a poor awareness of their bodies may benefit from looking in a full-length mirror at their movements.

ASSESSMENT

Can the children recognise and name the ribs, spine and skull? Can they explain why we are made of lots of small bones and not one large bone?

PLENARY

Ask the children to point to their own ribs, skull and spine. Ask some children to tell the others what they have noted about different joints. Those who have researched names for other bones can label the class skeleton for the others. Ask the class to explain why the skeleton is made of lots of small bones. Can they imagine what it would be like with one solid bone?

OUTCOMES

- Can recognise that the skeleton is made up of lots of different bones.
- Can recognise and name the skull, ribs and spine.
- Can understand why the skeleton is made of lots of different bones.
- Can make observations.

LINKS

PSHE: understanding of our own bodies.
Literacy: labelling a drawing.
Drama: exploring the movements of the body.

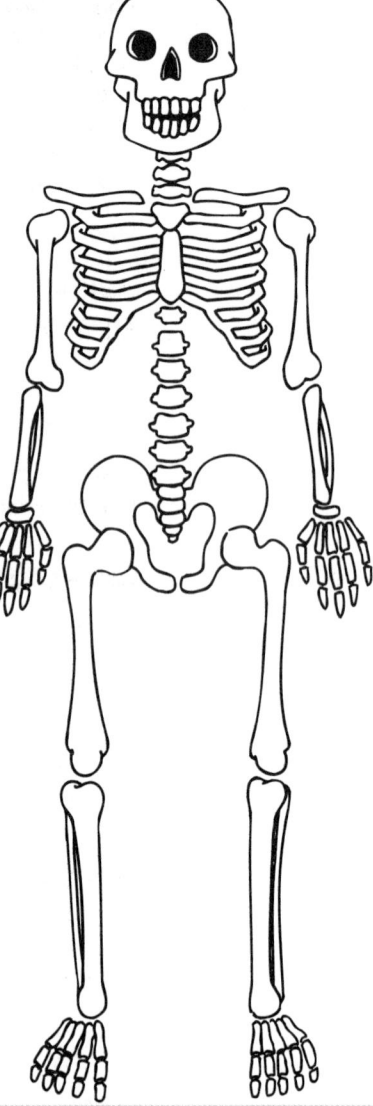

LESSON 3

OBJECTIVES

- To know that the skeleton grows from birth to adulthood.
- To plan a survey (on bone growth).
- To consider what sources of information they will use to answer questions.

RESOURCES

Main teaching activity: Photographs of people of different ages; photographs or X-rays showing bones from people of different ages (if available); a model skeleton, an enlarged copy of photocopiable page 24, a flip chart.
Group activities: 1. Writing materials, copies of photocopiable page 24 for each group.
2. Tape measures, scrap paper and pencils.

PREPARATION

Photocopy page 24 for each group and enlarge it to A3 for display or copy it on to the flip chart for the Main teaching activity.

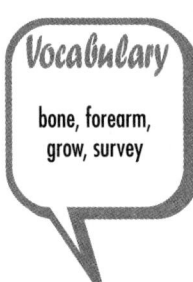

Vocabulary

bone, forearm, grow, survey

BACKGROUND

It is important that children do not think that fair testing is the only form of enquiry that is valid in science. Surveys are an important part of the range of enquiry skills they need to develop, particularly when investigating living things that cannot be controlled in fair tests. The data produced needs to be handled in different ways and helps children to understand the variation that exists between organisms.

The data collected could be entered into a database to be analysed, either in addition to or instead of the use of cards. The data to be collected needs to be discussed with the class, and suggestions for this are given on photocopiable page 24.

INTRODUCTION

Remind the children what they learned in the previous lesson. Show them the photographs of people of different ages. Ask: *How do you think their skeletons have changed?* (In size, strength and shape.) Give the children the opportunity here to talk about any personal experiences that relate to bone growth by asking: *Does anyone have anything they want to tell us about how bones grow?* For example, they may have had a broken leg, or have an older relative whose broken bone is taking a long time to mend; perhaps they have been told about having well-fitting shoes so that their feet can grow properly.

MAIN TEACHING ACTIVITY

Ask the children each to look at their own forearm. Show them the forearm bones on the model skeleton. Ask: *How do you think your forearm has changed since you were born? Do you expect it to change as you grow older?* (It should get longer and wider.) *How could we find out about how children's arms grow?* If the children do not suggest it then introduce the idea of a survey.

Display the A3 enlargement of photocopiable page 24 or the questions written on the flip chart for discussion. Read through the questions and give each group a copy of them (photocopiable page 24).

GROUP ACTIVITIES

1. Ask each group to go back to their table and discuss what they think about each of these questions, explaining that everyone's ideas will be taken into account, but the whole class will need to use the same method in the end.
2. Ask each child to measure the forearm of all the other children in their group and jot down the measurements on scrap paper. Ask: *Do you all have the same measurement for each person? Why?/Why not?* This will alert you to any children who need support with measuring and provide discussion points for the Plenary.

DIFFERENTIATION

Have mixed-attainment groups so that there are a variety of ideas discussed. Support any groups in need by asking questions such as: *Do you think all the children in Reception/Primary 1 have the same length forearms? How long would it take to measure the forearms of the whole class?*

ASSESSMENT

Do the children realise that bones grow from birth to adulthood? Do the children contribute to planning the survey? Do any children need extra input or support with measuring in the next lesson?

PLENARY

Discuss the questions, recording the class's decisions by each question on the flip chart. Ask: *Who shall we survey?* Emphasise that you will not be recording names so that people will not get embarrassed. Ask: *What ages shall we survey? Shall we survey boys, girls or both?* (Equal numbers.) *How many children?* (Ten from each year group?) *What information do we need to record?* (Age or year group, and length of forearm.) Ask: *How will we measure the forearm? Where from? Where to? Shall we measure the inside or outside of the arm? How accurate does our measuring have to be?* (To the nearest centimetre.) Ask: *What equipment do we need?* (Tape measures, paper and pencils for recording.)

Explain that the children will carry out the survey in the next lesson all using the same method as agreed here.

OUTCOMES

- Can state that the skeleton grows from birth to adulthood.
- Has participated in the planning of the survey.
- Can consider the information that needs to be collected to answer a question.

LINKS

PSHE: understanding how our bodies grow as we get older.
Maths: data-handling.

LESSON 4

OBJECTIVES

● To know that the skeleton grows from birth to adulthood.
● To carry out a survey of bone growth.
● To interpret the data from the survey.

RESOURCES

Main teaching activity: Large sheet of paper.
Group activities: 1. Small cards (5×7cm) in a different colour for each year group (or use coloured Post-it Notes), writing materials, tape measures. **2.** Small cards as for Group activity 1 with recorded data.

PREPARATION

Make sure you have arranged a time that is convenient to the other classes for your surveys.

Vocabulary

longest, range, shortest, survey, vary

BACKGROUND

The survey will produce data that is continuous – that is, the measurements could be anywhere along a continuous line. This kind of data is more difficult to handle than discrete data, for example eye colour, that can be represented as simple block graphs. The children can begin to understand how the data is distributed by representing it as shown opposite. The range of the data is the spread from the lowest measurement to the highest.

INTRODUCTION

Remind the children of the decisions they made in the previous lesson by returning to the flip chart and reviewing their decisions about the process of data collection.

MAIN TEACHING ACTIVITY

Allocate a year group for each group to survey. A good way for the children to record the data for later analysis is to record each person's data on a separate card, colour-coded for the different year groups.

Each group measures one or two of its own members to form the data for Year 4/Primary 5 and to practise measuring and recording the information before leaving the classroom.

GROUP ACTIVITIES

1. Each group visits another class to collect data.
2. Ask each group to put their cards in order from the shortest forearm to the longest forearm. Explain that this is the 'range'.

DIFFERENTIATION

Place the children in mixed-attainment groups for peer support.

ASSESSMENT

Have the children collected the data as agreed? Have they recorded it in the form that the class has agreed upon?

PLENARY

Ask each group in turn, starting with those who surveyed the youngest children, to come and write the length of the shortest and the longest forearm on the board. Ask the class to look at the numbers. Ask: *Do you notice anything about the numbers?* (They get bigger, but not in neat steps.) *Do all children who are in Year 6/Primary 7 have the same length of forearm?* (No.) *Why not?* (People are not all exactly the same, and they grow at different rates.) *Do you still think it is true that bones grow as children get older?* (Yes.)

The cards could then be made into a graph by writing the different forearm lengths along the bottom of a large sheet of paper (on the x axis). The children could stick the cards above these lengths to make a frequency graph. The spread of the different-coloured cards should show how the older children tend to have the longer forearms. This could form the basis of a display with questions around it such as: 'How long is the longest forearm in Year 5/Primary 6?', 'How many Year 6/Primary 7 children have a forearm longer than 20cm?'

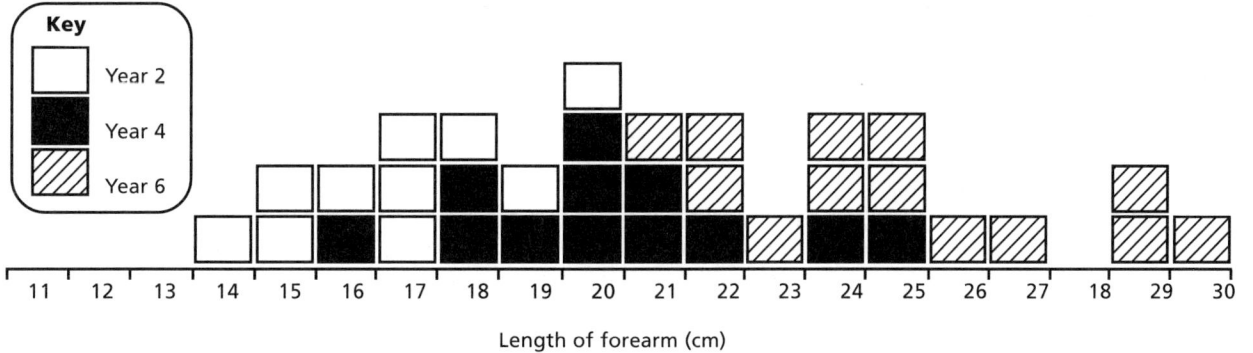

Key
Year 2
Year 4
Year 6

11 12 13 14 15 16 17 18 19 20 21 22 23 24 25 26 27 18 29 30

Length of forearm (cm)

OUTCOMES

● Can carry out a survey in collaboration with others.
● Can use the data from the survey to develop their ideas about bone growth.

LINKS

PSHE: understanding and accepting that people vary from one another.
Maths: data-handling.

LESSON 5

Objectives	● To know that a skeleton supports the body. ● To explore ideas by making models.
Resources	Straws, pipe cleaners, cotton wool, scissors, adhesive.
Main activity	Show the children how to join the straws together by using pipe cleaners cut in half. pipe cleaner straw The children design their own skeleton for an imaginary animal. Use cotton wool stuck onto the skeleton to represent body parts. Circulate, asking children how their straw skeletons support the animal they are making.
Differentiation	Mainly by outcome. Support children who are less dextrous with extra adult help.
Assessment	Can the children explain how a skeleton provides support?
Plenary	Show the children's models and discuss how the straws act like a skeleton. Say: *Imagine how animals made from only cotton wool might look.* Ask: *Could they stand up? Why not?*
Outcomes	● Can recognise that a skeleton provides support. ● Can use model making to explore ideas.

LESSON 6

OBJECTIVES

● To know that the skeleton supports and protects organs in the human body.
● To locate and name some of the organs of the body.
● To use secondary sources of information to answer questions.

RESOURCES

Main teaching activity: A model of a human torso or a commercially produced 'body apron': a tabard that a child wears with felt cut-outs of different body parts that are stuck on with Velcro; large labels for 'brain', 'heart', 'lungs', 'stomach', 'bladder', 'kidney', 'intestines'; Blu-Tack; double-sided sticky tape or Velcro as appropriate to attach labels.
Group activities: 1. Books on the body; prepared questions on cards, each inserted into the book that contains the answer. **2.** Drawing materials.

PREPARATION

Have the resources for the Main teaching activity to hand. Have the books and question cards ready on the tables. The exact questions will depend on the information available in the books provided for the groups. The following questions about the brain, heart, lungs, intestines, stomach, kidneys and bladder provide guidance:
- Make a list of things the brain helps us to do.
- Is the heart heart-shaped?
- How big is the heart?
- What does the heart do?
- What do we do with our lungs?
- What do we breathe?
- We breathe in air through our m - - - - and our n - - -.
- How long is the intestine?
- Whereabouts is your stomach?
- How does food get into your stomach?
- How many kidneys have we got?
- Are the kidneys at the back or the front of our bodies?
- What do we store in the bladder?

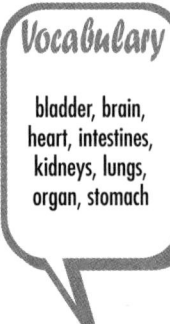

Vocabulary

bladder, brain, heart, intestines, kidneys, lungs, organ, stomach

BACKGROUND

Children have existing ideas about what is inside their bodies, as will be evident from Lesson 1 (page 12). Common ideas are that the heart is heart-shaped, and that food goes into the stomach and stops. Few children will have ideas about the intestine and kidneys by Year 4/Primary 5. This lesson is not intended to give the children a full understanding of the function of each of these organs, but to be a foundation for later work. This lesson could be linked with work in English on using information texts.

INTRODUCTION

Review the children's drawings from the initial assessment in Lesson 1. Ask the children what they think is inside their bodies. Make a list of the main organs (brain, heart, lungs, stomach, bladder, kidneys, intestines) on the board as the children suggest their ideas.

MAIN TEACHING ACTIVITY

Look at the model/body apron, asking children if they can name any parts. Add the labels in the correct places. Discuss briefly what each organ does, but do not go into details (see Preparation).

Explain that each group will study one organ and find out some information about it using books or CD-ROMs to report back to the rest of the class.

GROUP ACTIVITIES

1. Nominate one member of each group to act as scribe. Each group finds out the answers to the questions on the cards on their table. The question cards should be inserted into the books containing the answer.
2. Ask each group to present their findings as a simple poster with an annotated drawing. Make sure the poster is kept simple and is about communicating information, not decorative artwork – a time limit might help with this.

DIFFERENTIATION

Use groups based on literacy attainment. Support those with weaker literacy skills with teacher time; the brain is a good subject for them. Those with good literacy skills and good scientific understanding can research the kidneys, bladder or the lungs.

For some lower attaining groups, the cards can be inserted at the right page, other higher attaining children will be able to use the index or practise skimming skills.

ASSESSMENT

Can the children locate the different organs on their own bodies and on a model? Can they explain how the skeleton protects them?

PLENARY

Take the labels off the model of the body and put them back as each group presents their information. Ask the children: *What might happen if our organs got damaged?* (They might not work properly, we might have to go to hospital, we could die.) Ask: *What is covering the organs that helps to protect them?* (Skin and the skeleton.) *Which part of the skeleton protects the brain?* (The skull.) *Which part of the skeleton protects the heart and the lungs?* (The ribs.)

OUTCOMES

● Can name and locate some of the organs of the body.
● Can describe how the skeleton protects some of the internal organs.

LINKS

PSHE: understanding that we need functioning organs to keep us alive and healthy.
Literacy: use of information texts; labelling diagrams.

LESSON 7

OBJECTIVES

● To know that the action of muscles helps the body to move.
● To observe their own bodies closely.

RESOURCES

Main teaching activity: Equipment for model of an elbow joint: two rulers with holes in one end, two pop socks, an elastic band cut open, strong sticky tape (see illustration overleaf).
Group activities: 1. Mirrors, writing equipment. **2.** Equipment for model elbow as above.

PREPARATION

Have all the resources for the model elbow to hand.

Vocabulary
bone, muscle, pull, stretch

BACKGROUND

Muscles are attached to bones by tendons. They contract (shorten), pulling on the bones to cause movement. They can contract on their own, but they cannot relax unless they are stretched out by another muscle shortening elsewhere. This means that muscles are organised in 'antagonistic pairs'. Children at this stage don't need to know this term, but can begin to understand that when one muscle contracts, the other is stretched and vice versa. Ligaments help to hold joints together.

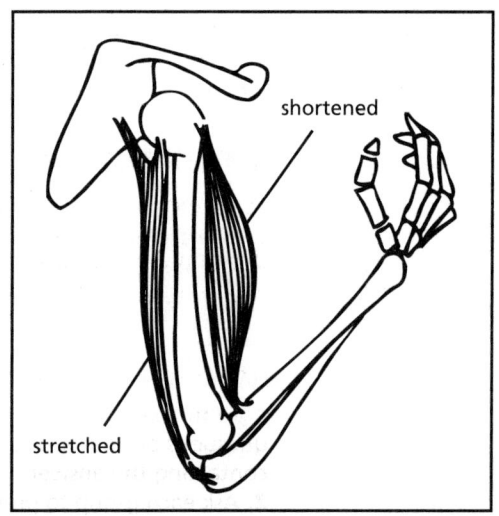

shortened

stretched

INTRODUCTION

Ask the children to tell you some things they have learned about the skeleton. List on the board or flip chart that it supports, protects and helps us to move. Ask the children what else we have that helps us to move. (The muscles help us to move.)

MAIN TEACHING ACTIVITY

Explain that you will make a model to help demonstrate how muscles work with the skeleton to make an arm move.

Ask the children to hold their right upper arm with one hand to keep it still. Ask them to move their forearm. Ask: *What directions can you move it in?* (Up and down.) Show the children the two rulers and explain that these are like the bones in your forearm and upper arm. Tie the rulers together using a cut elastic band through the holes at the ends. Explain that you have made a joint, like the joint at the elbow. Show how the rulers can move, forming the 'elbow'.

Show the pop socks and explain that these are like muscles because they can stretch in length and return to being short again. Tape one pop sock several centimetres from one end of both rulers, explaining that your muscles are joined onto your bones. Straighten out the rulers to represent a straight arm. The children can follow these movements with their own arms. Ask them to describe the pop sock 'muscle'. (It is stretched and long.) Explain that the muscle can make itself short and that this pulls up the forearm. Demonstrate while you explain.

Tell the children that although the muscle can make itself short, it cannot then make itself long again. Ask: *Can you think of a way of bringing the forearm down again?* (Use another

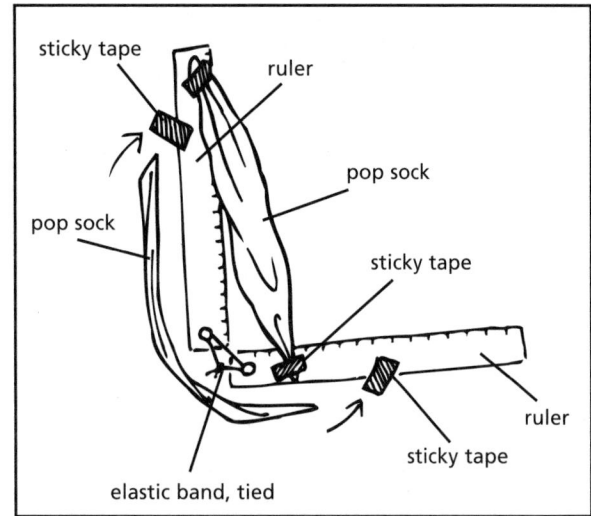

sticky tape
ruler
pop sock
pop sock
sticky tape
ruler
sticky tape
elastic band, tied

muscle.) Tape another pop sock onto the underside of the rulers and show how when this gets shorter the other 'muscle' is pulled long again and the forearm is brought down.

GROUP ACTIVITIES

1. Ask the children to observe and feel what happens to their muscles as they move their arms. When the muscles feel hard, they are short and are working at pulling a bone. When they feel soft, they have been stretched out. Ask the children to write in their own words and draw how muscles and bones work together to make us move.

2. Ask the children to work in pairs to make their own model elbow joints. Making effective pairs of muscles can be difficult, so initially limit the activity to making a model with a muscle to pull the arm up, extending it to a pair of muscles only if the first task has been successfully completed.

DIFFERENTIATION

For Group activity 1, write out the key vocabulary as a word bank to support those who are lower attainers in literacy. Expect more detailed descriptions from the higher attainers in science.

ASSESSMENT

In the children's work, do they show an understanding that muscles pull on bones to make them move?

PLENARY

Ask: *How does our skeleton help us?* (It gives support and protection and allows movement.) *How do our muscles help us to move?* (They pull on the bones.) *What tells the muscles to pull on the bones?* (Our brain.)

OUTCOMES

● Can explain that we need both skeleton and muscles to move.
● Can explain that muscles pull on the bones to move our limbs.
● Can observe themselves in a focused way.

LINKS

Unit 6: forces.
PE: movement.

LESSON 8

Objectives	● To know that when muscles work hard in exercise they also affect the body in other ways. ● To relate their work in science to PE.
Resources	A PE lesson.
Main activity	Ask the children what they will be using to help them move. (The skeleton and the muscles.). During the lesson, and as the children are cooling down, ask them to describe how they are feeling. (Tired, hot, out of breath and can feel the heart beating fast.)
Differentiation	Target questions to involve those children who are enthusiastic about sport and less so about science!
Assessment	Are the children able to describe the changes to their bodies? Can they make connections between their science work and the PE lesson?
Plenary	Back in class, ask the children: *When your muscles had to work hard to move you quickly, how did that make you feel? Does this link to anything else we have been learning?* (The heart and lungs are working hard, too.)
Outcomes	● Can describe how their body feels after exercise. ● Can relate their science work to PE.

ASSESSMENT
LESSON 9

OBJECTIVES
- To assess the children's knowledge and understanding of the skeletal system.
- To assess the children's ability to interpret survey data.

RESOURCES
Assessment activities: 1. A copy of photocopiable page 25 for each child, writing materials.
2. A copy of photocopiable page 26 for each child, writing materials.

INTRODUCTION
These Assessment activities should be considered alongside the ongoing assessment opportunities indicated throughout the unit when making a judgement about the level at which the child is working. If you are unsure what a child means by their response to a question, then discuss it with them afterwards.

The children could do Assessment activity 1 then Assessment activity 2 immediately afterwards, but it may be preferable to carry out each assessment on a separate occasion.

ASSESSMENT ACTIVITY 1
Give each child a copy of photocopiable page 25. Act as a reader and scribe for any children who need this support. You may wish to discuss the answers immediately so that the children are able to assess their own progress, and any questions can be addressed on the spot.

Answers
1. To support our body; To help us move; To protect some of our organs.
2a. The skull.
2b. The ribs.
2c. Labelled diagram.
3. It grows/The bones get bigger/longer.

Looking for levels
Most children should be able to answer these questions correctly. Some may have difficulty remembering the correct vocabulary. Questions 1 and 3 are the most important in demonstrating understanding of the key ideas.

ASSESSMENT ACTIVITY 2

This activity focuses on assessing children's data interpretation skills. Give each child a copy of photocopiable page 26. Ask them to answer the questions on their own. Make sure they realise that you are looking for evidence of thoughtful explanation, not the 'right' answer in this section.

Looking for levels

Most children should be able to answer questions 1 and 2. In question 3, some children may think that the children must be different ages because they have different-sized feet. Some may argue that Mark is younger because his feet are a lot smaller. Others may remember that there was a spread of forearm length in their earlier survey and so say that they could be the same age. These are all acceptable responses.

If the children are able to suggest a reason for their answer they are demonstrating that they can suggest an explanation for the data and are working at NC Level 3/Scottish Level C. Those who give more sophisticated explanations relating to scientific knowledge and understanding are working at NC Level 4/Scottish Level C/D in this aspect.

PLENARY

In relation to photocopiable page 26, it would be good to discuss the different interpretations of the data and allow different children to argue the

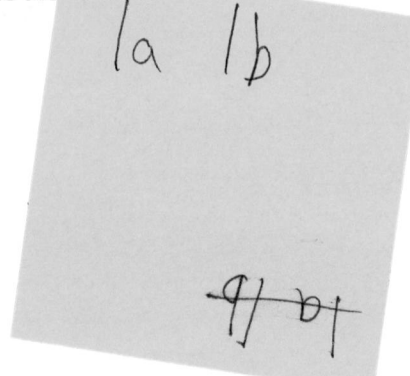

Name

My skeleton

skeleton

bone

joint

rib

skull

spine

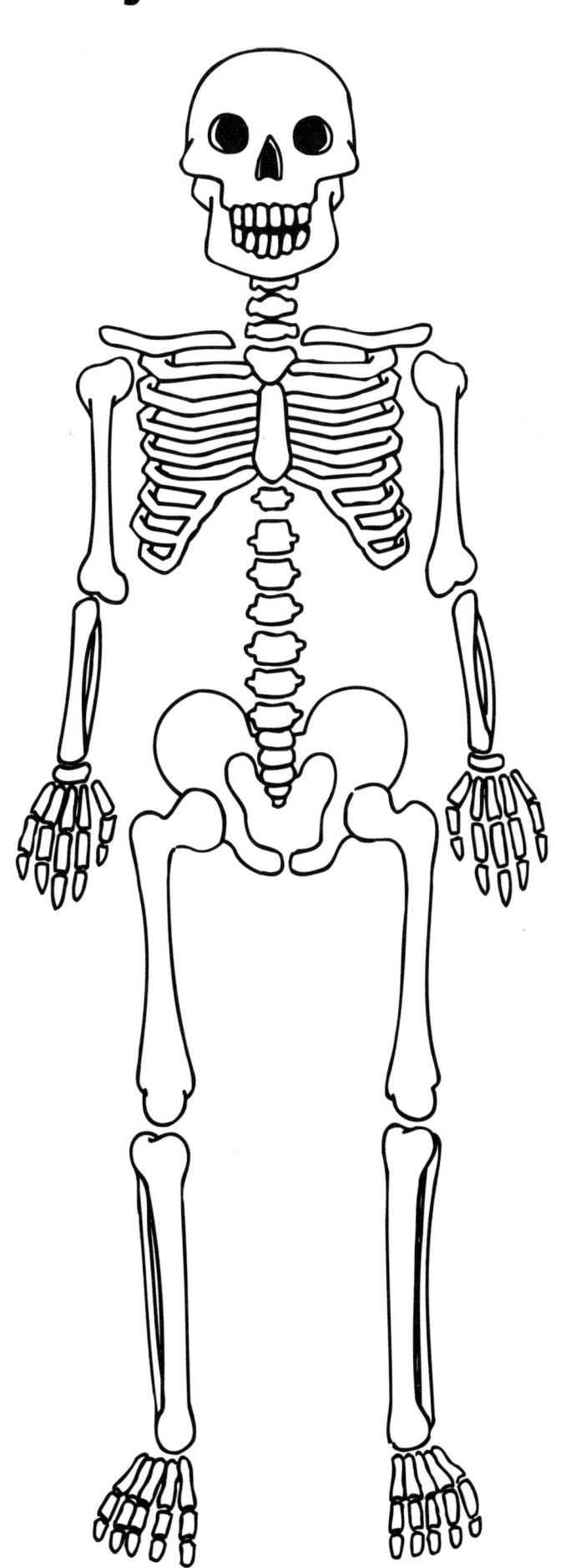

Planning a survey

Do children's forearms grow as they get older?

What ages shall we survey?

_____

Shall we survey boys, girls or both?

_____

How many children shall we survey?

_____

What information do we need to record?

_____

_____

How will we measure the forearm?

_____

_____

How accurate does our measuring have to be?

_____

_____

What equipment do we need?

_____

_____

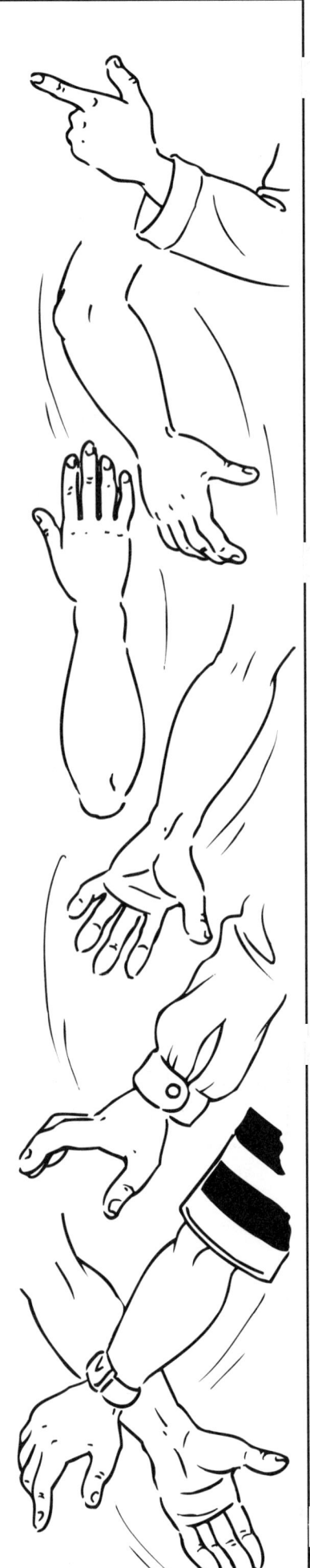

Name

How I move

1. Why do we need a skeleton?

✓ Tick the answers you agree with.

☐ To support our body

☐ To help us move

☐ To make us tall

☐ To protect some of our organs

☐ To make us heavy

☐ To protect our muscles

2a. Which part of the skeleton protects the brain?

_____

2b. Which part of the skeleton protects the heart and lungs?

_____

2c. Now label those two parts (a) and (b) on the drawing of the skeleton.

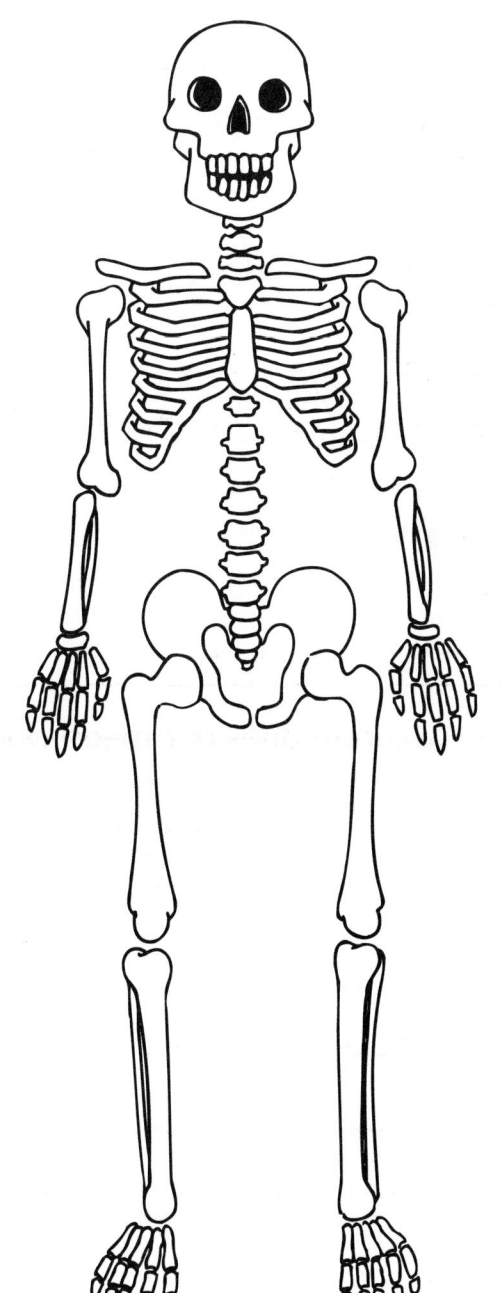

3. What happens to your skeleton as you get older?

_____

_____

_____

_____

_____

How I move

A group of children measured the length of their feet. The results are in the table below.

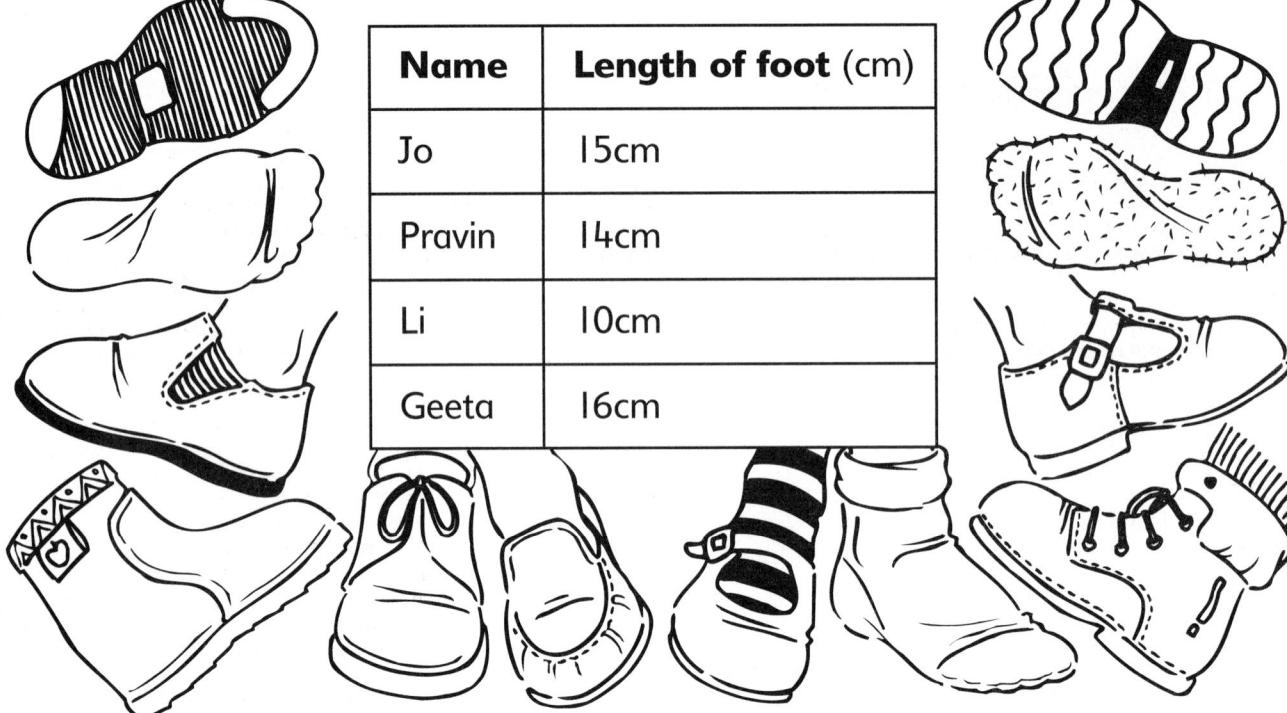

Name	Length of foot (cm)
Jo	15cm
Pravin	14cm
Li	10cm
Geeta	16cm

1. Who had the longest foot?

_____

2. Who had the shortest foot?

_____

3. Do you think these children are the same age?

_____

_____

4. Explain why you think that.

_____

_____

Different sorts of skeletons

ORGANISATION (9 LESSONS)

	OBJECTIVES	MAIN ACTIVITY	GROUP ACTIVITIES	PLENARY	OUTCOMES
LESSON 1	● To elicit children's existing understanding of groups of living things. ● To observe features of living things. ● To group living things according to observable features. ● To understand that a wide range of living things can be classified as animals or as plants.	Grouping pictures of plants and animals and identifying features common to each group.	Grouping and comparing photographs of living things.	Discussion on differences between plants and animals.	● Can sort living things according to observable features. ● Can explain criteria used for grouping. ● Can recognise the diversity of living things within the classification of plants and animals.
LESSON 2	● To know that bones have some features that can be compared. ● To make close observations recorded as drawings. ● To raise questions.	Using a feely box to enhance observation of bones.	Observational drawings of bones and raising questions about bones. Descriptive writing about the bones.	Considering the range of questions raised and how the answers might be found.	● Can compare the features of different bones. ● Can make careful observational drawings. ● Can raise scientific questions.
LESSON 3	● To know that some animals have skeletons of bones and some do not. ● To use secondary sources to answer questions.	Researching answers to questions raised using secondary sources.		Oral feedback of information gathered, recorded and made into a display.	● Can use secondary sources to answer a question. ● Can give examples of animals with skeletons of bones. ● Understand that not all animals have skeletons made of bones.
LESSON 4	● To know that animals can be grouped according to whether or not they have a backbone. ● To recognise similarities and differences between different groups of vertebrates. ● To compare and group items according to different criteria.	Classifying animals into those with and without backbones and identifying the groups: mammals, birds, fish, reptiles and amphibians.	Recording similarities and differences between pictures of animals and classifying animals with backbones as mammals, birds, fish, reptiles and amphibians.	Discussing similarities and differences identified and clarifying the group animals belong to.	● Can explain that animals can be grouped into those with and without backbones. ● Can recall the five different groups of animals with backbones. ● Can describe features that characterise members of the five groups.
LESSON 5	● To know how to use a simple key to identify vertebrates and plants. ● To carry out observations outside the classroom.	Using a simple key to identify local birds. Collecting plants to be identified and making a simple key by describing them.		Presenting keys made to the class.	● Can use a key to identify local animals. ● Can construct a simple key to identify local plants.
LESSON 6	● To know that some animals have a 'skeleton' of water.	Introducing the idea that some animals have a 'water skeleton' using a water-filled balloon.		Discussion on the limitations of a water skeleton.	● Can describe how water is used as a skeleton in some animals.
LESSON 7	● To know how to collect animals sensitively. ● To observe carefully. ● To know that some invertebrates have soft bodies and some have a skeleton on the outside.	Introduce the idea of an 'outside skeleton'. Demonstration of techniques for collecting small animals.	Collection and observational drawing of small animals.	Grouping collected animals according to their skeleton.	● Can observe closely. ● Can collect animals with respect for life. ● Can group a collection of invertebrates according to observable features. ● Can explain that there are different types of skeleton including an 'outside skeleton'.

ORGANISATION (9 LESSONS)

	OBJECTIVES	MAIN ACTIVITY	GROUP ACTIVITIES	PLENARY	OUTCOMES
LESSON 8	● To know how a decision tree key can be used to classify and identify animals.	Explaining how to use a decision tree to identify animals.	Using decision trees to identify pictures of animals.	Checking that the animals have been correctly identified.	● Can use a decision tree to identify invertebrates.

	OBJECTIVES	ACTIVITY 1	ACTIVITY 2
ASSESSMENT 9	● To assess the children's knowledge of the kinds of skeletons animals have and of the way animals are classified. ● To assess the children's ability to use a tree diagram to identify living things.	Grouping pictures of animals according to observable features and explaining reasons for the choice of grouping.	Pencil and paper test on types of skeletons, classifying animals and using decision trees.

LESSON 1

OBJECTIVES

● To elicit children's existing understanding of groups of living things.
● To observe features of living things.
● To group living things according to observable features.
● To understand that a wide range of living things can be classified as animals or as plants.

RESOURCES

Main teaching activity: A collection of photographs of living things with the name of the organism written clearly on the back (include a range of plants such as a small flowering plant, a fruiting deciduous tree such as an apple tree, a fruiting bush such as a blackberry; corn or grass, a vegetable plant, a fir tree, moss and a fern; and animals such as a snail, cow, spider, worm, snake, fish, bird, human), two labels of the words 'plants' and 'animals', two hoops.
Group activities: 1. Each group needs a set of photographs as above. (There are commercially produced photopacks or you can collect your own from magazines. *Junior Education* magazine [published by Scholastic] is a useful source of photographs.) **2.** Writing and drawing materials.

PREPARATION

Have the sets of photographs ready on the tables. It is a good idea to colour-code each set with a sticky label on the back in case they get mixed up. Have the card labels to hand.

Vocabulary

animal, group, plant, sort

BACKGROUND

Living things can be classified into 'kingdoms'. The two main kingdoms are plants and animals. Children often have their own meanings for these categories. For example, they may not see a tree as a plant, because their understanding is that a plant is something smaller. In everyday language the word 'animal' is frequently used to mean mammal, so children may not consider fish, birds, and insects as animals. Sometimes children do not realise that humans are animals too.
    This lesson is planned to find out what existing ideas the children have and to begin to develop and challenge these, so the Group activities come before the Main teaching activity. Ideas about classification will continue to be developed through the other lessons in this unit.

INTRODUCTION

Explain to the children that they are starting a new topic about animals and plants and that you are interested in finding out what ideas they have got about animals and plants.
    Hold up one photograph. Ask: *What can you tell me about this?* Accept all the children's ideas. Help them to focus on making careful observations by asking: *Can you describe the colours? What might it feel like?* Explain that you want them to look very carefully and thoughtfully at some photographs and to sort them into groups. Stress that there are no right answers and that they can group them as they choose.

GROUP ACTIVITIES

1. Ask the children to take one photograph from the collection, look carefully at it and describe to the rest of their group what they observe. Then ask them to sort the collection of photographs into groups. Circulate, asking the groups to explain why they have grouped them as they have and encouraging them to find different ways of grouping them, for example by colour, size, where they are found and so on.
2. Ask the children to record one of the ways they have sorted the collection in their own way.

DIFFERENTIATION

Let the children work in mixed-attainment groups so that they support each other through discussion. Some children may need individual questioning to help them to make careful observations and to group the photographs. Ask: *What do you notice about this photograph? Is there another photograph that you would put with it? Why have you chosen that one?* Some groups may need support to resolve disputes – explain that scientists often disagree with each other, but need to listen and try out each other's ideas.

MAIN TEACHING ACTIVITY

Have the class sitting in a circle on the carpet. Put out the two hoops and spread all the photographs around them. Explain that you are going to focus on one particular way of grouping them. Put the label 'plants' by one hoop and the label 'animals' by the other. Ask a child to choose a photograph to put in one of the hoops and to explain why they think it goes in that hoop. Continue, asking different children to do this, discussing reasons. You may need to introduce the idea that a snail, for example, is an animal and that a tree is a plant. Ask the children: *What have the animals got in common?* (For example, parts to help them move, parts to help them eat.) *What have the plants got in common?* (For example, green colour, they stay in one place.)

ASSESSMENT

Are the children able to give reasons for the way they have grouped the photographs? Can they correctly group the living things as plants or animals?

PLENARY

Ask the children to recap the different ways in which they sorted the photographs. Ask: *What did you need to do to sort them?* (Look carefully at each one.) Collect up all the photographs and go through them one at a time, at a fast pace, asking the children which hoop it should go into.

The collection of photographs sorted into plants and animals could be displayed on the wall as a record of the discussion and for the children to refer to.

OUTCOMES

- Can sort living things according to observable features.
- Can explain criteria used for grouping.
- Can recognise the diversity of living things within the classification of plants and animals.

LINKS

Maths: sorting and grouping.

LESSON 2

OBJECTIVES

- To know that bones have some features that can be compared.
- To make close observations recorded as drawings.
- To raise questions.

RESOURCES

Main teaching activity: An interesting bone, ideally an animal or bird skull, in a feely bag or box (a bag or box that a child can put their hand in to feel an object without seeing it).
Group activities: 1. A collection of sterilised bones including some bird and large fish bones as well as mammalian bones; a feely bag or box for each group, hand lenses, drawing materials, paper, cards with question words 'How', 'Why', 'Which', 'What', 'When', strips of card. **2.** Writing materials.

PREPARATION

Bones need to be sterilised by boiling for at least an hour before classroom use. Share the collection of bones between the feely bags. There should be at least one bone for each child.

BACKGROUND

Bones are sometimes seen as dead, solid objects. Close observation reveals that they have holes – some being large spaces inside the bone where the bone marrow was situated, some being small

channels where blood vessels travelled, and some being sponge-like spaces that make the bones lighter. The ends of bones can be examined to see how they might fit together as joints. Different bones can be compared and suggestions made as to which animal or which part of an animal they might have come from.

INTRODUCTION

Remind the children of the way they sorted living things by looking closely at them. Explain that in this lesson they will develop their observation skills further. Refer to the wall display of the groups of animals and plants and explain that for this lesson they will be exploring some different sorts of animals.

MAIN TEACHING ACTIVITY

Show the children the feely box or bag and ask for a volunteer to come and feel what is inside. Tell the volunteer that they must not say what they think it is, but only to describe what it feels like. Ask several other children to do the same. Then ask the other children: *What do you think it might be?* Ask the children who have felt the bone if they agree with the suggestions. Draw out the skull or bone with a dramatic flourish!

Explain that each group has some bones to explore. Demonstrate how to use a hand lens to observe details. Explain that they are going to make some drawings of the bones they observe.

GROUP ACTIVITIES

1. Each member of the group takes a turn to take a bone out of the feely bag, describing it to the rest of the group. Circulate and encourage the children to compare their bones by asking: *Is there anything the same about your bones? Is there anything that is different?* The children then work individually to observe and draw their chosen bone. Ask the children to annotate their drawings with questions. If this is an unfamiliar activity then stop the whole class and model it by writing some examples on the board. Refer them to the question cards on the table for support. Make sure that all the children have had the opportunity to feel the skull or bone from the Main teaching activity during this time. Leave it on display.
2. Ask the children to work in twos and threes to brainstorm descriptive words or phrases about the bones. These can include personal responses such as 'scary'. Ask the children to use these words as the basis for a poem or a piece of descriptive writing.

DIFFERENTIATION

Encourage children who are having difficulty raising questions by modelling them, asking such questions as: *I wonder what animal this comes from? Why does this bone have a hole here?* Children with weaker literacy skills can be supported in their recording by scribing their question onto a strip of card and cutting it up for the child to reassemble and copy.

Higher attaining children can be extended in their questioning by challenging them to use all the different question words twice.

ASSESSMENT

Do the children's drawings show evidence of careful observation? Can they describe similarities and differences between the bones? Have they raised questions about the bones?

PLENARY

Ask various children to tell the class one of their questions. Use a flip chart or piece of sugar paper to record a range of questions. Make sure that this includes: 'Do all animals have bones?' Ask: *How could we find out the answers to our questions?* (Use books or CD-ROMs, ask experts.) Explain that the children will be trying to find the answers in the next lesson.

OUTCOMES

● Can compare the features of different bones.
● Can make careful observational drawings.
● Can raise scientific questions.

LINKS

Unit 1 Ourselves: How I move.
Art: observational drawing.
English: writing questions.

LESSON 3

Objectives	● To know that some animals have skeletons of bones and some do not. ● To use secondary sources to answer questions.
Resources	Reference books and/or CD-ROMs on bones and skeletons including dinosaurs; strips of card in two colours; marker pens, writing materials.
Main activity	Based on the questions raised by the children in the previous lesson, and available resources, write questions on cards for different pairs of children to research (these can be duplicated). Examples of questions could include: 'Which animals have bones in their bodies?', 'What are bones made from?', 'How do we know that dinosaurs had bones?', 'Which animal did the bone come from?', 'Which part of the animal did the bone come from?' The children can research and make notes of the answers. Give them a time limit after which they need to be ready to report to the class.
Differentiation	Match the questions and research materials to children's interests and their ability to access the text containing the answers. Pair less-skilled readers with other children who can support them.
Assessment	Can the children find the answer to their question? Can they give examples of animals that have bones?
Plenary	Ask each child to present their information orally. Record their answers on different-coloured strips of card. This can be made into a temporary display. Ask the children: *Do all animals have bones?* (No, not all animals have bones.) *Can you give me an example of an animal that does have bones?* (Any mammal or bird, some reptiles and most fish.) If necessary, ask: *Do you think birds/fish/frogs/snakes have bones?* Refer the children to the wall display of animals and plants. Ask: *Can you think of any animals that don't have bones?* (Worms and caterpillars do not have bones.) Explain that the children will be thinking about what these animals have instead in later lessons.
Outcomes	● Can use secondary sources to answer a question. ● Can give examples of animals with skeletons of bones. ● Understand that not all animals have skeletons made of bones.

LESSON 4

OBJECTIVES
● To know that animals can be grouped according to whether or not they have a backbone.
● To recognise similarities and differences between different groups of vertebrates.
● To compare and group items according to different criteria.

RESOURCES
Main teaching activity: A collection of photographs as in Lesson 1 (see page 28); card labels of 'Animals with backbones', 'Animals without backbones', 'Reptiles', 'Amphibians', 'Birds', 'Fish' and 'Mammals'; a picture of a skeleton showing a backbone (perhaps in a book); additional photographs of animals from each of the five vertebrate groups.
Group activities: 1. Sets of photographs for each group (as in Lesson 1); writing materials; the writing frame from photocopiable page 39 (optional). **2.** Photocopiable page 40, writing materials.

PREPARATION
Remove the display of grouped pictures of animals and plants from Lesson 1 and put the photographs out on a table.

Vocabulary

amphibian, backbone, bird, fish, mammal, reptile

BACKGROUND
The animal kingdom is subdivided into animals with backbones (vertebrates) and animals without backbones (invertebrates). The vertebrates are subdivided again into mammals, birds, fish, amphibians and reptiles. Children can begin to become aware of these different groupings and how they help scientists to understand different animals.
    Mammals are characterised by the fact that they give birth to live young rather than laying eggs, they suckle their young and are hairy. Birds have feathers and wings. Fish have scales and can 'breathe' underwater. Amphibians, such as frogs, can live both in water and on land. Reptiles, such as lizards and snakes, have a scaly skin and mostly lay eggs; they breathe on land.

INTRODUCTION
With the children sitting in a circle ask them to think back to when they sorted all the photographs into animals and plants. Explain that you want to focus on animals again today, but

when you took the display down all the photographs got muddled up. Ask: *Can you help me to pick out all the animals from the collection?* Hold up each picture, allowing the children to call out 'animal' or 'plant'. Put the plants to one side and spread the animal photographs out in the middle of the circle.

MAIN TEACHING ACTIVITY

Ask: *What can you tell me about bones?* Listen to the children's answers, clarifying them if necessary.

Ask different children to point to an animal they think does have bones, then one they think does not have bones. Ask one child to sort the picture collection into those with and without bones. Ask the other children if they agree, and intervene to correct the groups if needed. Put the labels 'Animals with backbones' and 'Animals without backbones' on the relevant groups.

Explain that scientists are particularly interested in whether or not animals have a backbone. Show the class a picture of a skeleton and point out the backbone. Ask them to feel their own backbones and then each other's. Explain that today you are going to concentrate on the animals with backbones, and put the group without backbones to one side. Ask the children if they can name any of the photographs – they may use the family name 'bird', for example, or give its common specific name, such as 'kingfisher'. Explain that at the moment you are interested in the family name. Focus on each group in turn, putting the card with the correct family name by the photograph(s). Ask the children to describe the animal there (for example: 'It has feathers/is scaly/lives in the water'). You may need to introduce the terms 'amphibian' and 'mammal', and add to the children's descriptions by asking: *Does this animal lay eggs? Where does it live?* Hold up the new photographs one by one and ask: *Which family does this belong to? How do you know that?*

Ask a child to choose two different photographs. Write the names of the two animals on the board or flip chart. Ask: *Can you tell me something that is different about the animals?* Write: 'They are different in that _____'. Then ask: *Can you tell me something that is the same?* Write: 'They both _____'. Explain that the children will all be looking for similarities and differences between the animals in their group work, and recording it in the way you have just demonstrated.

GROUP ACTIVITIES

1. Ask the children to work in pairs. They choose two photographs and record similarities and differences in the way that you showed them. Photocopiable page 39 provides a writing frame.
2. Distribute copies of photocopiable page 40, which the children can work individually or in twos and threes.

DIFFERENTIATION

In Group activity 1, expect a different number of pairs of photographs to be compared according to the speed the children can work at. Expect more sophisticated comparisons from some children, and simple descriptions from others. Those with limited writing skills could record their comparisons on a ready-made writing frame (see photocopiable page 39).

ASSESSMENT

Can the children give examples of some animals that have backbones and some that do not? Can they describe similarities and differences between different animals? Can they describe the main features of each vertebrate group?

PLENARY

Ask pairs of children to hold up the photographs they compared and tell the class the similarities and differences they noted. Ask them to say which of the five groups their animals belong to. Ask the class to describe distinctive features of fish, reptiles, amphibians, birds and mammals. The set of pictures can be returned to the wall display with the new sub-groups shown.

OUTCOMES

- Can explain that animals can be grouped into those with and without backbones.
- Can recall the five different groups of animals with backbones.
- Can describe features that characterise members of the five groups.

LINKS

Maths: sorting and grouping.
Unit 1 Ourselves: note that humans are mammals.

LESSON 5

Objectives	● To know how to use a simple key to identify vertebrates and plants. ● To carry out observations outside the classroom.
Resources	A local park or similar space; a simple key on local birds requiring matching the bird with a picture and short description; sandwich bags for collecting plant material; adult helpers. (It is a good idea to visit the area in advance and to prepare a key that matches the range of birds that are actually found there.)

Main activity	Review the classification system so far understood – from animals to animals with backbones, to birds and so on, and explain that the next step is to identify particular sorts of birds.
	    Explain how to use the key, and that features such as colour, beak shape and size are important indicators.
	    Visit the local park or suitable outdoor space. Ask the children to sit quietly and identify the birds that they see using the key. Gather the class and review which birds have been spotted. Ask whether any were difficult to identify.
	    Give out the bags. Ask the children to collect six different sorts of plants within a group, for example leaves from different trees or flowers from different grasses, that they will use to make their own key later. Give clear guidance on any plants that are *not* to be collected.
	    Back in the classroom, the children can tape their specimens to a piece of paper and write a brief description. If the name is known then that can be included, but it is not essential – children could make up their own names.

Differentiation	The keys can be differentiated by changing the number of birds. Adult support can be provided for children needing extra guidance.
Assessment	Can the children use keys to correctly identify birds? Can they construct their own simple key?
Plenary	Children present their keys to the class. If you have access to a colour photocopier, a permanent record can be made by putting the paper with samples directly on to the copier. Digital cameras could also be used to record findings.
Outcomes	● Can use a key to identify local animals. ● Can construct a simple key to identify local plants.

LESSON 6

Objective	● To know that some animals have a 'skeleton' of water.
Resources	Snails, worms and slugs in transparent containers; long balloons filled with water; hanging masses, trays, writing materials.
Main activity	Review the children's ideas about animals with and without backbones. Ask the children if they can think of any animals that might not have backbones (jellyfish, spiders, ants, worms and so on). Explain that today they are going to focus on one group of animals without backbones: worms, slugs and snails. Give the children time to observe the animals. Ask them to think about how they move and what they might have instead of a skeleton. Discuss the children's ideas. Introduce the idea that these animals have a 'water skeleton'. Demonstrate how a balloon can be given a firm structure by filling it with water. Give the children time to feel the water-filled balloons and to try putting masses (weights) on them to show how water skeletons can support them. Ask the children: *Why do you think the snail has a shell too?* Discuss their ideas. Ask the children to record their ideas about worms, slugs and snails as annotated drawings. Release the creatures where they were found.
Differentiation	Support children with weaker writing skills by providing a bank of key words. Expect some children to offer more sophisticated explanations of how the water skeleton works.
Assessment	Can the children describe how a worm keeps its shape? Can they name some other animals that have a water skeleton?
Plenary	Ask the children: *Could humans have a water skeleton?* Discuss the limitations of a water skeleton: no joints, small range of movement, size and shape.
Outcome	● Can describe how water is used as a skeleton in some animals.

LESSON 7

OBJECTIVES
● To know how to collect animals sensitively.
● To observe carefully.
● To know that some invertebrates have soft bodies and some have a skeleton on the outside.

RESOURCES
Main teaching activity: A pooter, a paintbrush, a transparent container.
Group activities: 1. Transparent collecting containers, pooters, paintbrushes, hand lenses or other magnifiers, drawing and writing materials. **2.** Copies of photocopiable page 41 and 42, several dice (optional).

PREPARATION
Have the resources for the Main teaching activity to hand. Put the resources for the Group activities on the tables.

BACKGROUND
In Lesson 6, the children explored animals with 'hyrdostatic' or water skeletons. In this lesson they will be introduced to the idea that other invertebrates, such as spiders, millipedes and beetles, have an 'exoskeleton' – an 'outside skeleton'. The exoskeleton has joints. The children don't need to use the technical vocabulary – 'water' and 'outside' skeleton are sufficient at this stage.

INTRODUCTION
Ask: *What do we have that supports us and helps us to keep our shape?* (We have a skeleton.) *What is our skeleton made of?* (Our skeleton is made of bones.) Ask: *How do worms keep their shape?* (Worms have a water skeleton.) Remind the children that we divide animals into two groups: those with and those without a backbone. Ask: *Do slugs have a backbone?* (No, slugs do not have a backbone, they have a water skeleton.) *What about beetles, do you think they have a backbone? How do you think beetles keep their shape?* Allow the children to express their ideas and make suggestions.

MAIN TEACHING ACTIVITY
Introduce the idea that a beetle has a skeleton on the outside! It has a hard 'crunchy skin'. Explain that the class is going to collect some animals and look at them carefully to think about the kind of skeleton that they have.

> **Vocabulary**
>
> ant, beetle, caterpillar, centipede, insect, millipede, 'outside skeleton', slug, snail, spider, worm

Demonstrate how to use a pooter or the tip of a paintbrush to collect small creatures without damaging them. Discuss with the class how they should treat animals with respect. Set your expectations of behaviour and boundaries for where they can go to collect.

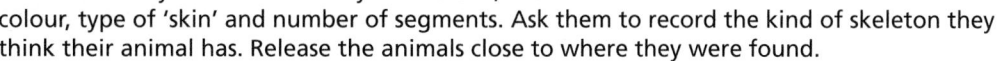

GROUP ACTIVITIES

1. Children collect one or two animals per group and return to the classroom to study them. Ask them to draw their animal carefully, using magnifiers to look at details. They can then write down any observations they have made, such as the colour, type of 'skin' and number of segments. Ask them to record the kind of skeleton they think their animal has. Release the animals close to where they were found.

2. Give the children a copy each of photocopiable page 41 which asks them to give descriptions of the pictures of animals using the word bank provided. An alternative or additional activity is for the children to play a game of 'Beetle' using photocopiable page 42.

DIFFERENTIATION

Expect more detailed descriptions from some children. Support children with weaker writing skills with a bank of key words.

ASSESSMENT

Do the children collect and release the animals with respect? Are the drawings good representations? Do the children refer to the type of skeleton in their descriptions?

PLENARY

Bring the class together. Write the names of the different animals that have been collected onto cards and stick them to the board. Ask the class: *Which of these animals could be grouped together?* Move the cards according to the children's suggestions. Make sure that one of the groupings is according to the kind of skeleton the animals have.

Ask: *Can you tell me some of the ways in which animals support their bodies?* (Some animals have a bone skeleton, some have a water skeleton, some have an outside skeleton.)

OUTCOMES

● Can observe closely.
● Can collect animals with respect for life.
● Can group a collection of invertebrates according to observable features.
● Can explain that there are different types of skeleton including an 'outside skeleton'.

LINKS

Art: observational drawing.

LESSON 8

OBJECTIVE
● To know how a decision tree key can be used to classify and identify animals.

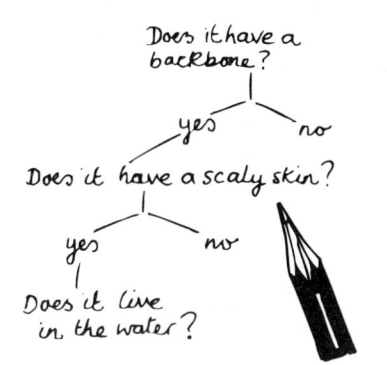

RESOURCES

Introduction: A decision tree copied on to a board or flip chart, as shown on the left, but modified to fit photographs from the collection used in Lesson 1.

Main teaching activity: Three cards with 'Yes' written on and three cards with 'No' written on; thin strips of card to represent lines; enlarged pictures from photocopiable page 43.

Group activity: Copies of photocopiable page 44 (one per pair of children).

PREPARATION

Enlarge the pictures from photocopiable 43 onto card and cut them out. Have the children sitting in a circle, but able to see a flip chart. Have the resources for the Introduction and Main teaching activity to hand.

BACKGROUND

Decision trees are fairly easy to use, but surprisingly difficult to construct, so, in this lesson, the process is done as a whole class and then the children use it to identify animals.

INTRODUCTION

Show the children the decision tree on the flip chart or board. Say that you are thinking of one of these animals: a snake, a rat, a sardine or a jellyfish, and they have to work out which one, using the decision tree. Tell the class to read out the first question: 'Does it have a backbone?' and answer 'Yes' or 'No'. Continue in the same way until they have identified the animal you were thinking of. Repeat this so that the children understand the structure. Ask one of the children to think of an animal and repeat it again.

MAIN TEACHING ACTIVITY

Put the pictures of the worm, the beetle, the spider and the slug from photocopiable page 43 out on the carpet. Explain that you are going to make a decision tree together. Ask a child to sort the pictures into two groups. Ask: *What is the difference between those groups?* Ask the children if they can think of a question with a yes/no answer to separate the groups. (They may need you to do this at first.) Write the question on a card and put thin strips of card running to 'Yes' and 'No' cards. For each picture, ask the question and place it in the appropriate group. Go to the smallest group and together think of another question that could separate the animals. Write it on the card and represent the tree on the carpet with card strips as before. Repeat this process for the other group, until each animal is identified separately and the pictures are all laid out. Now pick up the pictures and ask a child to take one of them. Together move through the decision tree to identify the animal.

GROUP ACTIVITY

Give each pair of children the decision tree on photocopiable page 44. Ask them to work in pairs, with one child asking the questions and the other answering. They change over roles each time an animal has been identified.

DIFFERENTIATION

Some children may find the decision tree difficult to follow. Help them by using the tree made as a class laid out on the floor and the child physically moving through the tree as yes/no decisions are made. Pair children who may need help with reading with other children who can support them.

Extend more able children by asking them to design their own decision trees for four animals of their own choice.

ASSESSMENT

Can the children successfully identify the animals using the decision tree?

PLENARY

Discuss each animal on photocopiable page 44 as a class to check that everyone agrees.

OUTCOME

● Can use a decision tree to identify invertebrates.

LINKS

Maths: data-handling.

ASSESSMENT

LESSON 9

OBJECTIVES
● To assess the children's knowledge of the kinds of skeletons animals have and of the way animals are classified.
● To assess the children's ability to use a tree diagram to identify living things.

RESOURCES

Assessment activities: 1. Copies of photocopiable page 45 scissors, glue, paper, writing materials. **2.** Copies of photocopiable page 46, writing materials.

INTRODUCTION

These Assessment activities should be considered alongside the ongoing assessment opportunities indicated throughout the unit when making a judgement about the level a child is working at. If you are unsure what a child means by their response to a question, then discuss it with them afterwards.

ASSESSMENT ACTIVITY 1

Give each child a copy of photocopiable page 45 and ask the children to cut out the pictures. Tell them to look carefully at each animal and then to sort them into groups by thinking about what their bodies are like. Explain that there is more than one good way to do the task. Ask the children to glue down the pictures and label each group to explain how they sorted them.

Looking for levels

Most children will be working at NC Level 3/Scottish Level C – they will have used observable features of the animals and clearly explained the criteria they have used for sorting on photocopiable page 45.

If they have used criteria based on personal experience, for example 'I like these/I don't like these', or have used very broad criteria such as 'big/small', this indicates working at Level 2/Scottish Level B.

Children working at NC Level 4/Scottish Level C/D will show that they have applied their knowledge and understanding, for example by classifying the animals as having backbones or not. The correct classification would be: without backbone – snail, spider, ladybird; with backbone – rabbit, fox, elephant (mammals), frog (amphibian), lizard, snake (reptile).

ASSESSMENT ACTIVITY 2

Give each child a copy of photocopiable page 46. You may wish to read the questions aloud to the whole class, or to administer the test by sitting with a small group, particularly if there are children who would have difficulty in reading the questions. This could be done while other children are completing Assessment activity 1.

Answers

1. Skeleton of bones: cat, baby, snake.
Water skeleton: worm, slug.
Outside skeleton: ladybird, wasp.
(1 mark for each correct answer.)
2. Look for answers that indicate an understanding that the skeleton supports or gives the body shape. They may also answer that it offers protection for soft body parts (2 marks).
3a. True; 3b. False; 3c. True; 3d. False; 3e. False; 3f. True; 3g. False (1 mark for each).
4. Decision tree: most children should correctly identify the pictures as a dragonfly and a centipede (2 marks).

Looking for levels

Most children will score over 12 out of the possible 18 marks, indicating Level 3 or Scottish Level C.

PLENARY

Assessment 1: Ask the children to show each other the different ways in which they grouped the animals and discuss this. Help children to understand the usefulness of the scientific classification by asking questions such as: *Will everyone know what you mean by 'big'? What other things do animals in this group have in common?*

Assessment 2: Discuss the answers to each question and, where possible, intervene to help children understand the reason a particular answer is correct.

Ask the children to think about what they have learned in this unit of work and give some examples. Can they suggest any ways in which their ideas have changed? You could return to the set of photographs used in Lesson 1 and use these to remind children of the ideas they had at the start of the unit. Explain that this is like being a scientist, because they are always learning and changing their ideas if they need to.

Name

Similarities and differences

My two animals are _____ and _____

They are different because _____

_____

_____

_____

_____

They are alike because they both _____

_____

_____

_____

_____

UNIT 2   ANIMALS & PLANTS

Name _____

Grouping animals with backbones

mammal   **bird**   **fish**   **reptile**   **amphibian**

The python belongs in the _____ group

because _____

_____ .

The mouse belongs in the _____ group

because _____

_____ .

The duck belongs in the _____ group

because _____

_____ .

Draw your own animal with a backbone and decide which group it belongs to.

The _____ belongs in the _____ group

because _____ .

Name

Describing minibeasts

Use the word bank to help you describe the animals in the boxes.
Remember to write in sentences.

> feelers   segments   shell   legs   eyes   body   wings   pattern
> head   stripes   spots   tail   water skeleton   outside skeleton
> one   two   three   four   five   six   seven   eight

The ladybird has _____

_____

_____

_____

The wasp has _____

_____

_____

_____

The grasshopper has _____

_____

_____

_____

The snail has _____

_____

_____

_____

Beetle

Take turns to roll the dice. You need a 6 to start so you can draw the body. Then add the other parts as you throw the dice. Remember, you can only put the feelers and eyes on when you have a head, and you need to have the right number to draw the part.

   The first person to draw a whole beetle shouts 'Beetle!'. Then you all stop and add up your total score for that game.

	Game 1	Game 2
head 5, eyes 1 each, feelers 2 each, legs 3 each, body 6, tail 4, Total 39		
Game 3	**Game 4**	**Game 5**
Game 6	**Game 7**	**Game 8**

Name

Make a decision tree

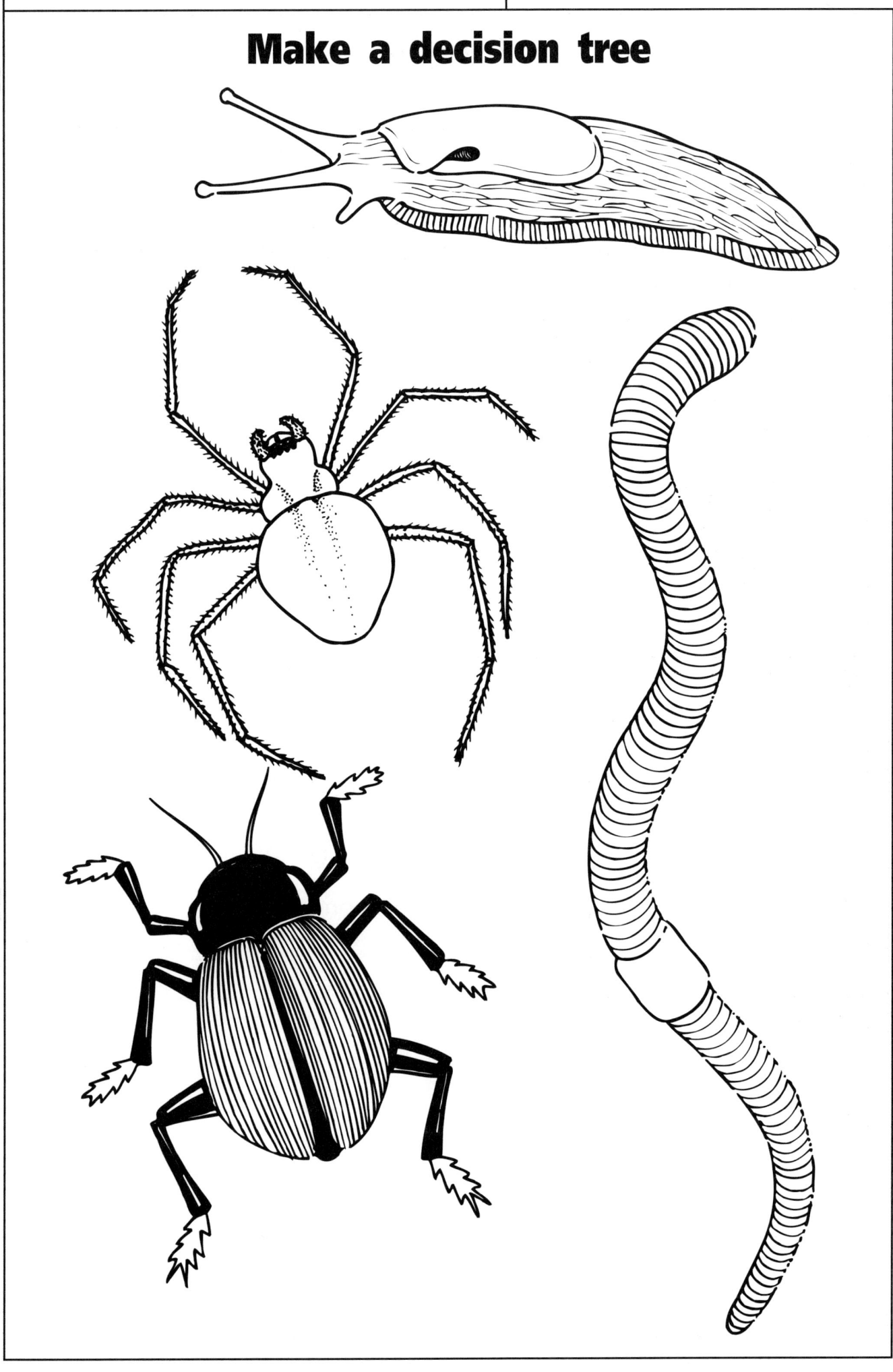

Decision tree

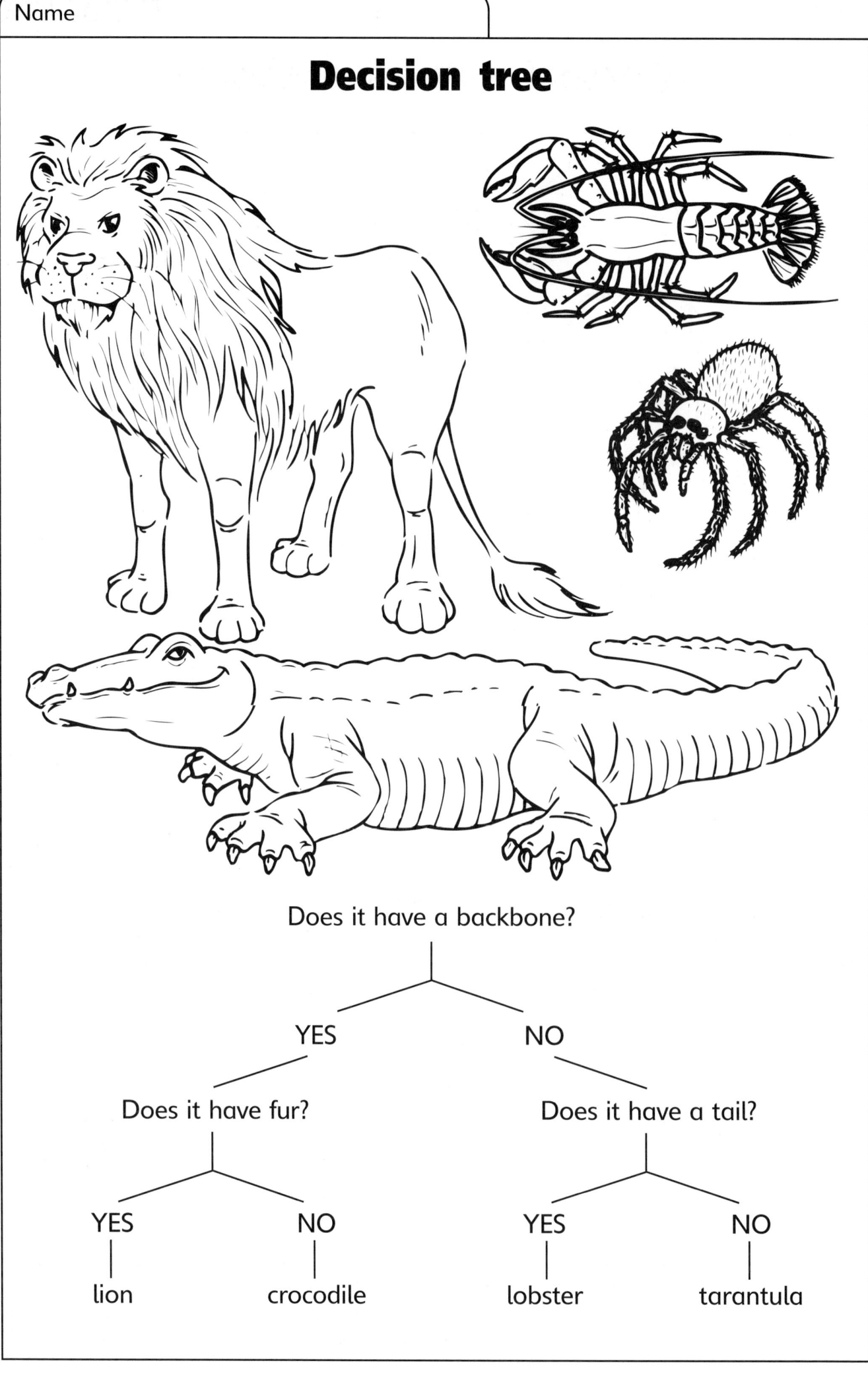

Does it have a backbone?

YES   NO

Does it have fur?   Does it have a tail?

YES   NO   YES   NO

lion   crocodile   lobster   tarantula

Different sorts of skeletons

Cut out these pictures and put the animals into groups. Stick them down and write next to each group why those animals go together.

Different sorts of skeletons

1. Draw a line from each animal to the sort of skeleton it has.

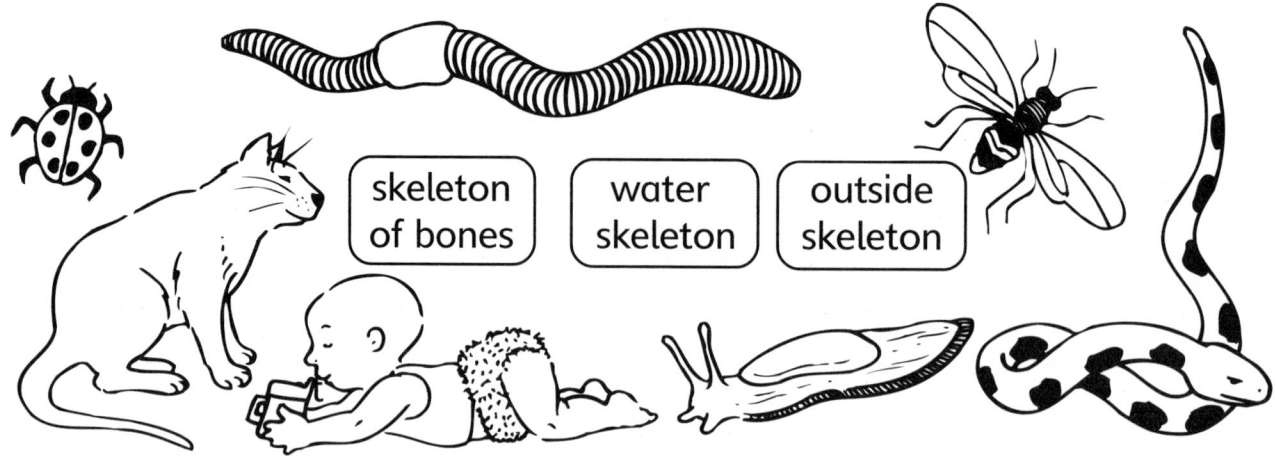

skeleton of bones | water skeleton | outside skeleton

2. Why do animals need a skeleton?

_____

_____

3. Put a tick in the correct box ✓

	True	False
a) A spider is an animal.		
b) Amphibians can only live in water.		
c) Fish and birds lay eggs.		
d) A beetle is a reptile.		
e) Worms have a backbone.		
f) Mammals have fur or hair.		
g) Humans are not animals.		

4. Use the tree diagram to find out the names of these two animals.

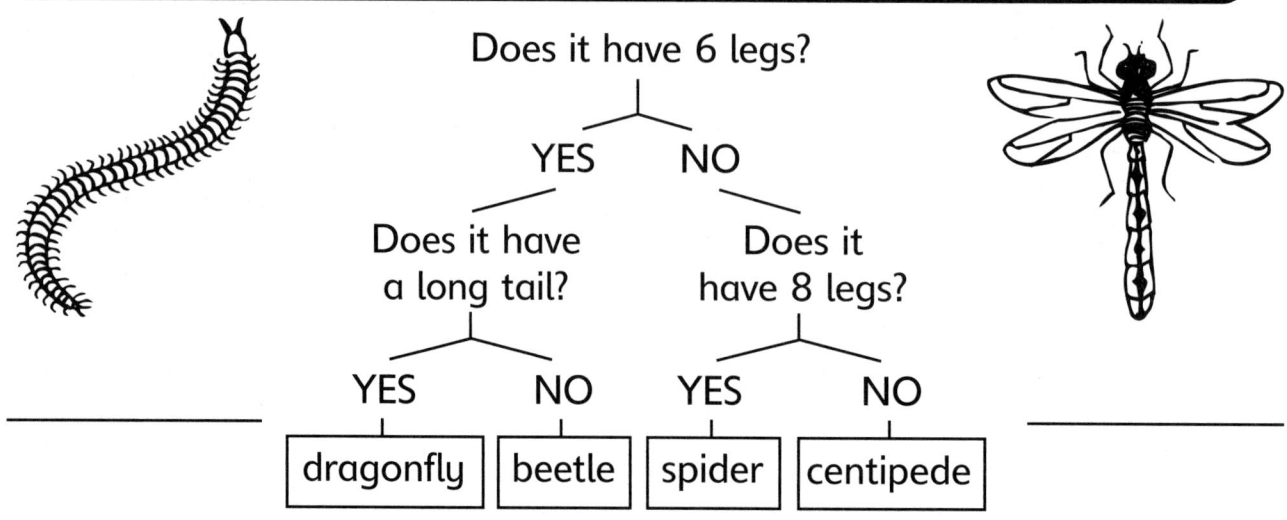

Does it have 6 legs?

YES   NO

Does it have a long tail?   Does it have 8 legs?

YES   NO   YES   NO

| dragonfly | beetle | spider | centipede |

UNIT 3

Habitats and food chains

ORGANISATION (17 LESSONS)

	OBJECTIVES	MAIN ACTIVITY	GROUP ACTIVITIES	PLENARY	OUTCOMES
LESSON 1	● To elicit children's ideas about living things. ● To know that there is a wide variety of organisms on the planet. ● To know that living things are called organisms.	Discussing what makes something 'living' Sorting a collection of living things into animals and plants.	Sorting a collection into 'living' and 'not living'.	Discussing the breadth of living things that exist.	● Teacher is aware of children's existing ideas about living things. ● Can give examples of a wide variety of organisms. ● Can understand the term 'organism'.
LESSON 2	● To know what the term 'habitat' means. ● To identify a variety of local habitats.	Discuss what living things need to stay alive and that they get them from their habitat.	Listing different habitats in the school grounds.	Considering the range of habitats within the school grounds.	● Can explain what the term 'habitat' means. ● Can identify a variety of local habitats.
LESSON 3	● To identify different physical aspects of habitats. ● To make observations and measurements of the physical conditions of two chosen habitats.	How to measure and record the physical nature of a habitat, such as light levels.	Observing and measuring physical nature of habitats within the school grounds. Presenting information as a book.	Discussing how the physical environment might affect the living things in a habitat.	● Can identify different physical aspects of habitats. ● Can make observations and measurements of the physical conditions of two chosen habitats.
LESSON 4	● To investigate the animals found in a particular habitat. ● To suggest reasons why animals are found in a certain habitat. ● To be able to choose appropriate equipment to collect an animal. ● To learn to collect animals carefully.	Demonstration of how to collect animals sensitively.	Collecting animals found in different habitats in the school grounds.	Relating the animals found in a habitat to the physical environment.	● Can collect animals carefully without damaging them. ● Can investigate the animals found in a particular habitat. ● Can choose appropriate equipment to collect an animal. ● Can suggest reasons why animals are found in a certain habitat.
LESSON 5	● To investigate the plants found in a certain habitat. ● To compare the numbers of different types of plant in the two habitats. ● To suggest reasons for differences in the plants that grow in different habitats. ● To devise their own record sheet.	Predicting how plants might vary in different habitats.	Carrying out a survey of plants growing in two different habitats.	Comparing plants found in two habitats and suggesting reasons for any differences.	● Can investigate the plants found in a certain habitat. ● Can compare the numbers of different types of plants in the two habitats. ● Can suggest reasons for differences in the plants that grow in different habitats. ● Can devise their own record sheet.
LESSON 6	● To communicate findings about the habitats investigated. ● To begin to explore the relationships between the physical aspects and the plants and animals living in a habitat.	Making a book to communicate their findings about two different habitats.		Sharing books that have been made.	● Can communicate findings. ● Can make suggestions about the relationships between the physical aspects and the plants and animals living in a habitat.
LESSON 7	● To know how to investigate the behaviour of an animal species. ● To understand the need for repeated tests. ● To pose their own questions for investigation.	Planning how to test animal preferences using choice chambers.	Carrying out tests of preference and recording results	Considering the need for repetition of tests.	● Can investigate the behaviour of an animal species. ● Can explain the need for repeated tests. ● Can put ideas for an investigation in the form of a question.

ORGANISATION (17 LESSONS)

	OBJECTIVES	MAIN ACTIVITY	GROUP ACTIVITIES	PLENARY	OUTCOMES
LESSON 8	● To know how to investigate the behaviour of birds. ● To make observations for a sustained period of time.	Observation of bird behaviour in a local area.		Discussing the most common behaviours observed.	● Can explain how to investigate the behaviour of birds. ● Can make observations for a sustained period of time.
LESSON 9	● To know that animals eat certain foods in a habitat. ● To use secondary sources to find information. ● To become familiar with a wider range of animals.	Explaining how to create a factfile card about animals in the UK and Ireland by using secondary sources of information.	Researching a particular animal using secondary sources.	Children report their research to the class.	● Can use secondary sources to find specific information. ● Can describe the eating habits of some animals found in the UK.
LESSON 10	● To know that animals in certain world habitats eat certain foods. ● To use secondary sources to answer questions.	Researching animals in world habitats using secondary sources.		Feeding back findings to the class.	● Can explain that animals in certain world habitats eat certain foods. ● Can use secondary sources to research the answers to questions.
LESSON 11	● To understand what is meant by a food chain. ● To know what the terms 'producer' and 'consumer' mean.	Explanation of the concepts of food chains, producers and consumers.	Constructing food chains from information cards.	Reinforcing how food chains are represented with arrows.	● Can make a food chain with one link. ● Can give examples of a producer and a consumer.
LESSON 12	● To be able to construct food chains with two links. ● To understand the terms 'predator' and 'prey'.	Reviewing ideas about food chains and identifying the prey and predator within examples of food chains.		Giving examples of prey and predators.	● Can construct food chains with two links. ● Can explain the terms 'predator' and 'prey'.
LESSON 13	● To understand the terms 'carnivore' and 'herbivore'. ● To understand that food chains are part of more complex food webs.	Explanation of the term 'food web'.	Constructing food webs from information on cards.	Discussing the complexity of food webs. Using terms 'carnivore', 'herbivore' and 'omnivore'.	● Can explain the terms 'carnivore' and 'herbivore'. ● Understand that food chains are part of more complex food webs.
LESSON 14	● To know that camouflage helps some animals to survive.	Read 'How the Leopard Got His Spots'; considering other examples of animal camouflage. Painting animals and background habitats.		Making an interactive display using the children's paintings.	● Can explain how camouflage helps some animals to survive.
LESSON 15	● To know that human activities can affect habitats. ● To communicate ideas effectively.	Discussing the impact of new paving on a grassy area on the food chain in that habitat.	Writing letters of protest about damage to habitats.	Discussing how humans can act to protect habitats.	● Can give examples of how human activities can affect habitats. ● Can communicate ideas effectively in the form of a letter.
LESSON 16	● To know that seasonal changes influence animals and plants in a habitat. ● To know that nature changes habitats. ● To understand some of our seasonal responses to help wildlife.	Considering a local habitat at different times of the year and how seasonal change affects living things.		Discussion on how natural processes as well as human influences can affect the animals in a habitat.	● To know that seasonal changes influence animals and plants in a habitat. ● To know that nature changes habitats. ● To understand some of our seasonal responses to help wildlife.

	OBJECTIVES		ACTIVITY 1	ACTIVITY 2
ASSESSMENT 17	● To assess children's understanding of the main groups of living things. ● To assess children's understanding of food chains. ● To assess children's understanding of habitats and how to study them. ● To assess children's ability to interpret data in the form of tables.		Pencil and paper test assessing children's classification of plants and animals, their interpretation of data and understanding of the impact of humans on animal life.	Assessment of children's understanding of food webs and use of terms such as 'prey'.

LESSON 1

OBJECTIVES

● To elicit children's ideas about living things.
● To know that there is a wide variety of organisms on the planet.
● To know that living things are called organisms.

RESOURCES

Main teaching activity: One collection as below; three hoops; card labels saying 'Living', 'Not living', 'Animal', 'Plant', 'Fungus'; flip chart and marker pens.
Group activity: A collection of living and non-living things for each group: a plant in a pot, the cut stem of a plant, a candle, a mushroom, a piece of wood, an apple, a stone, a crayon; pictures of a cat, a frog, a spider, a tree and a car.

PREPARATION

Have the resources for the Main teaching activity to hand. Put the collections for the Group activities on the tables.

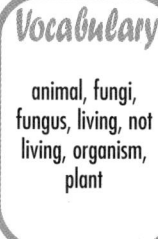

Vocabulary

animal, fungi, fungus, living, not living, organism, plant

BACKGROUND

Living things can be called organisms. Living things have the potential for growth, movement, feeding, respiration (using oxygen to get energy from food, which plants do as well as animals), excretion, sensitivity to stimuli (for example, a plant's response to light) and reproduction. It is not expected that the children should learn these as a list, but this will help inform your responses. Living things can be grouped into plants, animals, fungi and bacteria. At this stage children can focus on the groups of plants and animals, but can be introduced to the idea that fungi are a group on their own.

Children may use some of the characteristics to group items in a way that is not in line with the scientific definition of living, for example they may group the car or the candle as living because they move and 'eat' petrol or wax. The apple may give rise to some discussion. It is living, because it contains seeds that are part of the life cycle of the apple tree.

Be aware that some children will not consider a tree to be plant, as their idea of a plant may be that it is small, green and fleshy, not big and solid. Another common alternative idea is that only mammals are animals, so some children may incorrectly classify the spider and frog. The group discussion that will arise is the first way of questioning and challenging these ideas.

In this lesson, the Group activity comes first, as sorting the collection is important in orientating the children to the new topic and eliciting their existing ideas.

INTRODUCTION

Explain that you are beginning a new topic and you want to find out what ideas the children have already to help you know what to teach them next. Explain that the topic is all about living things and the places that they live. Give the children several minutes to explore the collection generally before setting the task.

GROUP ACTIVITY

Ask the groups to each sort their collection into things they think are 'living' and things they think are 'not living'. (Do not use the term 'dead'.) Ask them to record how they have sorted them in their own way. If the children are using pictures to record, however, ensure that they draw quick sketches that will not take too long. Ask for a written response to the question: *How do you know these things are living?*

Observe how the children have made their decisions and ask: *What made you decide to put that object in the 'living' group? How do you know that object is not living?*

MAIN TEACHING ACTIVITY

Bring the class to sit in a circle on the carpet. Have one of the collections in the centre. Choose a group to show the rest of the class how they sorted the collection, putting the items into the two labelled hoops. Ask: *Are there any items that other groups sorted differently?* Ask the children to explain the reasons for their choices. Encourage the children to discuss their ideas by asking: *Does anyone agree or disagree with that decision? Why?* Clarify ideas by explaining the reasons that scientists would use to decide which group they belong to.

Ask: *How do we know these things are living? What have they all got in common?* List the children's responses on the flip chart. Explain that all living things can be called 'organisms' and write the word on the flip chart. Put the non-living group to one side and ask: *Could we sort this 'living' group into smaller groups?* Let different children show the class how they would sort the collection. If it doesn't arise naturally, suggest that the collection could be sorted into 'plants' and 'animals'. At this point you may need to explain that the mushroom has a group of its own, and put it in the third hoop with the label 'fungi'. (You might also want to explain that 'fungus' is singular and 'fungi' plural.)

DIFFERENTIATION

Have mixed-attainment groups to encourage cross-fertilisation of ideas. Where you identify ideas that are different from the scientific ones, intervene by questioning and explain the scientific view. Support children's recording in the Group activity by providing a word bank with the names of the items in the collection. Extend more able children by asking them to pick out two items in the 'living' group and to list the things they have got in common.

ASSESSMENT

Have the children sorted the collection according to the scientific classification? Can they give examples of how we know something is alive? (For example, it feeds or it moves.) Can they give examples of plants and animals?

PLENARY

Ask: *Can you give me an example of an organism?* Ask several children for their suggestions. Ask: *Can you explain how we know if something is living or not? Can you give me some examples of plants and animals?* Encourage a diverse range of responses by praising unusual contributions.

OUTCOMES

- Teacher is aware of children's existing ideas about living things.
- Can give examples of a wide variety of organisms.
- Can understand the term 'organism'.

LINKS

Unit 2 Animals and plants: Lesson 1.
Maths: sorting and grouping.

LESSON 2

OBJECTIVES
- To know what the term 'habitat' means.
- To identify a variety of local habitats.

RESOURCES

Main teaching activity: Flip chart and marker pen, the page from the flip chart from Lesson 1 of the list of characteristics of living things.
Group activity: Clipboards, writing materials.

PREPARATION

Have the materials for the Main teaching activity ready and the children sitting on the floor in front of you.

Vocabulary

habitat, organism

BACKGROUND

A habitat is the place where an animal or plant lives. Each type of living thing is adapted to suit the habitat it lives in. There are several aspects to studying a habitat: the physical conditions of the habitat itself, the animals and plants that live there, and the relationships between the physical environment and the different living things. This includes considering how the organisms are suited to that particular habitat and the relationships between the different organisms, such as food chains.

INTRODUCTION

Return to the list compiled in the previous lesson of characteristics of living things and review it with the class.

MAIN TEACHING ACTIVITY

Now turn to a new sheet of the flip chart and, as a class, brainstorm a list of things that organisms need to stay alive, for example food, water, warmth, shelter, safety, air (oxygen). Ask: *Where do you get all the things you need to stay alive?* (From home, school and at the shops.) *Where do you think other living things might get everything they need?* Encourage children to give more specific answers by asking about certain animals: *Where does a spider/shark/blackbird/ daisy get what it needs to stay alive?*

Explain that the place where an animal lives and gets everything it needs to stay alive is called its habitat. Give some examples of different main habitats and ask children to add to the list: *Organisms might live in a pond, in the sea, in a wood, high on a mountain.*

Explain that these are 'big' habitats, but that there are little ones where different things may live too, such as under a rotting log, in a crack in a wall, on the branch of a tree. Tell the children that you are going to go for a walk around the school grounds and do the 'habitat challenge' – see how many different habitats they can find. Remember to set boundaries for exploration and agree a signal for when to regroup.

GROUP ACTIVITY

Ask the children to work in pairs to list on their clipboard as many different habitats as they can find.

DIFFERENTIATION

Pair children so that at least one of the two has good writing skills to facilitate recording. Expect some children to identify more obvious habitats and others to be very imaginative. Help children who are finding this difficult by encouraging them to imagine that they are an ant, a beetle, a bird, and think about what the school grounds would be like from their point of view.

ASSESSMENT

Can the children find examples of different habitats? Can they give examples of what an organism gets from their habitat to keep them alive?

PLENARY

Back in the classroom, ask the pairs to feed back some of their ideas to the whole class. Keep a list of these on the flip chart. As a class, go through the list and identify those which are 'tiny' habitats, such as under a leaf, and larger habitats such as the hedge. Choose several of the habitats and ask: *What might live here?*

OUTCOMES

- Can explain what the term 'habitat' means.
- Can identify a variety of local habitats.

LINKS

Unit 2 Animals and plants: Lessons 5 and 7.
Environmental issues: an awareness that different animals live in specific habitats.

LESSON 3

OBJECTIVES

- To identify different physical aspects of habitats.
- To make observations and measurements of the physical conditions of two chosen habitats.

RESOURCES

Main teaching activity: An electronic light sensor; an electronic temperature sensor, data-logging equipment or thermometers; the page of flip chart from Lesson 2, digital cameras.
Group activities: 1. Clipboards; copies of photocopiable page 69; writing materials. **2.** Writing materials, sugar paper books (see Preparation).

PREPARATION

Copy photocopiable page 69 for each group. Have card or sugar paper booklets made up so that the children can see the form in which their work will be presented.

BACKGROUND

It is a good idea for the work of Lessons 3, 4 and 5 to be presented in the form of a book about the habitats prepared by each group of three or four children. This is motivating and also provides a way in which children can learn from each other.

In this series of lessons, the children will explore two habitats that are easily accessible so that they can study them in some depth, comparing them as they go along.

The range of measuring equipment used will depend on what is available in each school, but this is an excellent opportunity to use data-logging equipment and electronic sensors to measure temperature and light levels.

Photographs (conventional or digital) provide a good record and means of communicating ideas about the habitats as they can be presented in the book with appropriate captions. Constraints on resources may mean that some groups use equipment such as thermometers or devise scales of their own (see Main teaching activity).

INTRODUCTION

Return to the flip chart from Lesson 2 and ask: *What do we mean by the word 'habitat'?* (It is a place where an organism lives.) Explain that over the next few science lessons the children are going to find out as much as they can about two habitats in the school grounds.

MAIN TEACHING ACTIVITY

Ask: *What might we notice or measure about the different habitats?* You may need to provide some examples to stimulate ideas (such as how dark or light it is, how damp or dry, how warm or cold, how windy, how sheltered or open, how low or high above the ground).

Demonstrate how to use the measuring equipment and digital camera. This will vary according to the precise equipment being used. (See Unit 4, Lesson 2 for a specific lesson on learning to use a thermometer.) As equipment is likely to be limited, explain that the different groups will take turns. Where specific measuring equipment is not available, the children could devise a scale, for example 0 = complete shade, 5 = full sunshine, so that they are beginning to quantify their observations.

GROUP ACTIVITIES

1. Ask each group to choose two different habitats within the school grounds to study. Each group needs to gather information about their chosen two habitats. Photocopiable page 69 may be used to support this process. It is also a good idea to take some photographs of the habitats. Circulate, ensuring that the measuring equipment is fairly shared and helping the children to use it. It may be best to move around with any particularly vulnerable equipment if this is the children's first experience with it. Ask questions such as: *Do you think the temperature will be the same all day? What might cause changes in the amount of light? Do all parts of your habitat have the same amount of shelter? How might the amount of moisture affect what lives here?*
2. Each group can then decide how best to present the information in their book. This might include mounted pictures and photographs with captions, questions and answers in speech bubbles. So page 1 might begin: 'What is it like in the hedge?', or 'What is it like in the flower bed?' and continue with a description, photos and measurements. Page 2 might begin: 'What lives in a hedge?' or 'What lives in a flower bed?', which could be added to the book as a result of Lesson 4. Starting these may form the basis of, or be continued in, subsequent lessons.

DIFFERENTIATION

Expect more and less accurate use of the measuring equipment and more and less detailed descriptions. Using mixed-attainment groups will support children who are less secure in collecting the information.

ASSESSMENT

Can the children describe physical aspects of their chosen habitat? Can they make measurements of some of these aspects? How accurate are their measurements? Can they begin to make suggestions as to how the physical aspects of the habitat may have an impact on the organisms that live there?

PLENARY

Ask the groups to feed back to the class what they have found out about one of their habitats. Encourage them to think about how the physical conditions might affect living things by asking questions such as: *How might the wind affect the plants that grow there? What do you think the shelter does for the plants and animals that live there? What sorts of living things might be suited to living in your habitat? Why do you think that?* Ask the children to compare their two habitats: *Did one have more light than the other? Do you think this might affect the things that can grow there?*

OUTCOMES

● Can identify different physical aspects of habitats.
● Can make observations and measurements of the physical conditions of two chosen habitats.

LINKS

Maths: measurement.
PSHE: environmental awareness.
Literacy: recording information.

LESSON 4

OBJECTIVES

● To investigate the animals found in a particular habitat.
● To suggest reasons why animals are found in a certain habitat.
● To be able to choose appropriate equipment to collect an animal.
● To learn to collect animals carefully.

RESOURCES

Main teaching activity: A pooter, a paintbrush, a flip chart and marker pen.
Group activities: 1. Photocopiable page 70; pooters, paintbrushes, nets; collecting pots, preferably transparent with magnifying lids; magnifiers; white scrap paper to use as a background for close observation; books and keys for identifying 'minibeasts'; a range of drawing materials. **2.** Photocopiable page 71, writing materials including coloured pencils.

PREPARATION

Have the resources for the Main teaching activity to hand. Have the resources for the Group activities on hand for the children to collect when they are outside.

Vocabulary

ant, aphid, beetle, butterfly, caterpillar, fly, ladybird, magnifier, millipede, moth, pooter, slug, snail, spider, woodlice, woodlouse

BACKGROUND

It is important that during this activity the children have a proper regard for the animals they collect so that they do so sensitively and without damaging them. A paintbrush can be used to lift small creatures, and a pooter can be used to collect even smaller ones (see Unit 2, page 35). The children themselves should return the animals to where they found them.

Drawing helps to focus observation and should be done with good quality materials, such as a range of pencils. The photocopiable page will structure note-taking, but is not intended to provide the end product which will be the book the group is making.

INTRODUCTION

Ask the children to think about their two habitats and predict what different animals they might find there. This provides an opportunity to remind individuals that insects, birds, and so on are all animals. Ask: *Why do you think you will find (snails) there?* (There is food for them; they have somewhere to hide from birds; they have been seen there before.)

MAIN TEACHING ACTIVITY

Explain that if the children are going to investigate animals it is important that they think about how they will treat the animals. Ask: *Can you tell me some things we should do, and some things we shouldn't when we look at animals?* On the flip chart write a list of 'Dos' and 'Don'ts' (see opposite).

Demonstrate how to use a pooter and a paintbrush to pick up a small animal without

Do handle animals carefully so you don't damage them.

Do put them back where you found them.

Don't keep the animals too long.

Don't hurt them in any way.

touching it. Demonstrate how to sweep a net across, hold the neck close and shake the contents gently into a container.

Explain that first the children should observe the habitat and make notes about any animals they see there, and then each child can choose one animal to bring inside to observe carefully and draw.

GROUP ACTIVITIES

1. Give each child a copy of photocopiable page 70. Ask the children to make observations of their habitats and complete the list of animals they find before choosing an animal to collect and selecting suitable collecting equipment. The animals can be brought inside to draw carefully. Encourage the children to use the magnifying equipment for closer observation. When the animal cannot be easily recognised, direct children to the keys and books to identify them. Remember to return the animals to the places they were taken from.
2. Give the children a copy of photocopiable page 71 and ask them to illustrate the 'Dos' and 'Don'ts' with a picture of children collecting and handling animals carefully using the equipment demonstrated.

DIFFERENTIATION

Children who have difficulty recording in writing can make quick sketches of the animals instead of listing them in words.

Support children with poorer observation skills by asking questions such as: *How many legs has it got? Can you see any wings? Can you describe its head? How does it move?* Some children could be extended by using magnifiers to do detailed observational drawing of particular parts of the animal.

ASSESSMENT

Do the children show sensitivity in their treatment of the animals? Can they describe the animals found in their chosen habitat? Are their observational drawings reasonably accurate? Can they make suggestions about why the animals may live in that particular habitat?

PLENARY

Sit the children in a circle holding their drawings. Ask a few children to describe their animals. Ask: *Why do you think you found a (snail) there? Where else might you find (snails)? What might that habitat give them that they need to stay alive?*

Play 'Silly habitats' – take it in turns to suggest an animal and an unlikely habitat, for example: 'I know a fish that lives in a tree!' 'I know a lion that lives in a pond!' and so on.

OUTCOMES

- Can collect animals carefully without damaging them.
- Can investigate the animals found in a particular habitat.
- Can choose appropriate equipment to collect an animal.
- Can suggest reasons why animals are found in a certain habitat.

LINKS

Environmental issues: respect for other living things.
Art: observational drawing.

LESSON 5

OBJECTIVES

- To investigate the plants found in a certain habitat.
- To compare the numbers of different types of plant in the two habitats.
- To suggest reasons for differences in the plants that grow in different habitats.
- To devise their own record sheet.

RESOURCES

Main teaching activity: Two hoops of different sizes, a flip chart or whiteboard and marker pens.
Group activities: 1. Writing materials. **2.** One hoop per group, writing materials, clipboards, adhesive tape, reference books and keys on plants.

PREPARATION

Copy the sample record chart below on to the flip chart. Have the resources for the Main teaching activity to hand. Have the resources for the Group activities ready to be taken outside.

Vocabulary

compare, fair test, hoop

BACKGROUND

In this lesson, children will begin to gain an appreciation of the diversity of plant life, even in places that at first glance seem to be just grass. They can draw on prior knowledge to help them make predictions about the kinds of plants that grow in different places and may begin to link this with the previous lessons' findings about the temperature, darkness, and so on, of each habitat.

It is good to extend children's knowledge of the names of different plants, but this should not become too threatening for you, and different strategies are recommended below for dealing with unknown plants. It is not expected that they will gain a detailed knowledge of which plants are suited to different conditions, but more that they begin to develop an awareness that the nature of the habitat will affect what can live there.

	Under tree	In playing field
daisies	1	6
clover	0	2
moss	Lots	2 patches
dandelion	0	1

INTRODUCTION

Recap the work done in the previous lesson on the animals found in the different habitats around the school and explain that this lesson will focus on plants that live in their chosen habitats.

MAIN TEACHING ACTIVITY

Write the descriptions of two habitats on the board, for example 'Under a large tree', 'In the middle of the playing field'. Ask: *What plants might we expect to find under the tree or in the field? What differences might there be in the plants that grow in each place? Why do you think that?* (Fewer plants might grow under the tree because it is dark; fewer might grow in the field because it is mown and trampled on; daisies might grow in the field but not under the tree because they like the sun.)

Write a prediction on the board to model this process. Ask: *How could we find out if our predictions are right?* (We can look.) Explain that to help them concentrate on one patch in their habitat, the children could put a hoop down and look at the plants that are growing inside the hoop. Hold up the large hoop and say: *Imagine I have put this on the field and I have counted six daisy plants.* Now take the smaller hoop and say: *Imagine that I put this hoop under the tree and I counted one daisy plant.* (If children find this difficult to visualise, then draw it on the board.) Ask: *Is this a fair test?* (No, it is not a fair test.) Ask: *Why not?* (Because you would be looking at different-sized areas.) *What must we do to make it a fair test?* (Use same-sized hoops.)

Show the children the example of recording on the flip chart (see above), explaining how the chart is organised into rows and columns. Ask questions such as: *How many daises did we find under the tree? How many clover plants were found in the field? Did we find any moss growing under the tree?* Explain that they might want to use this way of recording, or they might want to find their own way.

GROUP ACTIVITIES

1. Before going outside, ask the children to write down what they predict they will find and if they expect to find any differences in the plants in the two different habitats they are going to study.

2. When outside, the children can begin investigating the plants in each habitat and recording their findings. If children do not know the name of a particular plant, they could either draw it, or take a small sample of it and attach it to their notes with sticky tape. It may be possible to identify them either by asking an adult or using reference books. If not, they could name the plant themselves.

Discuss questions that arise as the children are working such as: *Do you count the number or flowers, or try to work out if they all belong to one plant? How do you record the number of grass plants?* (You estimate.) Ask: *Did you choose where you put your hoop, or did you just drop it down? Which would be fairer?* (Dropping, so that there is no pre-selection of 'interesting bits'.)

DIFFERENTIATION

More mathematically able children could make a more accurate estimate of the number of grass plants in an area by counting the number in a small area and multiplying by the number of those small areas that would fit into the hoop. Challenge children by asking them to link the physical aspects they recorded with the plants that grow there.

ASSESSMENT

Can the children record the different plants that they find? Can they devise a table to record quantitatively? Can they make comparisons between the two habitats and suggest reasons for the differences?

PLENARY

Return to the classroom and ask the children to write at least a sentence comparing what they found in the two different habitats. You may want to provide a structure for this, for example: 'We found _____ in both habitats, but we only found _____ in the _____ .We think this is because _____'. Ask: *Did you find any plants you didn't recognise? What did you do?* Ask the children to compare the different habitats by asking: *Did you find different plants in each habitat? Can you suggest why that might be?*

OUTCOMES

- Can investigate the plants found in a certain habitat.
- Can compare the numbers of different types of plant in the two habitats.
- Can suggest reasons for differences in the plants that grow in different habitats.
- Can devise their own record sheet.

LINKS

Unit 2 Animals and plants: using keys to identify plants.

LESSON 6

Objectives	● To communicate findings about the habitats investigated. ● To begin to explore the relationships between the physical aspects and the plants and animals living in a habitat.
Resources	Writing materials; ready-made books into which items can be glued; coloured paper and card; glue, scissors, photographs from Lesson 2; example pages on presentation, such as photographs mounted and with a caption, and questions in speech bubbles.

Main activity	Ask the children to have their notes and records about their habitats with them. Recap the three previous lessons, noting the three aspects they gathered information on: physical aspects, plants and animals. Ask: *Do you think there are any connections between these three things?* Listen to the children's ideas, intervening with further questions when necessary (for example, 'I think the snails like it better in the long grass'. *Why do you think they prefer the long grass? Does it give protection? Does it provide food?*)
	    Ask each group to work collaboratively to make a book about the two habitats they studied. They can present it as they wish, but they need to cover the three different parts of their investigation. Provide some examples of how they might set out their work.
	    As the children work, help them to make connections by asking questions such as: *Why do you think the woodlice live there, but not there? What kinds of places do you think dandelions grow best in?*

Differentiation	Some children will need extra support with the writing, for example scribing, extra adult support, use of a computer for redrafting. Some groups will need support to work collaboratively.
Assessment	Have the children communicated their findings clearly and presented them well? Are they making connections between the physical conditions, plants and animals in a habitat?
Plenary	The books can be shared with each other, each group showing one of their pages. The books could be taken to another class and the children could share their books and new expertise with younger children.
Outcomes	● Can communicate findings. ● Can make suggestions about the relationships between the physical aspects and the plants and animals living in a habitat.

LESSON 7

OBJECTIVES

● To know how to investigate the behaviour of an animal species.
● To understand the need for repeated tests.
● To pose their own questions for investigation.

RESOURCES

Main teaching activity: A transparent container with one end containing dry sand and one end containing wet sand; a separate container of woodlice.
Group activities: 1. Containers such as ice-cream tubs; card and sticky tape; water, soil or sand; a range of foodstuffs, for example apple or lettuce; a range of 'smells', for example peppermint, vanilla essence, lavender oil (diluted with water, as undiluted essential oils could damage children's skin), antiseptic liquid (for example Dettol diluted with water); cotton buds. **2.** Writing materials.

PREPARATION

Have the resources for the Group activities prepared, but keep them to one side where the children can collect them. Have the resources for the Main teaching activity to hand.

Vocabulary

behaviour, choice, prefer, respond

BACKGROUND

Investigating living things has particular issues associated with it. For ethical reasons, the tests that can be done on animals must not involve cruelty and should keep disturbance to the animal to a minimum. The tests suggested here can be carried out quickly and the animals returned to their natural environment at the end of the lesson.

INTRODUCTION

Revise the code of conduct for how to collect and treat animals, reminding the children that they should be treated with respect.

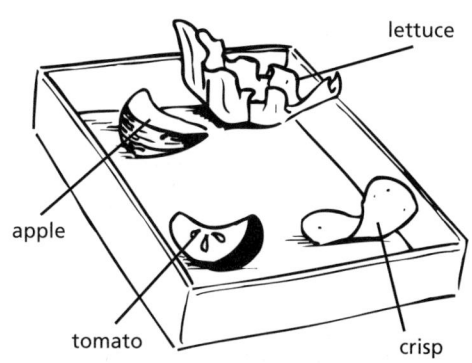

lettuce

apple

tomato

crisp

Dark/light choice

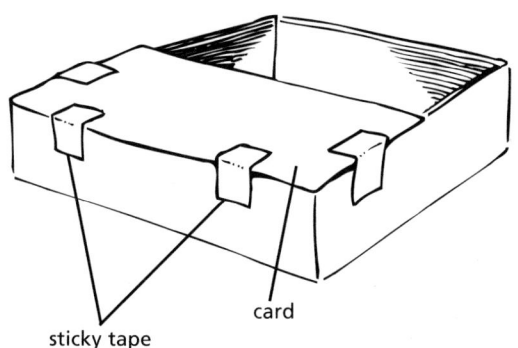

sticky tape

card

MAIN TEACHING ACTIVITY

Show the children the container with wet and dry sand. Explain that the question you are investigating is: 'Do woodlice prefer wet or dry conditions?' Write this question on the board or flip chart. Put one woodlouse into the container and ask the children to observe it. Ask: *What do you notice about it?*

When the woodlouse has made some movement, perhaps to the dry sand, ask: *Can we say that woodlice prefer dry conditions from this test?* (No, it may be chance that the woodlouse went to one end; other woodlice may behave differently.) Ask: *How could we improve this test so that we can be more sure of our results?* (Try it with more woodlice and observe over a longer period of time to see if they stay in one area in preference to the other.) Put the rest of the woodlice in the container and set it to one side.

Explain that the children will be able to carry out their own tests of this kind on animals that they collect. Give the children some examples of other preference tests they could try, such as the sorts of food or whether dark or light is preferred. Suggest that they might like to try out some of their ideas about their chosen habitats. For example, if they think there are snails there because they like the grass, they could try putting grass and some other sorts of leaves in and see which the snails prefer. Alternatively, they could investigate whether different animals respond to smells by holding scented cotton buds near to the animals and noting their response.

GROUP ACTIVITIES

1. Small groups collect animals and bring them back to the classroom. The groups set up and carry out their tests. Ask the children to record their results as follows:
Our question:
Drawing of our test:
What we found out:

2. Ask the children to choose an animal to write about 'A Day in the Life of...' from the animal's point of view, for example, 'Hello, My name is Sammy Snail. When I woke up this morning I felt hungry, so I set off to find a leaf to munch. On the way...'

DIFFERENTIATION

Support children who are having difficulty in framing questions by providing examples for them to adapt to their own interests.

Encourage more mathematically able children to quantify their results, for example '5 out of 8 woodlice chose the dark side, which is more than half'.

ASSESSMENT

Can the children carry out an investigation into animal behaviour? Can they give a reason for repeating the test or having more than one animal? Have they put the focus for their investigation in the form of a question?

PLENARY

Ask each group what their question was, then ask: *What was the answer to your question?* Some groups may not have reached a definite answer, and may need reassurance that this is a normal part of the process of science.

OUTCOMES

- Can investigate the behaviour of an animal species.
- Can explain the need for repeated tests.
- Can put ideas for an investigation in the form of a question.

LINKS

PSHE: ethics of using animals in scientific tests.

LESSON 8

Objectives	• To know how to investigate the behaviour of birds. • To make observations for a sustained period of time.
Resources	An area where birds can be observed, such as a local park; clipboards and writing materials; an identification guide to common birds (optional); prepared observation sheets (one for each child and some spares, plus an enlarged copy to use in the Main teaching activity).
Main activity	Review the ways used to explore the behaviour of small animals. Ask: *Could we use the same approach to finding out about birds?* (No, it would be cruel and impractical: it is better to observe birds in their natural environment.) Ask: *How could we find out about bird behaviour?* (Observe and make notes.) Explain that one way of being more focused is to decide in advance what the bird might be doing and have a list to tick as we watch. Show the children the enlarged recording sheet and explain how it is to be used. Explain the meaning of terms such as 'preening'. The blank spaces are for the children's own ideas. Discuss the need to be very quiet and still and to have good concentration. Children go outside and observe a bird for up to 10 minutes. If the bird flies away another sheet can be started. Name of bird: <table><tr><td>Behaviour</td><td>How often</td></tr><tr><td>feeding</td><td></td></tr><tr><td>preening</td><td></td></tr><tr><td>singing</td><td></td></tr><tr><td>flying</td><td></td></tr><tr><td></td><td></td></tr><tr><td></td><td></td></tr></table> There are some spaces for your own ideas.
Differentiation	Some children could be shown how to use tally marks instead of ticks on the record sheet. Children with poor concentration will benefit from sitting near the teacher and observing alongside.
Assessment	Are the children able to make sustained observations? Is their own behaviour conducive to making observations? Can they explain why they have taken this approach to investigating bird behaviour?
Plenary	The children can feed back to the class the most common behaviours they observed. Discuss what they have seen.
Outcomes	• Can explain how to investigate the behaviour of birds. • Can make observations for a sustained period of time.

LESSON 9

OBJECTIVES
● To know that animals eat certain foods in a habitat.
● To use secondary sources to find information.
● To become familiar with a wider range of animals.

RESOURCES
Main teaching activity: An A5-sized ring binder, 'factfile' headings written on a flip chart.
Group activities: 1. A range of books and resources about animals in local habitats (for example, *Investigating Minibeasts* cards, available from Technology Teaching Systems (see page 10); relevant CD-ROMs; 'factfile' pages made from photocopiable page 72, writing materials.
2. Photocopiable page 73, writing materials.

PREPARATION
Make the 'factfile' pages by copying photocopiable page 72 onto card, cutting in half and hole-punching. Put some of the cards into the ring binder and put the rest on the tables for the Group activities. Write the headings of the factfile cards onto the board or flip chart for the Main teaching activity. The following are possible lists of animals:
● dragonfly, frog, minnow, newt, otter, pike
● grasshopper, ladybird, slug, snail, spider, woodlouse
● adder, hare, kestrel, slow-worm, squirrel, weasel
● bat, fieldmouse, grass snake, shrew, toad, vole
● blackbird, blue-tit, cuckoo, robin, sparrow, thrush
● badger, fox, hedgehog, mole, owl, rabbit.
These lists need to be checked against available resources, and written on cards for each table. Put the relevant secondary sources on the table with the appropriate list. Identify any texts particularly suitable for more or less able readers and put them near the children they will be best matched to.

Vocabulary

See lists of animals in Preparation section.

BACKGROUND
It is important that the use of secondary sources is focused so that children process information rather than merely repeat it. The lesson described here could be integrated into a Literacy Hour (in England and Wales) if the learning objectives are appropriate, or attention could be drawn to skills learned in the Literacy Hour that could be applied in the science lesson. Preparation in matching secondary sources to the children's reading level will be required, but this will ensure that children do not become frustrated during the lesson and that they have a positive experience of using information texts.
    Children are often very enthusiastic about miniature factfiles, and this activity gives them the chance to make their own.

INTRODUCTION
Show the children the folder for the factfile and explain that they are each going to make a page on a particular animal. If any children have factfiles of their own, they could show them to the class.

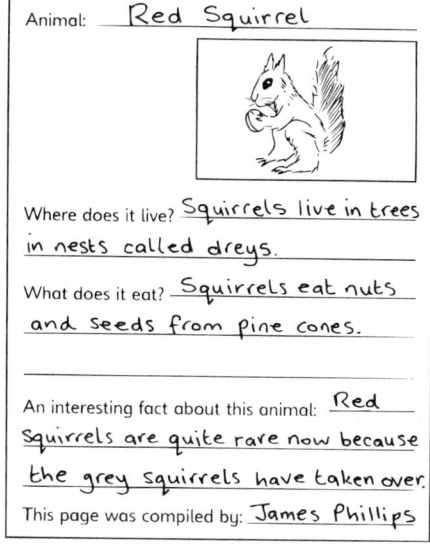

Animal: Red Squirrel

Where does it live? Squirrels live in trees in nests called dreys.

What does it eat? Squirrels eat nuts and seeds from pine cones.

An interesting fact about this animal: Red Squirrels are quite rare now because the grey squirrels have taken over.

This page was compiled by: James Phillips

MAIN TEACHING ACTIVITY
Look at the layout of the factfile card. Explain that the children will first need to find out information using the secondary sources and making notes, then they will carefully write the information onto the factfile card. If appropriate, revise skimming and scanning a text for information and the use of contents and index pages with one example such as the rabbit.
    Explain that each table will have a selection of animals to choose from to make sure that the same animal isn't researched twice.

GROUP ACTIVITIES
1. Ask the children to make notes on scrap paper as they find the answers to the questions and any interesting facts. Encourage skimming to identify the food and habitat, and then more careful reading for interesting information.

Once the information has been gathered it can be written onto the factfile (in sentences) and lastly, a picture of the animal can be drawn in the box.

2. The wordsearch on photocopiable page 73 may be useful as an independent activity, releasing you to support particular groups in their research. The solution is shown below.

DIFFERENTIATION

The lists have been ordered from more difficult to easier on the basis of familiarity. However, the main means of differentiation is the matching of the level of text difficulty with the reading level of the children in each group. For children with poor reading skills, identify a particular text and animal that they have responsibility for researching. Children with more advanced reading skills could gather information from several sources and draw it together and compare it.

Some children may research more than one animal; others could be invited to make an index or design a cover for the file.

ASSESSMENT

Can the children use the secondary sources to locate information about their animal? Can they describe the eating habits of their chosen animal?

E	A	R	W	I	G	W	Y	L	F	R
G	R	A	S	S	H	O	P	P	E	R
S	Y	F	O	X	Q	R	H	T	O	M
Q	M	O	L	E	S	M	N	R	E	B
U	B	E	E	X	H	A	A	E	S	E
I	W	L	W	O	R	P	A	D	U	E
R	B	A	D	G	E	R	N	I	O	T
R	P	L	H	A	W	K	T	P	M	L
E	W	O	O	D	L	O	U	S	E	E
L	B	U	G	Z	L	I	A	N	S	X

PLENARY

Ask each child to briefly report back to the class what they have discovered about where their chosen animal lives and what it eats. Put their card into the factfile as they report. The factfile can be made available for individual reading and may be drawn upon in subsequent lessons.

OUTCOMES
● Can use secondary sources to find specific information.
● Can describe the eating habits of some animals found in the UK.

LINKS

English: non-fiction texts, information finding (*100 Literacy Hours: Year 4*, Scholastic, ISBN: 0-590-53916-7, has an activity teaching children to make notes from a text on spiders).

LESSON 10

Objectives	● To know that animals in certain world habitats eat certain foods. ● To use secondary sources to answer questions.
Resources	A range of secondary sources: books, CD-ROMs and so on; writing materials.

Main activity	Explain that in this lesson the children will be learning about animals anywhere in the world.
	    Draw three columns on the flip chart and put the headings: 'What I already know'; 'My question'; 'What I have found out' on each column. Model the process by choosing an animal, for example the tiger, and asking the class: *What do you already know about tigers?* Write their response in the first column. Next ask: *What would you like to find out about tigers? What questions about tigers have you got?* Write these in the second column. Include 'What do tigers eat?' Model skimming and scanning to try to answer the questions. Explain that the children may not be able to answer all the questions, but should find the answers to those they can.
	    Ask the children to work in pairs or threes to list what they already know and raise questions. Ask the children to include 'What do they eat?', even if they think they already know. Each group researches their animal and records what they have found in the last column of the grid. This could be carried out as a group activity in a Literacy Hour to reduce the demand on resources.

Differentiation	Work in groups where at least one child has good writing skills and can act as scribe for the group. Target texts for lower- and higher-attaining readers appropriately. Expect some groups to answer only one or two questions at a basic level and others to have a range of detailed answers.
Assessment	Can the children give examples of foods eaten by animals from around the world? Can they use secondary sources to try to answer their questions?
Plenary	Ask the groups to feed back what they have found out about what the animals eat. Ask: *Why do you think different animals eat different food?*
Outcomes	● Can explain that animals in certain world habitats eat certain foods. ● Can use secondary sources to research the answers to questions.

LESSON 11

OBJECTIVES
● To understand what is meant by a food chain.
● To know what the terms 'producer' and 'consumer' mean.

RESOURCES
Main teaching activity: A loaf of sliced bread; samples or pictures of flour, wheat and corn; flip chart and marker pens.
Group activities: 1. Writing materials, sets of cards made from photocopiable page 74.
2. Musical instruments (optional).
Plenary: Card labels saying 'Consumers' and 'Producers'; Blu-Tack.

PREPARATION
Copy photocopiable page 74 onto card and cut up as a set for each group. (Using different coloured card helps to stop the sets getting mixed up. They could be laminated for future use.) Cut the slices of bread into quarters.

Vocabulary

consumer, food chain, producer

BACKGROUND
As the children have not yet been introduced to the idea that plants make their own food, they may find that there are some difficult concepts in this lesson. The idea that plants make their own food is introduced, but this does not require a discussion of photosynthesis. These ideas will be further developed in Year 6/Primary 7. Focus instead on the idea of the green plants being the first living thing in every food chain – they don't 'eat' anything. The idea is introduced that plants get their energy from the Sun, relating this to previous work on plant growth when the children became aware of a plant's need for light. The term 'food chain' is introduced and also the terms 'producer' and 'consumer'. All green plants are producers, because they make their own food by photosynthesis. Other living things get their energy by eating other living things, so they are called consumers.

This lesson draws together a great deal of prior knowledge and children will vary in their understanding about what different foods are made from and how they are produced. Discussing experiences of cooking can help them relate the ingredients to the end product.

INTRODUCTION
Give each child a piece of bread to eat. As they eat it ask them to think about where their food comes from. (Be aware of and sensitive to children who are vegetarian or with specific dietary needs, such as coeliacs needing gluten-free bread.)

MAIN TEACHING ACTIVITY
Ask: *Where do we (humans) get our energy from?* (We get energy from our food.) *What different things do we eat?* List children's suggestions on the flip chart. Take one of the suggestions and trace it backwards along its food chain until you reach a green plant. Record this on the board as you go along. (Do not show arrows at this stage as this may cause confusion when proper food chains are constructed.) To help children understand the processes in food production show them samples of flour, wheat and corn as these are mentioned.

Ask: *What does a chicken eat to get its energy?* (It eats corn or wheat.) *Does the wheat eat anything to get energy?* (No, wheat gets its energy from the Sun and makes its own food.) Ask: *What is cheese made from?* (Cheese is made from milk.) *Where does the milk come from?* (Milk comes from a cow, or a sheep or a goat.) *What does the cow eat to get its energy?* (A cow eats grass.) *Does the grass eat anything to get its energy?* (No, grass gets its energy from the Sun and makes its own food.) Repeat this for various different foods.

Go down the list and ask: *What is at the beginning of this chain?* Draw a circle around each of the producers. Ask: *What have these got in common?* (They are all plants.) Explain that following the food as it goes from plants into animals and then into other animals is called a 'food chain'. Draw a food chain on the board in the form: corn → chicken → human. Ask: *Which direction are the arrows going in?* Explain that they always go that way because they are showing the journey of the energy in the food.

GROUP ACTIVITIES

1. Give the children the information cards (photocopiable page 74) and ask them to draw their own food chains using that information.

2. Ask groups to represent one of the food chains through drama. They could mime the different plants and animals or play a musical instrument for each organism, adding a new instrument as something eats it. The resulting compositon will show how there is a part of each living thing within its consumer.

DIFFERENTIATION

Some children's enquiries can be extended by asking them to construct their own food chains for animals that they have researched. The class factfile will also be a useful source of information.

ASSESSMENT

Can the children construct a simple food chain, using the arrows correctly? Can they give examples of producers and consumers?

PLENARY

Go through each card, showing on the flip chart the correct way to write the food chain. Write them one above the other. Ask children to add any that they have found from their own research.

Explain that the green plants are all known as producers because they produce their own food. Blu-Tack the card with the word 'producers' on it above the list of green plants. Explain that the animals are all called consumers because they eat (or consume) the green plants. Blu-Tack the card with 'consumers' written on it above the list of animals.

OUTCOMES

● Can make a food chain with one link.
● Can give examples of a producer and a consumer.

LINKS

PSHE: choices about eating.

LESSON 12

Objectives	● To be able to construct food chains with two links.
	● To understand the terms 'predator' and 'prey'.
Resources	Writing materials; a set of a pair of cards for each group: 1. *Foxes eat rabbits, Rabbits eat grass*; 2. *Common bats eat flies, Flies eat dead plants*; 3. *Hedgehogs eat slugs, Slugs eat plants*; 4. *Otters eat fish, Fish eat pond weed*; 5. *Badgers eat mice, Mice eat seeds*; 6. *Grass snakes eat frogs, Frogs eat flies.*
Main activity	Recap the previous lesson by looking at the flip chart from the Plenary of Lesson 11 and asking the children to give examples of a producer and a consumer. Explain that in this lesson you will be learning about more complicated food chains. Put the following example of a food chain on the board or flip chart: corn ➡ vole ➡ owl. Ask: *Which is the producer?* (The corn is the producer.) *Which are the consumers?* Explain that there are now two sets of consumers. Introduce the terms 'prey' and 'predator'. Ask the children to write food chains using the six sets of cards as sources of information. Ask them to identify the prey and predator in each case and write 'predator' or 'prey' in brackets near the right animal. Remind them that the predator eats the prey, and to use arrows to show where the food is going.
Differentiation	Some children's enquiries may be extended by researching their own food chains from a range of secondary sources of information.
Assessment	Can the children construct the food chains accurately from the information given? Can they correctly identify prey and predators?
Plenary	Go through the examples of food chains on the cards, asking the children to identify the prey and predators in each case. Card 6 may give rise to interesting discussion as the frog is both prey and predator.
Outcomes	● Can construct food chains with two links.
	● Can explain the terms 'predator' and 'prey'.

LESSON 13

OBJECTIVES

● To understand the terms 'carnivore' and 'herbivore'.
● To understand that food chains are part of more complex food webs.

RESOURCES

Main teaching activity: Flip chart or board and marker pens.
Group activity: Sets of cards from photocopiable page 75; sugar paper, pencils, glue, felt-tipped pens.

PREPARATION

Copy photocopiable page 75 onto card and cut out the cards. Each group needs a set. (It helps prevent sets being muddled if each is copied onto different-coloured card. The sets could be laminated for future use.)

Vocabulary

carnivore, food web, herbivore, omnivore

BACKGROUND

Food chains can be very complex, as many animals have more than one common source of food. In any habitat there will be complex food webs, rather than simple chains that show the feeding relationships between all the living things in a habitat. This lesson provides an important basis for understanding how all the elements of a habitat are inter-related so that later they will consider how changing one element will have an impact on all the others. The terms 'carnivore' (eats meat only), 'herbivore' (eats only plants) and 'omnivore' (eats a mixed diet) are introduced.

This lesson depends on the children's experiences in the Group activity, so the Main teaching activity is short but the Plenary is long.

INTRODUCTION

Ask: *What do we mean by a food chain? Can anyone give us any examples of a food chain?* Ask a number of children to respond to get a good variety of living things mentioned.

MAIN TEACHING ACTIVITY

Ask: *Are some animals eaten by more than one predator? What different living things eat slugs?* (Birds, foxes, hedgehogs, badgers and so on eat slugs.) *What different living things eat grass?* (Deer, rabbits, cows, sheep, and so on eat grass.) Explain that although food chains are a useful idea, the real picture is more complicated. Introduce the term 'food web' to describe the complicated links between the different feeding relationships. Explain that the task the children are going to do may seem frustrating at times, but this will help them to understand what is going on in a habitat and they should persevere.

GROUP ACTIVITY

As a collaborative Group activity, using the cards provided on photocopiable page 75, ask each group to work out the food web provided and represent it by showing arrows to link the food with what eats it. This is best done by spreading the cards out on sugar paper and drawing the links in pencil first, only gluing down the cards and marking the arrows in pen when the children are satisfied of the correct links. Suggest that all the cards that do not 'eat' anything are lined up across the bottom of the sugar paper.

DIFFERENTIATION

Have the children working in mixed-attainment groups so that they can support each other.

ASSESSMENT

Can the children give examples where a living thing provides food for more than one consumer? Can they find examples of carnivores, herbivores and omnivores?

PLENARY

Ask the groups to show their sheets of sugar paper. Reassure them that there is more than one correct way of setting it out. Ask: *What made that activity difficult to do?* (It is complicated.) Using the groups' photocopiable pages, ask the children to pick out food chains within the web, for example berries are eaten by mice which are eaten by snakes which are eaten by badgers.

Explain that some animals eat only plants – they are called herbivores; some animals eat only meat – they are called carnivores; and some animals eat a mixture of both – they are called omnivores. Write these terms on a board or flip chart.

Ask the children if they can pick out examples of each type using their food webs (for example, the fox and the grass snake are carnivores; the vole and the rabbit are herbivores; and the badger is an omnivore). *Can you think of any other examples from your general experience?* (For example, lions are carnivores; cows are herbivores.) Ask: *What are humans?* (Humans are omnivores.)

OUTCOMES

● Can explain the terms 'carnivore' and 'herbivore'.
● Understand that food chains are part of more complex food webs.

LINKS

Environmental issues: awareness of the dependence of animals on plants (see page 115 of *100 Literacy Hours: Year 4* (Scholastic, ISBN 0-590-53916-7), for 'Old Praise Song of the Crocodile').

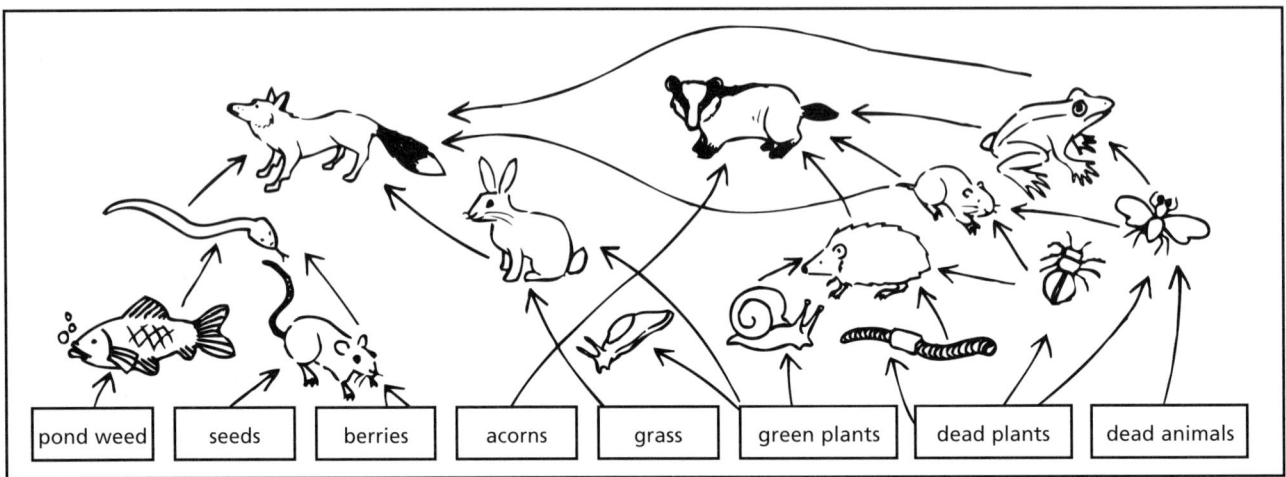

| pond weed | seeds | berries | acorns | grass | green plants | dead plants | dead animals |

LESSON 14

Objective	● To know that camouflage helps some animals to survive.
Resources	A copy of 'How the Leopard Got His Spots' by Rudyard Kipling; photographs of animals in their natural habitats, drawing and painting materials, card, lolly sticks.
Main activity	Read 'How the Leopard Got His Spots' and discuss the way the animals changed their skin to blend into the background. (You may need to emphasise that this is only a story and not a real account of either leopards or Ethiopians.) Introduce the term 'camouflage'. Ask: *Have you heard this word before?* Some children may have encountered it in a military context or in camouflage prints for fashion clothes. Explain how camouflage on tanks and soldiers' clothes does the same job as camouflage of animals. Relate it to the work on food chains by explaining that it helps prey hide from predators. Ask: *Can you think of any examples of camouflage from your own work on habitats?* (Grasshoppers are green; snails have striped shells.) Some animals use bright colours instead to suggest to possible predators that they are poisonous. Look at some photographs of animals in their natural habitats, such as lions on dry savannah or a crocodile floating in a river, and discuss how they are camouflaged. Ask children to work in groups to paint different habitat backgrounds. This could be related to the local habitats they studied and the photographs used as a basis for the paintings. On separate pieces of card, the children can then draw or paint different animals, mount them on lolly sticks and test them by holding them against the different backgrounds.
Differentiation	If the term 'camouflage' seems new to children, target them with questions about the photographs such as: *Can you describe in what way this animal is suited to its habitat? How will its colouring make it harder for predators to catch it?*
Assessment	Can the children explain how the colouring of animals helps to protect them from predators? Can they give examples of how animals are camouflaged?
Plenary	The children can show each other their paintings and how the animals look against the different backgrounds. The paintings could be made into an interactive display in which children can try holding the animals against different backgrounds.
Outcome	● Can explain how camouflage helps some animals to survive.

LESSON 15

OBJECTIVES

- To know that human activities can affect habitats.
- To communicate ideas effectively.

RESOURCES

Main teaching activity: An enlarged copy of photocopiable page 76; a flip chart or board and marker pens.
Group activities: 1. The habitat books made in earlier lessons in the unit; sugar paper and felt-tipped pens; writing materials. **2.** Writing materials.

PREPARATION

Enlarge photocopiable page 76 so that the whole class can read it.

Vocabulary

affect, effect, habitat, protect

BACKGROUND

This lesson asks children to consider the effects that humans may have on the environment. It brings together the work on individual habitats and ideas about food chains as children imagine the impact of changes on the different living things in a habitat. Children sometimes find it hard to grasp why animals can't just 'move somewhere else' or 'eat something different' when their habitats are destroyed or damaged. This can be addressed by helping them think about where the animals would move to – and the impact on the living things already there.

This lesson would be best linked with work in English on persuasive writing and/or letter writing, as this lesson focuses on the scientific content rather than on how to structure a letter and present a point of view.

INTRODUCTION

Ask the children to think about the two habitats they studied earlier in this unit. It would be appropriate for each group to spend five minutes looking at the book they have made.

MAIN TEACHING ACTIVITY

Ask: *What things might humans do that could change a habitat?* (They might trample on it; cut long grass short; cut down a tree; dig up bushes; spray it with weedkiller; put down slug pellets.) Make a list of the ideas the children have on the board or flip chart and introduce some more suggestions if necessary.

Explain that the children are going to think about one example together, then each group will think about their own habitats. Give the example of putting paving slabs down on an area of the school field that has long grass. Ask: *What living things might that affect?* Help the children to apply their understanding of food chains, for example: *So you are saying that there won't be anywhere for the snails to live. What animals eat snails?* (Thrushes and other birds eat snails.) *So what effect will the paving have on the thrushes?* (They will have less food, so will have to go elsewhere and some may not survive.) (The plight of the thrush is developed in *100 Science Lessons: Year 5/Primary 6,* and touched on again in *Year 6/Primary 7*.) Together, read the copy of photocopiable page 76.

GROUP ACTIVITIES

1. Ask each group to decide on a change that humans could make to one of their habitats and to collaboratively brainstorm the effects it might have on the habitat. These ideas can be recorded on sugar paper. Then, individually, each child can write a letter of protest to the relevant people, explaining the impact the change might have on their habitat.

2. The children could imagine the headteacher's response to the letter on photocopiable page 76 and write back to Kate Lucas 'in role'. This may help the children's understanding of conflicting points of view.

DIFFERENTIATION

Some support for the initial ideas about damage to the habitat will come from working as a group, but you may need to spend more time discussing the possibilities with some groups than others. Some children may need support with the writing – a writing frame for the letter could be provided for them, or they could work with another child or adult assistant.

ASSESSMENT

Can the children make suggestions about the impact of the imagined damage to the habitat? Can they give examples of living things that would suffer? Are they able to communicate these ideas in the form of a letter?

PLENARY

Ask some of the children from each group to read their letters to the rest of the class. Ask: *What things can humans do to help protect habitats?* (Leave corners of lawn unmown to grow wild; protect areas of the countryside; set up areas in towns for wildlife.)

OUTCOMES

● Can give examples of how human activities can affect habitats.
● Can communicate ideas effectively in the form of a letter.

LINKS

Literacy: letter-writing, persuasive writing.

LESSON 16

Objectives	● To know that seasonal changes influence animals and plants in a habitat. ● To know that nature changes habitats. ● To understand some of our seasonal responses to help wildlife.	
Resources	A camera, photographs of the same habitat at different times of the year.	
Main activity	The best way to meet this learning objective is to visit the same area, such as a school conservation area or a park, at different times during the school year, observing and taking photographs. If this is not possible, then a collection of photographs of the same place at different times of the year can be used to promote discussion. 　Ask: *What has changed about the habitat?* (Leaves are falling; there is new growth, and so on.) *How might the temperature/sunlight affect the plants? How might it affect the animals? What might happen if there isn't much rain? When is there a lot of food for animals? At what times of year is there very little food?* 　Introduce the idea of some animals gathering food for the winter, for example squirrels, and some hibernating, for example hedgehogs. Ask: *How can we help birds survive when it is winter and there isn't much food for them?* 　Ask the children to write an imaginary diary page for an animal at a certain time of year. Try to get a range of different animals and times of year across the class.	
Differentiation	Some children could write collaboratively to support their ideas for writing and/or their writing skills.	
Assessment	Can the children describe seasonal changes? Can they give examples of how seasonal changes may influence plants and animals? Can they suggest how humans can help protect living things?	
Plenary	Ask some children to read examples of their diary entries to the rest of the class. Discuss how there are natural challenges to the lives of plants and animals as well as the effect of humans on the environment.	
Outcomes	● Can give examples of how habitats change during the seasons. ● Can describe how seasonal changes influence animals and plants in a habitat. ● Can give examples of how humans and the seasons can affect living things.	

LESSON 17

OBJECTIVES
- To assess children's understanding of the main groups of living things.
- To assess children's understanding of food chains.
- To assess children's understanding of habitats and how to study them.
- To assess children's ability to interpret data in the form of tables.

RESOURCES

Assessment activities: 1. A copy of photocopiable page 77 for each child, writing materials. **2.** Photocopiable page 78 for each child, writing materials.

INTRODUCTION

These Assessment activities should be considered alongside the ongoing assessment opportunities indicated throughout the unit when making a judgement about which level the child is working at. If you are unsure what a child means by their response to a question, then discuss it with them afterwards.

ASSESSMENT ACTIVITY 1

Give each child a copy of photocopiable page 77 to work through individually.

Answers
1a. snails
1b. 0
1c. ladybirds
1d. 5
1e. 3
1f. accept sensible suggestions, for example: shelter; more food; less trampled.
1g. accept sensible suggestions, for example: protection from birds; food plants grow there.
2. Possible rules for collecting animals could be: don't hurt the animals; put them back; don't keep them long; handle them carefully.

Looking for levels
The majority of children would be expected to get questions 1a to 1e correct, achieving Level 3/Scottish Level C. The last two questions require a greater level of understanding of habitats and indicate children working at Level 4/Scottish Level C/D. Poor performance in question 1 may indicate that further work on interpretation of data is required.

Most children will be able to suggest rules that show a respect for living things. Some may take this further and relate it to food chains or wider environmental issues.

ASSESSMENT ACTIVITY 2

Work with a group of children at a time using photocopiable page 78. Ask them to work through the first question individually, then in groups give them a moment to look at the food web on their copy of the photocopiable sheet. Ask the following questions and note children's responses. If you need to explain the terms such as 'predator', then do so, noting when the concept is secure, but the relevant vocabulary is not yet being used. Repeat the questions with different examples to give more children the opportunity to answer. Target questions at individuals rather than allowing more confident children to dominate.

Ask: *What sort of diagram have you got in front of you? What is it?* (It is a food web/chain.)
What does the _____ *eat?* (Do several examples to include all children.)
What is the prey of the _____ *?*
Name a predator of _____.
Can you tell me one producer?
Can you tell me the name of a consumer?
A 'carnivore' is an animal that eats only meat. Can you give me an example of a carnivore?
(Repeat for herbivore.)

Answers

1. oak tree: plant
   owl: animal
   mushroom: fungus
   ant: animal
   human: animal
   dandelion: plant
   fox: animal
   woodlouse: animal
   toadstool: fungus
   moss: plant
   grass: plant

Looking for levels

Children working at Level 3/Scottish Level C will get about two-thirds of the answers to question 1 on photocopiable page 78 correct, but may be confused in some particular examples. If all the answers are correct, it suggests that the children are working at Level 4/Scottish Level D.

For the questions about the food web, if the children can describe the feeding relationships and recognise that food moves up a chain from the green plants, but are not using the terms confidently, this indicates Level 3/Scottish Level C If they are using the correct terminology with understanding, this indicates achievement at Level 4/Scottish Level C/D. Less able children may recognise that animals need to eat, but find it hard to understand links in the food chain that are not direct, such as the relationship between the fox and grass.

PLENARY

Go through the test with the children, explaining the correct answers. Ask the class as a whole to give some examples of food chains and predator–prey relationships.

Ask the children to reflect on what they have learned during this topic. Have they changed their ideas? Ask: *What did we do that helped you to learn more?* (Observation, surveys, tests, discussion, asking questions and using secondary sources to answer.) Explain that scientists are always learning and that this sometimes means they are changing their ideas too.

Name

Habitat investigators 1

Collect information about your chosen habitats.

	Habitat 1	Habitat 2
Description (for example, recently mown grass on a playing field)		
Amount of light (for example, whether it is shaded or in the sun)		
Temperature (for example, how warm or cold it is)		
Moisture (for example, how damp or dry it is)		
Shelter (for example, whether it is in the wind or sheltered)		

The last three rows are left blank for your own ideas.

Name

Habitat investigators 2

Investigate some animals in your chosen habitats.

	Habitat 1	Habitat 2
List of all the animals I found there		
Animal I have chosen to collect		
Where exactly the animal was found (for example, on the stem of the bush in the hedge)		
Notes about the animal		
Drawing of the animal		

Collecting animals

Illustrate these rules with pictures showing how to collect animals carefully.

Do handle animals carefully so you don't damage them.

Do put them back where you found them.

Don't keep the animals too long.

Don't hurt them in any way.

Factfile

Animal: _____

Where does it live? _____

What does it eat? _____

An interesting fact about this animal: _____

This page was compiled by: _____

Animal: _____

Where does it live? _____

What does it eat? _____

An interesting fact about this animal: _____

This page was compiled by: _____

Name

Animal wordsearch

Find the names of these animals in the grid.

ant	earwig	mole	snail
badger	fly	moth	spider
bee	fox	mouse	squirrel
beetle	grasshopper	owl	woodlouse
bug	hawk	shrew	worm

E	A	R	W	I	G	W	Y	L	F	R
G	R	A	S	S	H	O	P	P	E	R
S	Y	F	O	X	Q	R	H	T	O	M
Q	M	O	L	E	S	M	N	R	E	B
U	B	E	E	X	H	A	A	E	S	E
I	W	L	W	O	R	P	A	D	U	E
R	B	A	D	G	E	R	N	I	O	T
R	P	L	H	A	W	K	T	P	M	L
E	W	O	O	D	L	O	U	S	E	E
L	B	U	G	Z	L	I	A	N	S	X

Name

Food chains

Make a food chain with one arrow for each of these animals. The first one has been done for you.

Rabbits eat grass.

Rabbits ◄——— grass.

Bullfinches eat berries.

_____

Deer eat shoots from trees.

Red squirrels eat hazelnuts.

_____

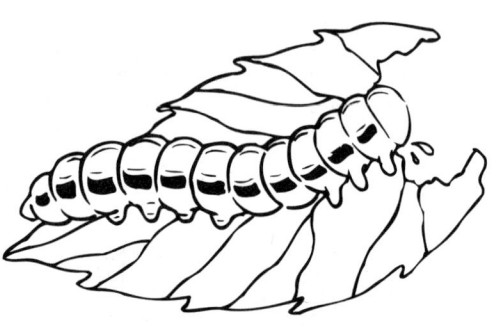

Caterpillars eat leaves.

Voles eat corn.

_____

Fish eat pond weed.

_____

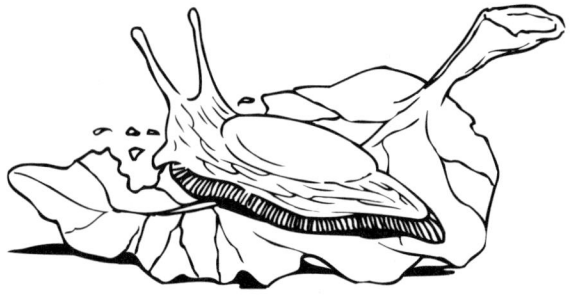

Slugs eat green plants.

_____

Name

Food web

I am a fox.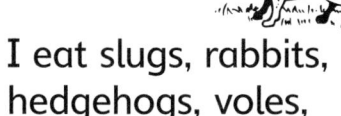

I eat slugs, rabbits, hedgehogs, voles, frogs and snakes.

I am a grass snake.

I eat fish and mice.

Green plants

I am a badger.

I eat voles, frogs, hedgehogs, snakes and acorns.

I am a snail.

I eat green plants.

Dead plants

I am a slug.

I eat green plants.

I am a beetle.

I eat dead plants.

Dead animals

I am a rabbit.

I eat grass and other green plants.

I am an earthworm.

I eat dead plants.

Grass

I am a hedgehog.

I eat snails and worms and beetles.

I am a fly.

I eat dead animals and plants.

Acorns

I am a vole.

I eat beetles and flies.

I am a fish.

I eat pond weed.

Berries

I am a frog.

I eat flies, worms and slugs.

I am a mouse.

I eat berries and seeds.

Seeds

Pond weed
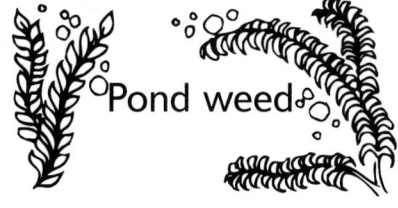

Protest letter

18th September

Kate Lucas

Class 4M

Fairways Primary School

The Headteacher

Dear Mrs Hayward

I am writing to you about the new pavement that is going to be built along the edge of the school field.

I am very worried because I think it will destroy the habitat of the snails, because they need long grass for food and protection. If there is nowhere for the snails to live then we might not have so many different sorts of birds, like thrushes, that eat snails.

Please will you think about this and if the pavement has to be built, could we have a different part of the field that does not get mown so that long grass can grow there instead?

Yours sincerely

Kate Lucas

Kate Lucas

Habitats and food chains

Gemma, Matthew and Sunita studied a wall and an area of concrete in their playground. They recorded their information in a table.

Animals	How many we found on the wall	How many we found on the concrete
snails	8	1
woodlice	6	2
ants	5	6
ladybirds	1	0
spiders	4	0

1 a) Which animal were there most of on the wall? _____

b) How many spiders did they find on the concrete? _____

c) Which animals were there least of on the wall? _____

d) How many different sorts of animal did they find on the wall? _____

e) How many different sorts of animal did they find on the concrete? _____

f) Why do you think there were more different animals on the wall than on the concrete? _____

g) The snails were found in the cracks in the wall. Why do you think they were there? _____

2. The children decided to take some animals back into the classroom.

Write down two rules for the children to follow when they collect the animals:

a) _____

b) _____

Habitats and food chains

Tick the box ✓ to say whether the living thing is a plant, animal or a fungus.

	Plant	Animal	Fungus
oak tree			
owl			
mushroom			
ant			
human			
dandelion			
fox			
woodlouse			
toadstool			
moss			
grass			

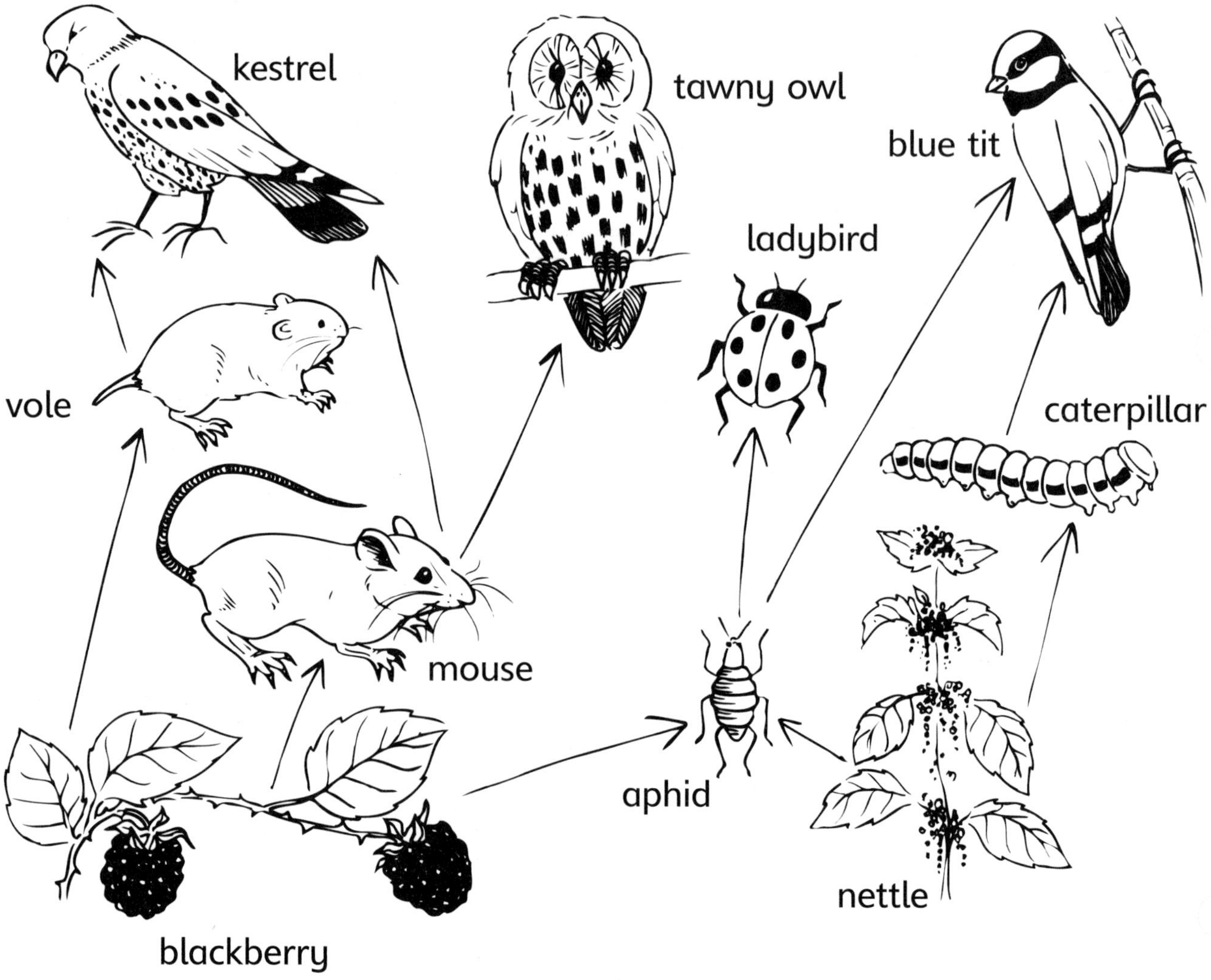

kestrel

tawny owl

blue tit

ladybird

vole

caterpillar

mouse

aphid

nettle

blackberry

Warm liquids and cool solids

ORGANISATION (18 LESSONS)

	OBJECTIVES	MAIN ACTIVITY	GROUP ACTIVITIES	PLENARY	OUTCOMES
LESSON 1	● To elicit children's existing understanding about materials. ● To develop observation and sorting skills.	Exploring a collection of items and considering the materials they are made from and their uses.	Choosing items from the collection and describing them in detail.	Discussion about 'big ideas' that this unit focuses on.	● Teacher awareness of children's existing ideas about materials. ● Can observe and sort a collection.
LESSON 2	● To know that the thermometer is an instrument for measuring temperature. ● To measure temperature using standard units with an appropriate degree of accuracy.	Demonstration of how to measure temperature using a thermometer.	Measuring the temperature of different things.	Discussion about the measurements taken and suggestions about the reasons for differences in temperature.	● Understand that temperature is a measure of hotness and coldness. ● Realise that temperature can be measured using a thermometer. ● Can read a thermometer with a reasonable amount of accuracy. ● Can read a pictorial representation of a thermometer.
LESSON 3	● To know that there are variations of temperature in a room. ● To use thermometers in an investigation. ● To describe and suggest explanations for findings.	Measuring the temperature in different parts of the room.		Suggesting reasons for their findings.	● Can use thermometers in the context of an investigation. ● Can describe their findings using appropriate vocabulary. ● Can suggest possible explanations for variations in temperature.
LESSON 4	● To know that the heat insulation property of materials can be compared by investigation. ● To know how to express predictions. ● To know how to record in a simple table. ● To know how to transfer information from a table to a bar chart.	Discussion about how to slow down the melting of an 'ice pop'. Support in planning a fair test and presenting results as a bar chart.	Planning and carrying out a test to find which material is best for slowing the melting. Presenting results as a bar chart.	Generalise from results about what materials are good insulators.	● Understand that different materials have different insulating properties and that these can be investigated to make predictions. ● To know what 'insulator' means in relation to materials and temperature. ● Can construct their own tables and bar charts from a model provided. ● Can make predictions and suggest explanations.
LESSON 5	● To know that the heat insulation property of materials can be compared by investigation. ● To design a table to record results. ● To carry out measurements with a reasonable degree of accuracy and record them in a table. ● To compare the results of two investigations.	Model the process of giving reasons for predictions about which material will keep water hot the longest.	Carrying out a fair test, devising a table to record results and considering results against predictions.	Relating materials which were good at keeping the ice cold to materials which were good at keeping the water hot.	● Can devise a table independently. ● Can compare the results of two investigations. ● Understand that some materials are better thermal insulators than others.
LESSON 6	● To know that different materials conduct heat differently. ● To observe using the sense of touch. ● To consider fair testing. ● To be able to identify possible safety risks. ● To relate the properties of materials to their uses. ● To work collaboratively.	Predicting what would happen to different spoons put in hot water. Fair testing. Considering safety aspects of the test.	Testing what happens to spoons of different materials in hot water. Exploring a collection of other protective items such as oven gloves.	Discuss how the properties of the materials are related to their use.	● Know that heat can travel through some materials more easily than others and to know some examples of this. ● Understand how the test was made fair. ● Is aware of some risks associated with heat and can suggest action that can be taken to reduce the risk. ● Can work collaboratively in a group.

ORGANISATION (18 LESSONS)

	OBJECTIVES	MAIN ACTIVITY	GROUP ACTIVITIES	PLENARY	OUTCOMES
LESSON 7	● To know that materials with good thermal conduction or insulation properties can have uses.	Write and draw about examples of everyday items that make use of thermal insulation properties.		Reinforce the idea that heat can travel through some materials more easily than others.	● Can describe some uses of materials with good thermal conductance. ● Can describe some uses of materials with poor thermal conductance.
LESSON 8	● To know that some materials can be classified as solids and some as liquids. ● To be able to describe some of the properties of solids and liquids. ● Classifying and recording classification as Venn diagrams.	Comparing two materials: water and wood.	Sorting the collection of solids and liquids and recording as a Venn diagram.	Considering the meaning of the terms 'solid' and 'liquid'.	● Can group solids and liquids. ● Can explain the criteria for sorting solids and liquids. ● Are aware of the terms 'solid' and 'liquid'.
LESSON 9	● To reinforce ideas about the properties of solids and liquids using drama. ● To work collaboratively.	Miming Plasticine being pulled and pushed to form new shapes.		Performing mimes to each other.	● Understand the difference between solids and liquids in terms of flow and holding shape. ● Can work collaboratively in a group.
LESSON 10	● To know that a liquid has a constant volume, but that its shape depends on that of its container. ● To be able to measure the volume of a liquid.	Demonstration and experience of measuring the volume of an amount of liquid.		Discussion about liquids maintaining volume while being poured into different containers.	● Can measure volumes of liquids accurately. ● Understand that the volume remains constant, even though the shape changes.
LESSON 11	● To know that solids made of very small particles behave in some ways like liquids.	Observation of sugar and flour being poured. Are they solid or liquid?	Pouring different solids with small particles. Observation of particles using magnifiers	Clarification that some solids with small particles can be poured, but they are not liquids.	● Know that solids made of very small particles behave in some ways like liquids.
LESSON 12	● To know that a solid can be changed into a liquid by melting. ● To know that a liquid can be changed into a solid by freezing. ● To know that melting and freezing can be reversed, and are the reverse of each other. ● To make predictions. ● To practise observation skills.	Demonstration of how to heat materials safely.	Observation of how materials change as they are heated and then left to cool.	Introduction of the idea of a reversible change.	● Can describe how water can be turned into ice and ice into water. ● Can describe how some materials have to be warmed to melt. ● Can make predictions. ● Can observe carefully.
LESSON 13	● To know that different solids melt at different temperatures. ● To know that some solids will melt at very high temperatures. ● To be able to raise questions. ● To use secondary sources of information to answer questions.	Use of secondary sources to consider examples of solids (for example, metal/rock melting at very high temperatures.		Discussion about different materials melting at different temperatures.	● Can recognise that different materials melt at different temperatures. ● Can recognise that metal needs a high temperature to melt and rock an extremely high temperature to melt. ● Can raise questions. ● Can use secondary sources to research answers.
LESSON 14	● To know that materials can be mixed together and separated. ● To know that mixtures can be separated by using differences in properties of materials.	Demonstration of different ways to separate mixtures by using a magnet, sieving and floating.	Children are challenged to separate different mixtures.	Discussion on how a knowledge of differences in properties of the materials allows them to be separated.	● Can recognise that some materials can be mixed. ● Can devise ways to separate materials. ● Can explain how sieving, floating and magnets can be used to separate materials.

ORGANISATION (18 LESSONS)

	OBJECTIVES	MAIN ACTIVITY	GROUP ACTIVITIES	PLENARY	OUTCOMES
LESSON 15	● To know that changes occur when some solids are added to water. ● To know that some solids dissolve in water and some don't. ● To devise and carry out a fair test. ● To apply skills of measurement of volumes of water.	Observing salt dissolving. Introducing a test to find out which materials dissolve. Using a table to record predictions and test results.	Carrying out investigations into which materials dissolve.	Modelling how to present findings clearly.	● Can recognise that some materials dissolve when mixed with water and some don't. ● Can devise a test. ● Can record predictions and findings.
LESSON 16	● To know that an undissolved solid can be separated from a liquid by filtering. ● To present findings and suggest explanations.	Demonstration of filtration with kitchen paper.	Groups investigate the best papers to filter a mixture of sand and water. Recording focuses on suggesting explanations for their results.	Imagining that the filter paper might have very small holes in it that let the water through.	● Can recognise the properties of a material that make it a good filter. ● Can recognise that filtering is a way of separating an undissolved solid from a liquid. ● Can suggest explanations for their findings.
LESSON 17	● To know that a dissolved substance cannot be separated from water by filtering. ● To be able to suggest possible explanations.	Filtering salt and sugar solutions and tasting to show the sugar/salt is still there.		Suggesting reasons why the sugar and salt were not filtered out.	● Can recognise that a dissolved substance cannot be separated from water by filtering. ● Can suggest explanations based on previous experience and ideas.

	OBJECTIVES	ACTIVITY 1	ACTIVITY 2
LESSON 18	● To assess children's understanding of properties of materials. ● To assess their understanding of how to carry out a fair test.	Children identify things that are 'unfair' about a test you have set up to investigate which sweets dissolve most quickly.	Pencil and paper test assessing reading a thermometer, uses of materials for thermal insulation and separating mixtures.

LESSON 1

OBJECTIVES

● To elicit children's existing understanding about materials.
● To develop observation and sorting skills.

RESOURCES

Main teaching activity: Board or flip chart, marker pens.
Group activities: 1. Collections of items made from different materials (one collection for each group), though they do not need to be the same; a bin-liner per group.

PREPARATION

The collections should include a wide range of items, for example a metal saucepan, a woollen glove, a plastic beaker, aluminium foil, a cereal box, a paper fastener, a plastic glove, cotton wool, a plastic bottle, a reel of thread. Try to include a few particularly interesting items, such as a glass pebble, a soft toy, an African wooden spoon. Put each group's collection into a bin-liner and put them out on the tables.

BACKGROUND

This activity will help you to find out what the children's existing ideas about materials are. It will help the children to make links with previous ideas and provide a thought-provoking start point to the unit. The word 'material' is commonly used to mean fabric. This lesson also provides an opportunity for children to learn/revise how the term 'material' is used in science.

Vocabulary

fabric, glass, materials, metal, paper, plastic, wood

INTRODUCTION

Ask the groups to explore their collection by taking it in turns to take out an item from the bag and describe it to the rest of the group. Encourage children to go beyond the obvious by saying three things about each item. Then ask the groups to sort their collection in as many different ways as they can, for example things used in the kitchen, things made from metal. Ask each group to choose one item and bring it to the carpet.

MAIN TEACHING ACTIVITY

Sit the children in a circle and ask each group to put their item in the centre. Pick one object and ask: *Can you tell me anything about this?* If these ideas don't arise from the children's comments, then follow up by asking: *What material is this made from? What do you think it is for? Why might it be made of that material?* Repeat this for each of the other objects.

Explain that in science the word 'material' means the 'stuff' that something is made from, such as glass, plastic, metal, or cotton.

GROUP ACTIVITIES

1. Ask each child to choose one item at a time from their collection, do a sketch of it and write down everything they can about it. This could be in the form of a table as shown.

2. Ask the children to work in groups of three or four. They take turns to think of an item and the others have 20 questions to work out what it is. Encourage them to ask questions about the materials it is made from and what it is used for.

Object	My ideas about it
Woollen glove	This is a glove. It is good for keeping your hand warm when it is winter. It is knitted.

DIFFERENTIATION

As this is an initial assessment, the differentiation will be mainly by outcome. However, less confident children may want to begin with the item that has already been discussed. Also, children with poorer writing skills can be supported by your scribing of their ideas.

ASSESSMENT

Some children may give a limited description of the materials the objects are made from, such as 'it's metal'. For these children, an important part of subsequent lessons will be helping them to observe different properties of materials. Others may be able to describe some of the properties, such as, 'it's hard, it's heavy'. These children can be targeted with questions to help them think more about the ways in which people use different materials to perform different functions. Other children may already be making links between the properties of the material and its use, and for them, the unit will broaden their experiences and help them to learn about specific properties such as insulation which they may not be aware of.

PLENARY

Explain that for the rest of the unit you are going to be finding out more about different materials and that there are three big questions to keep in mind when the children are learning about materials. Write these onto the board or flip chart:
- *What are the materials like?*
- *What do they do?*
- *How can we use them?*

OUTCOMES

- Teacher awareness of children's existing ideas about materials.
- Can observe and sort a collection.

LINKS

English: description.
Maths: sorting.

LESSON 2

OBJECTIVES

● To know that the thermometer is an instrument for measuring temperature.
● To measure using standard units with an appropriate degree of accuracy.

RESOURCES

Main teaching activity: Several ice cubes; a covered hot water bottle (not too hot); a spirit-filled thermometer (avoid clinical mercury thermometers: not only is mercury poisonous, but they will break at temperatures above 40°C); a picture of a giant thermometer drawn on a flip chart (see below); a red marker pen; a transparent plastic container.
Group activities: 1. Spirit-filled thermometers; a thermos flask of hot, but not boiling, water; ice cubes; containers; woolly fabric; photocopiable page 103 (for less able children). **2.** Photocopiable page 104, differentiated by drawing in the spirit 'lines' to the nearest 10, 5 or 1°C.

Vocabulary

Celsius, cold, degrees, hot, temperature, thermometer

BACKGROUND

Temperature can be understood by considering the idea that all matter is made of tiny particles. Temperature is a measure of how fast the particles are moving, of how much energy they have; the faster they are moving, the more energy and the higher the temperature. Children often think that coldness is a property itself, rather than thinking about it as an absence of heat.

Children do not need to know about particles at Key Stage 2, but having this understanding may help you avoid using phrases such as 'letting the cold air in', which are scientifically untrue.

Temperature is measured in degrees Celsius (°C). The melting–freezing point of water is 0°C and the boiling point is 100°C. Room temperature is generally around 23°C and everything in a room will be at room temperature unless it has its own heat source. One source of confusion is that when we feel things by touching them, they may feel cold or warm, even though they are actually at room temperature. This is because some materials, like metals, conduct the heat from our bodies away quickly, leaving our skin feeling cold. In comparison, a material like polystyrene – which is a good insulator – feels warm, as little of our body heat is drawn away.

A thermometer works by the liquid inside it, for example spirit or mercury, expanding as it is heated and contracting as it cools.

PREPARATION

Draw the thermometer opposite on the flip chart and have it where the children can see it clearly. Copy photocopiable page 103 for lower-attaining children. Differentiate a copy of photocopiable page 104 before copying it further by drawing lines to nearest 10°C (easiest for lower-attaining children), to the nearest 5°C, or the nearest 1°C (for higher-attaining children).

INTRODUCTION

Have the children sitting in a circle. Pass around some ice cubes and a covered hot water bottle. Ask the children to describe what they feel like. Introduce the word 'temperature' and ask the children what they think it means. Ask the children how they could measure the temperature of the ice and hot water, introducing the idea of a thermometer if necessary. Help the children to relate their own experiences of thermometers, such as when they were ill. Explain that in this lesson they will learn to use thermometers, and this will help them to investigate materials.

MAIN TEACHING ACTIVITY

Show the children a spirit-filled thermometer, explaining that it is fragile and must be handled with care.

Using the drawing of the thermometer show the children how the scale is arranged and explain that temperature is measured in degrees Celsius. Draw a red line up to 10°C and ask the children what temperature that represents. Increase the line to 30°C and ask again. Draw the line to 35°C and help them to work out what it would represent. Do the same for approximately 47°C and further examples.

Pour some warm water from the thermos flask into a transparent container and show the children that you need to wait for the line to stop moving and keep the thermometer in the water while you read the temperature. Remember that this is different from what they will have experienced with clinical thermometers. Point out that you do not have to shake the thermometer to make the line go down again.

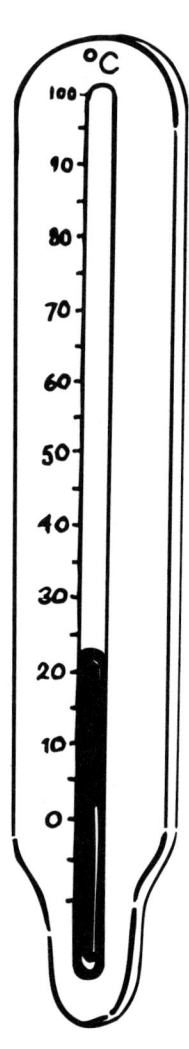

GROUP ACTIVITIES

1. Working in pairs, ask the children to find the temperatures of the different things. Encourage them to feel them with their fingers as well. While they are doing the first few items you can put out containers of warm and icy water. Children can take ownership by trying out some ideas of their own, but warn against putting thermometers in their mouths. Give less able children support with photocopiable page 103.

2. Give each child a differentiated copy of photocopiable page 104. Ask them to read the temperatures indicated on the drawings.

DIFFERENTIATION

In the Group activities, most children will be able to devise their own table for recording the measurements, but some will need support with this for which you can use photocopiable page 103. Expect differing degrees of accuracy in measurement.

ASSESSMENT

Observe the accuracy of the children's practical measurement skills. Most should be able to read to the nearest 10°C, and many will be able to read to the nearest 5°C. Are their readings from the pictures of the thermometers correct? Can the children demonstrate their understanding of temperature by predicting whether it will go up or down when the thermometer is moved between substances?

PLENARY

Ask what the children think the word 'temperature' means. Ask: *Were there any surprises?* (Perhaps that the woolly fabric isn't warm.) *What temperature was the icy water?* (Should be 0°C if the thermometers are accurate.) *Can it ever get colder than 0°C?* (Below 0°C, it will be ice.) *Did everyone get exactly the same measurements?* (Probably not.) *What might affect the accuracy?* (Thermometers, care with reading or letting the level of spirit adjust.) Ask: *How could you change the temperature of something?* (For example warming with an oven or radiator.)

OUTCOMES

- Understand that temperature is a measure of hotness and coldness.
- Realise that temperature can be measured using a thermometer.
- Can read a thermometer with a reasonable amount of accuracy.
- Can read a pictorial representation of a thermometer.

LINKS

Maths: measurement, using scales.

LESSON 3

Objectives	● To know that there are variations of temperature in a room. ● To use thermometers in an investigation. ● To describe and suggest explanations for findings.
Resources	Thermometers.
Main activity	Review how to use a thermometer. Make predictions about the room temperature. Ask the children: *Do you think the room will be the same temperature all over? What parts of the room could we try?* The children take temperatures in different parts of the classroom, for example in the Sun, near the door, near a radiator. They measure the temperature in the same place during the course of the day and record their measurements.
Differentiation	Expect different accuracy of measurement, with most children measuring to the nearest 5°C, but with mathematically able children estimating to 1°C, and the mathematically less able measuring to the nearest 10°C.
Assessment	Have the children been able to use the thermometers independently? Can they describe their findings? Can they suggest possible explanations that are consistent with their findings?
Plenary	Look at the measurements taken during the day. First ask the children to describe what they found and then to suggest possible explanations for it.
Outcomes	● Can use thermometers in the context of an investigation. ● Can describe their findings using appropriate vocabulary. ● Can suggest possible explanations for variations in temperature.

LESSON 4

OBJECTIVES
- To know that the heat insulation property of materials can be compared by investigation.
- To know how to express predictions.
- To know how to record in a simple table.
- To know how to transfer information from a table to a bar chart.

RESOURCES

Main teaching activity: A frozen 'ice pop', two ice cubes, a large wad of newspaper, a small piece of fabric, equal-sized pieces of newspaper and fabric.
Group activities: 1. A collection of materials including fur fabric, woolly fabric, bubble wrap, tin foil, newspaper, plastics, timers, hand lenses, ice cubes (use very small ice cubes if you want to speed up the test!) **2.** Optional copies of photocopiable pages 105 and 106. **3.** Reference books or copies of photocopiable page 107.

Vocabulary

bar chart, frozen, insulator, material, melt, table

BACKGROUND

Different materials have different thermal insulation properties. Because of their own, everyday experiences of putting on more clothes when it is cold, children often think that covering something will make it warmer. They may need teacher intervention to help them distinguish things that produce their own heat from things that do not. Even for those who have grasped how, for example, wrapping a baked potato keeps it warm for longer can have their ideas challenged by wrapping an ice cube because they expect the wrapping to warm it up. For some children the explanation of their results will be that the wrapping keeps the cold *in*, rather than the scientific version that the wrapping keeps the heat of the room *out*. Be prepared for a long wait – a well-wrapped ice cube can take over an hour to melt!

In this lesson, whole-class interactive teaching is interspersed with two practical Group activities for the children. This enables the teacher to keep a tight focus on the skills being taught, modelling them step by step.

INTRODUCTION

Show the children a frozen 'ice pop'. Ask them to imagine that they had bought an ice pop to give to their friend, but their friend lived quite a long way away. Ask the children what might happen to the ice pop on the way, allowing them to use their own words. This will provide formative assessment of the children's existing ideas for the teacher to build on.

MAIN TEACHING ACTIVITY – PART 1

Can the children think of anything that could help stop the ice pop from melting? The children can draw on their own experience to make suggestions. Say that people sometimes wrapped ice-cream blocks up in newspaper to take them home from the shops. Do the children think that would work? What else could they try?

Explain that ice pops are too big and expensive to use for a test, but that the children can test their ideas using ice cubes. Wrap one ice cube in a huge wad of newspaper and another in a tiny piece of woolly fabric. Ask: *Is that a good test?* Remind the class of the importance of fair testing. Now wrap the ice cubes in similar-sized pieces of the two materials. Ask different children to predict which ice cube they think will take the longest to melt. Ask them to give a reason for their answers. On the flip chart or board, model predicting with a reason: 'I think the ice cube wrapped in _____ will melt fastest because _____. I think that the ice cube wrapped in _____ will melt slowest because _____.'

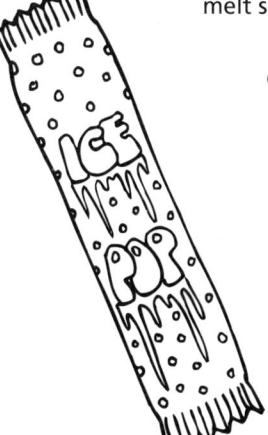

GROUP ACTIVITIES

1. Ask the children, in groups of three, to select from a range of materials the three that they would like to test. Ask them to record their predictions with reasons as you have shown. Have hand lenses available to encourage close observation of the materials.

MAIN TEACHING ACTIVITY – PART 2

Bring the class back together. Ask the children how they will know how long the ice cubes take to melt. Discuss the use of timers. How often will they check the ice cubes? Ten intervals would be appropriate. Together, devise a table to record this or use photocopiable page 105.

GROUP ACTIVITIES

2. The children construct their own tables, or use photocopiable page 105 and carry out the test, recording their results.

3. It may be useful to have another simple ongoing activity during this time, perhaps reading relevant non-fiction books on materials or doing the wordsearch provided on photocopiable page 106. The solution is shown below.

MAIN TEACHING ACTIVITY – PART 3

Explain to the class how to represent their results as a bar chart (based on photocopiable page 107 if wished). Each child can then construct their own using squared paper or a copy of photocopiable page 107.

DIFFERENTIATION

Use ready-made blanks of tables and graphs (photocopiable pages 105 and 107 to support children with weaker recording skills. Extend the more mathematically able by asking them to devise their own tables and graphs independently.

ASSESSMENT

Have the children expressed their predictions and explanations clearly? Have they been able to construct and use the table accurately? Can they transfer their own results to a bar chart?

PLENARY

Ask the groups to report back to the class on their findings. Were their results as they predicted? Ask the children to explain why some materials were better than others, for example they were thicker, they trapped air. Can any generalisations be made? Introduce the term 'a good insulator'. Ask the children to explain how they think the materials worked to slow down the melting.

OUTCOMES

● Understand that different materials have different insulating properties and that these can be investigated to make predictions.
● To know what 'insulator' means in relation to materials and temperature.
● Can construct their own tables and bar charts from a model provided.
● Can make predictions and suggest explanations.

LINKS

Unit 5 Electricity: comparing thermal insulators with electrical insulators.
Maths: data-handling.

LESSON 5

OBJECTIVES

● To know that the heat insulation property of materials can be compared by investigation.
● To design a table to record results.
● To carry out measurements with a reasonable degree of accuracy and record them in a table.
● To compare the results of two investigations.

RESOURCES

Main teaching activity: A collection of materials including fur fabric, woolly fabric, bubble wrap, tin foil, newspaper, plastics and timers.
Group activities: 1. Thermometers; a collection of materials as above; hot (not boiling) water; bottles to put the hot water in, such as small plastic fizzy drink bottles; containers to stand the bottles in, such as plastic beakers. **2.** A collection of assorted fabrics (a rag bag); scissors; glue.

PREPARATION

The recording could be made into a sugar paper class book, with each group contributing one A4 page to be stuck in. Prepare the book in advance so the children have some idea of the end product.

Vocabulary

insulator, material, table

BACKGROUND

Different materials have different thermal insulation properties. A good insulator does not allow much heat to travel through it so the heat tends to stay where it is. This means that a good insulator will keep hot water hot and keep ice cold! Children may not find this an easy concept. By comparing the results of this investigation into which material is best at keeping things warm, with the results of the previous investigation in Lesson 2 – keeping an ice cube cold – they will begin to see that what appears to be two different properties of materials is actually the same thing. Be careful with your own language and don't talk about 'keeping the cold out'; instead say 'keeping the heat in'.

INTRODUCTION

Show the class a baby bottle with some warm milk in it. Explain that the baby's dad wants to take the baby out on a trip on a cool day, but the baby will need some warm milk when they are out. Ask the class: *What will happen to the warm milk dad has prepared?* (It will cool down.) Say: *He doesn't have a thermos flask or camp stove.* Ask: *We are going to think of a way dad can keep the milk warm for longer.* Ask the children: *How would you keep yourselves warm on a cold day?* (Wear warm clothes.) *What materials do you think would be best for keeping the baby's milk warm?* The children may draw on other experiences such as polystyrene foam or aluminium dishes that they have had take-away meals in.

MAIN TEACHING ACTIVITY

Show the class the collection, and ask several children to select a material they think would be good and give a reason for their choice. Model writing on the flip chart: *I think the woolly fabric will be good because jumpers keep you warm.*

Show the class the bottles they are going to use for the test. Demonstrate how the small bottle will be stood in the container, the chosen material put around it, and then the bottle filled with hot water. Ask the children: *How could you measure the temperature of the water?* (With a thermometer.) Explain that you want them to devise their own tables for recording their results, remembering what they have done in previous investigations. Stress that there is more than one right way of doing this. If you are making a class book, show the children where their work will be stuck in.

GROUP ACTIVITIES

1. The children can work in pairs or threes. Ask them to choose one material from the collection that they think will be good at keeping the water warm and one that they think will not be so good. Ask them to record their choices in this format: *I think that the _____ will be good at keeping the water warm because _____ and the _____ will not be as good because _____.*

The children should then set up their two bottles. When they are ready and they have designed a table to record the results, help them to put hot water in the bottles and they can begin recording the temperature.

Ask the children to write what they found out in the format: *We found out that the _____ kept the water hot for longer than the _____. We think this is because _____. This is/is not what we predicted.*

2. Ask the children in their groups to draw pictures of children on a hot day and a cold day, wearing appropriate clothes. They choose swatches of fabric from the collection and stick these alongside the drawing with arrows to indicate which item of clothing they would be suitable for. They should explain in terms of their insulating properties whether heat is being kept in or out.

DIFFERENTIATION

For some children, recording the temperature of one bottle of water will be sufficiently demanding practically. Some may need support in drawing up a table of results. Those previously identified as needing support with the accuracy of their measurement can be targeted for help with their measuring skills.

Children with more advanced investigative skills could compare three samples of materials to test a more sophisticated hypothesis. (For example: *We think thick materials are better than thin ones.*) The explanations expected from some children will be at a higher level by being based on the nature of the material rather than previous experience. (For example: *I think this bubble wrap is good because of the air trapped inside it.*) This can be supported by providing hand lenses or ×20 magnifiers to encourage the children to consider the structure of the material more closely.

ASSESSMENT

Are the children able to construct and use a table that is appropriate for the experiment? Can they relate this test to the previous one on ice cubes?

PLENARY

Ask each group which material kept the water warm the longest and which cooled the most quickly. Record these answers in two lists on the board or flip chart. Pointing to the first list, ask the class: *Is there anything you notice about this?* (The same materials are repeated; they are thicker; they have air spaces.) Do the same for the other list. It may be possible to make some generalisations. (For example: *We found that thick fabrics are better than thin ones, except for the newspaper, but that was scrunched up.*)

Ask the children to think back to the investigation into keeping an ice cube frozen. *Which material was best at keeping the ice cube cold?* It is likely that the best materials in each case are the same. Ask the children: *Why could these materials be good at keeping things hot and keeping them cold?* The children may respond by saying that coldness and heat can't get through these materials. This is a good basis for developing ideas about insulation, and for some children that is enough. Develop their ideas by explaining that coldness is not a separate thing, but that things are cold when they haven't got much heat – we do not have a separate way of measuring coldness, a thermometer measures the amount of heat. If heat cannot get through a material very well (for example, a material that was a good thermal insulator in both experiments), then the heat is kept in the hot water, or the room can't warm up the ice.

OUTCOMES

● Can devise a table independently.
● Can compare the results of two investigations.
● Understand that some materials are better thermal insulators than others.

LINKS

Design and technology: choosing appropriate materials.

LESSON 6

OBJECTIVES

● To know that different materials conduct heat differently.
● To observe using the sense of touch.
● To consider fair testing.
● To be able to identify possible safety risks.
● To relate the properties of materials to their uses.
● To work collaboratively.

RESOURCES

Main teaching activity: A collection of spoons made from different materials.
Group activities: 1. Stable bowls for hot water; collections of various spoons made from different materials – you can include different spoons made from the same material (do test the spoons first – some plastic ones melt at surprisingly low temperatures. You will need to show the children how to carry out the test safely.); a source of hot (not boiling) water; sugar paper and felt-tipped pens; strip thermometers (if available). **2.** Drawing materials and paper.

PREPARATION

Set up the tables for the Group activities, keeping one collection of spoons to hand. Sit the children around you.

Vocabulary

cold, heat, hotter, less hot, metal, plastic, travel, warm, wood

BACKGROUND

Heat can travel through some materials more easily than others. Those materials that heat can travel through easily, for example metal, are known as good thermal conductors (and poor thermal insulators). Those that heat cannot travel through easily are poor conductors (and good insulators), for example wood and plastic. Helping children to make the connection between these two apparently different properties of conduction and insulation will help to develop their understanding of heat, as well as their experience of materials.

The investigative focus is on fair testing and so to limit the number of things the children need to think about, the temperature of the spoons is judged by touch, rather than measured. However, if you have strip thermometers available, these could be used to extend the activity.

Using hot water could pose a safety risk, so it is important that safe ways of conducting the test are made clear.

INTRODUCTION

Show the children the collection of spoons. Ask a child to choose one spoon and describe it, if necessary asking questions to prompt: *What is it made of? What would you use it for?* Ask different children to do the same for other spoons from the collection. Ask the children: *Why do we need to have different sorts of spoons?* This will help to set the activity in a real context so the children can relate it to their previous experience. It will also enable you to find out what ideas they already have so these can be developed and particular children targeted during the activity.

MAIN TEACHING ACTIVITY

Ask the children: *What do you think would happen if we put these spoons into hot water?* The children may draw on previous experience to answer, for example knowing that a spoon gets hot in a cup of tea. Ask the children: *Will the same thing happen to all the different spoons?* Again the children may draw on previous experiences of cooking. Help them to focus on what will happen to the temperature of the handles. Ask: *How could we test that?* (Put them in hot water and feel how hot they get.) Ask: *How can we make sure it is a fair test?* (Put all the spoons in the hot water at the same time.)

Explain that the children will work in groups. Ask them to record their predictions of what will happen to each spoon and then test and record what does happen. Remind the children how to record results in the form of a table. Explain that each group will feed back to the rest of the class what they have found out.

Ask the children: *Are there any dangers with this test?* (Hot water might injure; hot spoons might burn skin.) *How can we make sure that we are safe?* (Have sensible behaviour; just lightly touch each spoon rather than grabbing it.) Demonstrate how they should quickly and lightly touch each spoon until they are sure it is not too hot.

GROUP ACTIVITIES

1. The children work in groups of up to six children, recording on sugar paper what they predict will happen to each spoon, then testing and recording it. Circulate, asking groups to give reasons for their predictions, focusing on those who did not participate earlier. Check that they are working safely. Encourage *all* children to feel the temperature of the spoon handles.
2. Ask the children to make a safety poster by drawing things in the home that might be very hot and should not be touched.

DIFFERENTIATION

Target questions at children who seemed less sure initially, asking them to name and describe the different materials and what happens to each one. Ask them about the different spoons used in their own homes. Extend children who seem confident with the concept by asking them to relate this test to previous investigations into insulation properties of materials. Children could also be extended by asking them to use strip thermometers to measure the temperature of the spoon handles.

ASSESSMENT

Are the children able to relate the property of thermal insulation to different materials, comparing them with each other? Do they show understanding of the need for a fair test? Have they worked collaboratively? Can they relate the property of thermal conductance to thermal insulation? Can they suggest any safety tips for cooking?

PLENARY

Each group will feed back to the class. Discuss whether everyone found the same thing. To summarise, ask: *Which materials let the heat through really easily? Which materials didn't let much heat go through them? What material would you use to make a handle for a spoon to stir a pot of soup? Why do you think teaspoons are often made of metal?* (Metal is easier to shape – can be made smaller, with a hollowed part.) *What could we do to be safer in the kitchen?* (Choose spoons with wooden or plastic handles; don't leave metal spoons in hot things.) *Can anyone think of any other examples of materials we use to stop us getting burned?* (Oven gloves, hot water bottle cover, barbecue tongs, handles on cups.)

To finish, play a game: in a circle each child suggests a nonsense item, such as a paper saucepan or a metal scarf. This is a fun way of making the point that materials can be used for particular purposes because of their properties.

OUTCOMES

● Know that heat can travel through some materials more easily than others and to know some examples of this.
● Understand how the test was made fair.
● Is aware of some risks associated with heat and can suggest action that can be taken to reduce the risk.
● Can work collaboratively in a group.

LINKS

PSHE: collaborative working; safety in the home.

LESSON 7

Objective	● To know that materials with good thermal conduction or insulation properties can have uses.
Resources	An oven glove, a scarf, a cool box, a sock, a wooden spoon, a table mat, a tea cosy, a radiator in the room, a metal saucepan.
Main activity	Review Lesson 6 on thermal conductivity of different spoons. Discuss other occasions when we might need to keep something cold or hot. Use the resources to stimulate and discuss ideas, encouraging children to contribute their own experiences. Ask children to choose two items and draw them, writing to explain how they work to keep/make something hot or cold.
Differentiation	Support children with poorer writing skills by scribing for them or providing words. Extend children who are secure with the idea that different materials have different thermal properties by asking them to suggest reasons why some materials may be better than others at keeping heat in.
Assessment	In their writing, do the children show that they are aware that different materials have different thermal properties? Do they refer to heat being able to get through/ not get through different materials?
Plenary	Ask several children to read what they have written. *Does everyone agree?* Reinforce the idea that heat can travel through some materials more easily than through others, and we can use this to help us.
Outcomes	● Can describe some uses of materials with good thermal conductance. ● Can describe some uses of materials with poor thermal conductance.

LESSON 8

OBJECTIVES

● To know that some materials can be classified as solids and some as liquids.
● To be able to describe some of the properties of solids and liquids.
● Classifying and recording classification as Venn diagrams.

RESOURCES

Main teaching activity: A block of wood; a cup of water and container to pour it into; two card labels with the words 'Solid' and 'Liquid' written on them; Plasticine, a paper clip.
Group activities: 1 and 2. Each group needs a collection of solids and liquids: for example, washing-up liquid, golden syrup, orange squash, water, bubble bath, vegetable oil, paper, card, rigid and flexible plastics, wood, stone, metal (for example, a paper clip), a glass marble, fabric, a sponge, chalk; transparent containers for liquids; plastic hoops; sugar paper; marker pens; drawing materials.

PREPARATION

Set up a collection on each group's table. Have the wood and water for the Main teaching activity to hand. Have the names of the materials in the collection written as a word bank for the children – either on the board or on cards.

BACKGROUND

Materials can be classified as solids, liquids and gases. Gases are difficult to understand at Year 4/Primary 5, as they cannot be observed directly, so the focus here is on solids and liquids. Solids keep their shape; liquids can be poured and take up the shape of their containers. Children sometimes find it hard to grasp that solids don't have to be 'solid' in the everyday sense of the word – so paper and sponge are solids. They may find it hard to classify viscous liquids such as

Vocabulary

hard, liquid, pour, runny, shape, soft, solid

golden syrup, which pour slowly. Interestingly, glass is actually a liquid that pours very slowly! Old church windows are thicker at the bottom than at the top!

Although Key Stage 2/Primary 4–7 children do not need to know about particle theory, it is useful for a teacher to know that in a solid the particles are held together by strong bonds and they are organised into a particular structure. In a liquid, although there is some attraction between the particles, they are free to move around and are not held together in particular ways. Drama can be used to model this without going into detail (see Lesson 9).

INTRODUCTION

Pass around the block of wood and the water. Ask the children: *What words can you use to describe the wood/water?* (Rough, hard, wet.) *What differences are there between the wood and the water?* (Runny/hard, strong/weak.)

MAIN TEACHING ACTIVITY

Explain that you will be asking each group to sort their collection of materials in different ways, looking for things the different materials have in common and for differences between them.

GROUP ACTIVITIES

1. The groups sort the collection in as many ways as possible, for example by colour, where they come from, their uses. They may well decide on solid/liquid as a category independently. If not, then ask the group to consider it by asking: *What happens to the materials when you move them about? Could you sort them according to those you can pour?* Encourage the children to use the hoops to sort the items into two groups. Ask the children to record this on the sugar paper as a Venn diagram.
2. Ask the children to choose two items from the collection and record ways in which they are different and ways in which they are similar.

DIFFERENTIATION

Children with poorer writing skills can record pictorially, or use the word bank to support their writing. Extend children who manage this task easily by encouraging them to add their own suggestions of objects that could go into each group, using a different coloured pen.

ASSESSMENT

Can the children group the items according to whether they are solid or liquid? Can they explain the criteria for sorting as solid or liquid? Can they record in the form of a Venn diagram?

PLENARY

Bring the children together in a circle on the carpet. Put out the two hoops and place two liquids in one and two solids in another. Invite children to put another two objects in each. Ask them: *What do all these solids have in common?* (They have a certain shape; they cannot be poured.) *What do all these liquids have in common*? (They take the shape of the container; they can be poured.) These criteria could be made more explicit by writing them up on a board or flip chart. Explain that there are names – 'solid' and 'liquid' – that describe these groups and put the relevant name card by each hoop. Ask the children: *Were there any things in your collection that you were not sure about?* Discuss their ideas, for example about fabric or golden syrup, ensuring that they are classified correctly. Explain that 'solid' has a special meaning in science that is different from its everyday meaning. Ask the children: *Can you think of any more things we could put in the solid/liquid groups?* If possible, they can get the objects and put them in the appropriate hoops. Show the children some Plasticine and ask them: *Which hoop should this go in?* Ask them to give reasons. Explain that you can change the shape of a solid by pushing or pulling it. Demonstrate this with the Plasticine and also with a piece of wire such as a paper clip.

OUTCOMES
- Can group solids and liquids.
- Can explain the criteria for sorting solids and liquids.
- Are aware of the terms 'solid' and 'liquid'.

LINKS
English: descriptive vocabulary.
Maths: classification, Venn diagrams.

LESSON 9

Objectives	● To reinforce ideas about the properties of solids and liquids using drama. ● To work collaboratively.
Resources	Time in the hall; either the collection of solids and liquids as in Lesson 8 or cards with the names of the items in the collection; two contrasting pieces of music (optional).
Main activity	As a warm-up, in pairs, one child mimes being a ball of Plasticine being pulled and twisted into a new shape by their partner. Groups then make solid shapes suggested by the collection of objects then, still in groups, mime liquids being poured: first golden syrup, then water. Use music to support this, if appropriate.
Differentiation	Groups who manage this successfully could be extended by adding relevant vocabulary as a chant. Children who find collaborative work difficult will benefit from pairing and grouping with supportive children.
Assessment	Do the movements of the groups demonstrate an understanding of the properties of solids and liquids? Can the children work collaboratively?
Plenary	Groups perform one of their mimes for a solid or liquid – the rest of the class guess which one. Review the characteristics of solids and liquids.
Outcomes	● Understand the difference between solids and liquids in terms of flow and holding shape. ● Can work collaboratively in a group.

LESSON 10

Objectives	● To know that a liquid has a constant volume, but that its shape depends on that of its container. ● To be able to measure the volume of a liquid.
Resources	Water; a variety of containers including calibrated beakers or measuring cylinders; water baths/tanks.
Main activity	Demonstrate to the children how to measure out a particular volume of water with a good degree of accuracy and how to measure the volume of water held by a container. Introduce units of measurement of volume – cubic centimetres. Children measure out a certain volume of water (this will need to be appropriate for the containers available) and explore pouring it into different containers. They check that the volume has not changed by measuring it again.
Differentiation	Expect different degrees of accuracy in measurement according to mathematical attainment. Less mathematically able children may need to measure in non-standard units, such as 'up to the line'.
Assessment	Can the children explain that the volume remains the same, even though the water is poured into different containers? Can they measure the volume with a reasonable degree of accuracy?
Plenary	Discuss the process, asking children what happened to the shape and volume of the water as they poured it between the various containers.
Outcomes	● Can measure volumes of liquids accurately. ● Understand that the volume remains constant, even though the shape changes.

LESSON 11

OBJECTIVE

● To know that solids made of very small particles behave in some ways like liquids.

RESOURCES

Main teaching activity: A collection of solids and liquids as in Lesson 7; two hoops; two card labels with 'Solid' and 'Liquid' written on them; flour, sugar, lentils in transparent containers; other containers to pour into.
Group activities: 1. Flour, salt, rice, sand, lentils in containers; other containers to pour into.
2. Writing and drawing materials.

PREPARATION

Have the resources available to one side. Have the children sitting in a circle.

Vocabulary

container, liquid, pour, shape, solid

BACKGROUND

In previous lessons, the characteristic of liquids as materials that can be poured is an idea that has been developed with the children. Sometimes solids can be poured too, when they are made of small particles, such as sugar or flour. This can be a source of confusion for children when classifying solids and liquids.

INTRODUCTION

Put the two hoops in the centre and place one of the card labels 'Solids' and 'Liquids' by each. To review previous learning, go around the circle asking each child to take an item from the collection and put it in the relevant hoop. Ask the children: *What can you tell me about a solid/ liquid?* Make sure that the idea that liquids can be poured is raised.

MAIN TEACHING ACTIVITY

Show the class some flour. Pour it from container to container and ask: *Which hoop should this go in?* Ask the children to explain the reasons for their answers. Leave the question unresolved and show the children some sugar, pouring it between containers. Ask: *Which hoop should this go in?* Again invite suggestions and reasons from the children. Then show the children one lentil and ask: *Is this a solid or a liquid?* The children will probably say 'a solid'. Then pour lentils between containers and ask which hoop they should go in. Put them into the 'Solids' hoop and then go back to the sugar, then the flour, putting them all into the 'Solids' hoop. Explain that sometimes solids can be poured when they are in lots of small pieces.

GROUP ACTIVITIES

1. Give the children time to explore pouring different solids between containers for themselves. Circulate and ask the children to describe how the solids fall into the container: *Do they take its shape? Do they go into all the corners?* Have hand lenses/×20 magnifiers available so that the children can look in detail at the flour and sugar.
2. Ask the children to do an annotated drawing of two of the solids describing their observations and explaining how they pour.

DIFFERENTIATION

Some children may need support with writing. Some children could be extended by inviting them to imagine the particles made from smaller and smaller pieces, as a precursor to particle theory.

ASSESSMENT

In their annotated drawings, are the children clear that it is a solid that is being poured? Do their observations show they realise that the solid will not take the shape of the container on its own as a liquid would?

PLENARY

Gather the children together. Pour some water into a transparent container and ask the children to observe carefully. Then do the same with one of the 'pourable' solids. Ask: *What differences did you notice between the two?* (The solid settled in a cone shape in the bottom of the container, while the liquid took the shape of the container.) Make sure that the children are aware of the difference. Finish by holding up each 'pourable' solid and asking if it is a solid or a liquid.

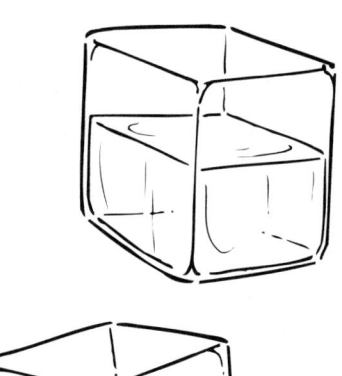
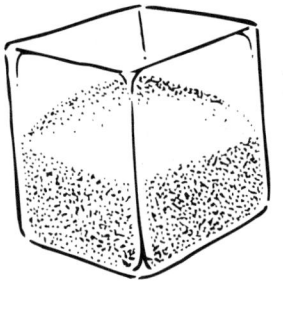
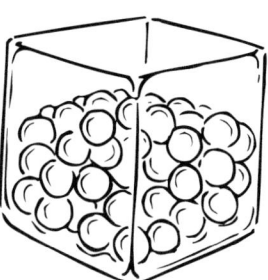

OUTCOME

● Know that solids made of very small particles behave in some ways like liquids.

LINKS

Unit 4 Materials: Lessons 7 and 8.

LESSON 12

OBJECTIVES

- To know that a solid can be changed into a liquid by melting.
- To know that a liquid can be changed into a solid by freezing.
- To know that melting and freezing can be reversed, and are the reverse of each other.
- To make predictions.
- To practise observation skills.

RESOURCES

Main teaching activity: A chocolate bar that has been allowed to melt and solidify again; chocolate, butter, ice cubes, candle wax, a heating system (these are commercially available or you can devise your own using tealights on saucers; the materials to be heated are put in foil dishes resting on a cylinder of chicken wire, or held in spoons with insulated handles. Ensure that the class follow safety instructions, as the foil dishes or spoons get very hot); matches (kept by the teacher).
Group activities: 1. Chocolate, butter, ice cubes, candle wax, a heating system as above, matches (kept by the teacher). **2.** Photocopiable page 108.

PREPARATION

Set up the tables for the Group activities. It is a good idea to have the materials to be heated ready-sorted, but kept in a cool box until the last moment. Have a flip chart or board ready to draw the table of results.

Vocabulary

freeze, heat, liquid, melt, reversible, solid, solidify

BACKGROUND

At a particular temperature, called the freezing point or melting point, solids change into liquids or liquids change into solids. To melt a solid it has to be given more energy (heat), and to freeze a liquid it has to have energy taken away. Children may need plenty of practical experience to appreciate that the substance is the same material, but in a different state. Often melting and dissolving are confused. When something melts, heat makes the particles vibrate faster and breaks down the bonds between them. They are still held together, but much more weakly. When something dissolves, a solvent (such as water) gets in between the particles. The children do not need to know about particle theory, but this may be helpful in clarifying your own understanding.

INTRODUCTION

Show the children the misshapen chocolate bar and ask them what they think might have happened to it. Ask the children what other experiences they have had of melting (for example ice, snow, ice cream, candle wax, butter). Draw out the role of heat in each example.

MAIN TEACHING ACTIVITY

Explain that the children are going to explore how different materials melt. Show them the materials in the collection. Demonstrate how to use the heating system safely. Ask the children to draw up a table with four columns to record the name of the material, their prediction of what will happen to each material and a description of what actually happens. The last column is for a description of what happens to the material as it cools.

GROUP ACTIVITIES

So that each group's heating materials can be closely supervised, a second Group activity is provided. Alternatively, extra adult support (classroom assistants) could each work with a group.
1. The children make their prediction, then heat each material in turn, recording their observations. The materials can then be left to cool and further observations recorded.
2. Ask the children to complete photocopiable page 108 on reversible and irreversible changes.

DIFFERENTIATION

Support less confident children's writing with word banks.

ASSESSMENT

Can the children describe how these materials need heat to melt? Can the children describe how ice can be turned into water and water into ice? Are their observations detailed and clearly recorded?

PLENARY

Consider each material and discuss the children's observations of what happened when it was heated and left to cool. Ask: *What has changed about the materials after cooling and what has stayed the same?* Emphasise that although the shape may have changed the material is still the same. If they got too hot some materials may have burned instead of melting and this may need clarification. Ask the children: *How could we get the water back into an ice cube?* Introduce the term 'reversible'.

OUTCOMES

- Can describe how water can be turned into ice and ice into water.
- Can describe how some materials have to be warmed to melt.
- Can make predictions.
- Can observe carefully.

LINKS

Design and echnology: cooking activities.

LESSON 13

Objectives	● To know that different solids melt at different temperatures. ● To know that some solids will melt at very high temperatures. ● To be able to raise questions. ● To use secondary sources of information to answer questions.
Resources	A metal object; a rock (preferably an igneous rock such as granite); video clips showing volcanoes and metal in a molten state poured into moulds and solidifying; secondary sources (such as books, CD-ROMs, the Internet) on processing metals and volcanic activity.
Main activity	Ask the children whether the rock and metal are solid or liquid. *Could they be melted into a liquid? How?* Discuss the children's ideas. Divide a flip chart into two columns. Down one side, list questions that the children raise as a result of the discussion. Keep the questions focused on melting/freezing of rocks and metals. Show the video clips. Ask: *What was needed to melt the metal and the rock?* (Very high temperatures were needed.) If you are able to answer any of the questions from the video clips, then record the information in the second column. In groups, use other secondary sources to try to answer the other questions. These could be presented in the form of 'question and answer' speech bubbles and made into a wall display.
Differentiation	Ensure that children with reading difficulties have access to pictorial sources. Challenge others to ask and answer questions of their own.
Assesment	Can the children offer explanations for how metal objects might be made that show an awareness of melting at high temperatures and moulding? Can they state that even rock can melt at high enough temperatures?
Plenary	Feed back any answers that have been found. Reinforce the idea that most things can melt, but that some need very high temperatures to do so. Can the children suggest how coins might be made? (They are discs cut out of warm sheet metal and stamped with the design.)
Outcomes	● Can recognise that different materials melt at different temperatures. ● Can recognise that metal needs a high temperature to melt and rock an extremely high temperature to melt. ● Can raise questions. ● Can use secondary sources to research answers.

LESSON 14

OBJECTIVES

- To know that materials can be mixed together and separated.
- To know that mixtures can be separated by using differences in properties of materials.

RESOURCES

Introduction: A puppet character.
Main teaching activity: A mixture of flour and pins; a magnet; a mixture of macaroni and rice; a colander; a mixture of gravel and lentils; a tank or bowl of water, a sieve.
Group activities: 1. Mixtures of: flour, rice and beans; dried peas and sand; pieces of plastic and paper clips; a good selection of sieves and colanders; a tank or bowl of water; a magnet. **2.** Children's recipe books; question cards, for example 'What goes together to make flapjack?' 'What goes together to make chapatti?', according to the content of the recipe books; writing materials and paper.

PREPARATION

Set up the tables for the Group activities. Ensure the resources for the Main teaching activity are to hand and all the children can see. Perhaps they could sit in a circle and the demonstrations could take place in the centre.

Vocabulary

colander, float, magnet, mixture, separate, sieve, sink

BACKGROUND

Different materials can be put together. If they can be separated again, for example muesli, then it is a mixture. This is unlike when different materials have been combined to make new materials, like a cake, when the individual parts cannot be separated. In order to separate a mixture you need to know the different properties of each material. For example, magnetic materials can easily be separated from non-magnetic materials by using a magnet. Particles of different sizes can be separated by sieving and filtering. In filtering, the liquid goes through the holes, but any solid stays behind in the filter. If one substance floats and the other sinks, that provides another means of separation. Children are unlikely to come to these ideas on their own, so show them some techniques that they can apply to problem-solving situations.

INTRODUCTION

Introduce the children to a puppet character. Tell them this 'naughty puppet' has mixed together lots of different things. Could the children help to separate them again?

MAIN TEACHING ACTIVITY

First demonstrate how to separate flour and pins using a magnet. Tell the children that the naughty puppet put pins in his Granny's flour jar as a joke, but this was very dangerous. Imagine what would happen if his Granny had made a cake with it! Show the children the equipment you are going to use and ask them: *How could we use this to separate this mixture?* When you have separated the mixture ask: *What was different about those materials that helped us to separate them?*

Then demonstrate how to separate macaroni and rice using a colander. Tell the children that the puppet hates rice pudding, but loves macaroni cheese, so he thought he would try mixing them and see if he liked that! Show the children the equipment you are going to use and ask them: *How could we use this to separate this mixture?* When you have separated the mixture, ask: *What was different about those materials that helped us to separate them?*

Lastly, demonstrate how to separate gravel and lentils by floating and sinking. Tell the children that the puppet spilled the lentils outside, scraped up the mixture of lentils and gravel and put it back in the jar hoping no one would notice! Again, show the children the equipment you are going to use and ask them: *How could we use this to separate this mixture?* When you have separated the mixture, ask: *What was different about those materials that helped us to separate them?*

GROUP ACTIVITIES

1. Challenge the children to separate different mixtures: flour, rice and beans; dried peas and sand; pieces of plastic and paper clips. Let them find their own solutions – there is more than one possibility. Ask them to record in drawing and writing how they separated the mixtures.
2. Ask the children to take a 'What goes together to make...' card and list all the ingredients on paper.

DIFFERENTIATION

Some children may need suggestions to prevent them becoming frustrated. Children who have successfully completed the task could be challenged to think of a mixture for other children to sort out – they must have a method in mind!

ASSESSMENT

Can the children devise ways to separate the mixtures? Can they explain how their methods work by using the properties of the materials?

PLENARY

Ask the groups to feed back some of the methods they used to separate the mixtures. Focus on the properties of the materials by asking questions such as: *How did the sieve separate the flour and rice? Why did putting the plastic and paper clips into water separate them?*

Ask the class if they can think of any real-life situation in which mixtures may need to be separated. If it doesn't arise, ask them to consider how rubbish could be sorted for recycling.

Ask if we can always separate materials from a mixture. (No, for example cakes or chapattis.)

OUTCOMES

- Can recognise that some materials can be mixed.
- Can devise ways to separate materials.
- Can explain how sieving, floating and magnets can be used to separate materials.

LESSON 15

OBJECTIVES

- To know that changes occur when some solids are added to water.
- To know that some solids dissolve in water and some don't.
- To devise and carry out a fair test.
- To apply skills of measurement of volumes of water.

RESOURCES

Main teaching activity: A transparent container of salty water; a transparent container of water; salt; a spoon; drinking straws cut into four.
Group activity: Transparent containers; calibrated beakers/measuring cylinders; spoons; labelled samples of salt, granulated sugar, sand, cornflour, wax flakes (available for batik from craft suppliers) and rice.

PREPARATION

Have the resources for the Group activity ready on the tables and have the resources for the Main teaching activity to hand.

Vocabulary

dissolve, settle, solid, volume

BACKGROUND

Some solids dissolve in water – they are soluble. When it has dissolved you can no longer see the solid. The water molecules have got between the particles of the solid and it is dispersed through the water. Children may describe the solid as having 'disappeared', and it is a good idea to explore their ideas about where they think it has gone. Sometimes, most of the solid will dissolve, but some will be left on the bottom. Sometimes, the solid will mix with the water, but not dissolve, forming a cloudy 'suspension' (school paint, for example). If a solid does not dissolve, it is insoluble in water. Because of these factors it is not always easy for children to decide if the solid has truly dissolved and this may need some discussion during the investigation.

Confusion between melting and dissolving is common, and children may well articulate ideas that express this. Focus their attention on the differences between the two – dissolving needs a liquid (usually water) and melting needs heat.

INTRODUCTION

Show the children a transparent container of the salt solution. Ask them to describe it. (It is watery, clear, transparent.) Now pass it around and ask each child to taste it by dipping in a cut up bit of a drinking straw (not by sucking!) Ask them to describe what it tastes like. (It tastes salty.) Ask: *What do you think might be in the water?* (There is salt in the water.) *Why can't we see it?* This is an opportunity to elicit the children's ideas about dissolving in order to develop them.

Tell the children that for safety reasons they must not taste clear liquids to find out what they are in normal circumstances – a clear liquid is not always water.

MAIN TEACHING ACTIVITY

If the children have not already used the term 'dissolve', then introduce it. Show the children some salt and ask: *What do you think would happen if we poured some water on this?* (The salt would dissolve.) Pour the water on and allow the children to observe the salt dissolving. Ask a child to give a 'commentary' on what they observe happening. Ask: *Can you think of anything else that dissolves in water?* (Sugar dissolves in tea.) *Can you think of anything that doesn't dissolve when you put water on it?*

Explain that the children are going to investigate the question: 'Which materials dissolve in water and which do not?' Write this question on the board. Explain that you want the children to decide how to carry out the investigation for themselves, but that you will be looking out to see if they have made it a fair test, and that you expect them to record their predictions and what happens. Show them how to use tables to record their predictions and results, drawing a table on the board as a model.

Do not at this stage discuss how to make it a fair test; this will be part of the Group activity.

Material	Prediction	Result

GROUP ACTIVITY

To enable all the children to consider the planning of the test they need to work in small groups: pairs or threes. Allow the children to begin discussing and carrying out their test. They are not expected to record the rest of their planning for the whole test in detail, as this would take too long. Circulate and ask: *How are you making this a fair test?* (By using the same amount of water and solid.) Intervene to help the children adjust their test if necessary, repeating parts if they need to.

DIFFERENTIATION

For some children, it will be enough to keep just one variable constant, for example they may put in the same amount of water, but not consider having the same amount of solid. For those children who need extension, you can ask them to consider how to keep a wider range of variables constant (to include the way they are stirring and for what length of time).

Some children may judge the amount of water by eye, others will measure it more accurately using the equipment provided. More accurate measurements of the amount of solid can be made by using level teaspoonfuls.

ASSESSMENT

Can the children keep variables constant to make it a fair test? How independently can they do this? Make notes about this as you circulate and question each group. Can they use the recording system for predictions and their results? Do they use the equipment to measure volumes of water?

PLENARY

Discuss each item in the collection – did it dissolve or not? If there are any disagreements then ask each group to explain why they think they are right. Summarise by writing on the board: *We found out that _____ dissolves in water and _____ does not dissolve in water.* This models how to present findings clearly.

OUTCOMES

● Can recognise that some materials dissolve when mixed with water and some do not.
● Can devise a test.
● Can record predictions and findings.

LINKS

Maths: measurement of volume.

LESSON 16

OBJECTIVES

● To know that an undissolved solid can be separated from a liquid by filtering.
● To present findings and suggest explanations.

RESOURCES

Main teaching activity: A sieve; a mixture of flour and lentils; a mixture of sand and water.
Group activities: 1. Containers; funnels; a collection of materials, including J-cloths, kitchen paper, loosely woven fabric, washed nylon tights, coffee filter paper, scientific filter paper; water; jugs/beakers; scissors; sand. **2.** Hand lenses or ×20 magnifiers; writing materials.

PREPARATION

Have the resources for the Main teaching activity to hand and ensure that all the children can see. Set up the tables for the Group activities, including word banks for children who need them.

Vocabulary

filter, filter paper, funnel, liquid, solid

BACKGROUND

An undissolved solid can be separated from water by filtering it. The filter works like a fine sieve, trapping the particles of solid and letting the water run through it. To help the children understand how it works, relate it to the work done in Lesson 12 on separating mixtures using sieves and colanders.

Children may have difficulty in moving from descriptions of what happens to explanations of *why* things may be happening. Being explicit about the use of the word 'because' helps to develop this.

As the investigative focus of this lesson is presenting findings and explaining, this is what children are asked to record and they are shown a way of carrying out the test so that there is not a long planning time. The children will revisit separating, including filtering (see *100 Science Lessons: Year 6/Primary 7*); so this is only an introduction to these scientific skills.

INTRODUCTION

Show the children the mixture of flour and lentils and ask them to think back to the lesson when they separated mixtures. Ask: *What could we use to separate the flour and lentils?* (A sieve.) Show the sand and water mixture and ask: *What can you tell me about this?* (The sand has sunk to the bottom, it has not dissolved.) *How could the sand and water be separated?* (With a sieve.)

MAIN TEACHING ACTIVITY

Demonstrate pouring the sand and water mixture through the sieve. Some may be trapped, but small grains of sand will go through. Ask: *How could we make sure that none of the sand gets left in the water?* (Get a sieve with smaller holes!) Explain that instead of a sieve, the children could use different materials. Demonstrate how they could test different materials by putting a piece of kitchen paper in a funnel over a beaker. Introduce the term 'filter'. Pose the question: *Which material is the best for filtering sand from water?*

Explain that you want the groups to find out which is the best material and which is the worst. You also want them to think about why each is good or bad and to try to explain it.

GROUP ACTIVITIES

1. The groups carry out the investigation. They do not need to write down how they carried out the test, but they do need to present their findings. Under the title 'What we found out', they could stick down samples of the materials they investigated, describe their effectiveness as sand filters and suggest a possible explanation for why some were better than others.
2. Ask the children to use the magnifiers to look at the materials carefully. Ask them to make drawings of what the materials look like under the magnifiers.

DIFFERENTIATION

Provide a word bank to support writing explanations. This could include useful phrases such as: 'better than', 'worse than', 'I think this is because . . .' Children could be asked to draw a diagram of what they think is happening to help extend their explanations.

ASSESSMENT

Do the children realise that filtering can be used to separate the sand from the water? Can they suggest possible explanations? Do they realise that the materials have small holes in, even though these may not be visible to the naked eye?

PLENARY

Ask the groups to feed back their findings and suggested explanations to the others. Ask: *If we had a powerful magnifier, what might we see in the filter papers?* (Holes.) Remind the children how this relates to the colander and the sieve they used in Lesson 12.

OUTCOMES

● Can recognise the properties of a material that make it a good filter.
● Can recognise that filtering is a way of separating an undissolved solid from a liquid.
● Can suggest explanations for their findings.

LINKS

English: explaining.

LESSON 17

Objectives	● To know that a dissolved substance cannot be separated from water by filtering. ● To be able to suggest possible explanations.
Resources	Sand, salt, sugar, cut up drinking straws, very clean containers, a funnel, filter paper.
Main activity	Review lessons on dissolving different materials and on separating undissolved solids by filtering. Demonstrate filtering sand from water using a filter paper as a reminder. Dissolve some sugar in water and pour through a filter. The children can taste the filtrate by dipping in their drinking straws. Repeat with the salt.
Differentiation	Expect more and less sophisticated explanations.
Assessment	Do the children realise that the filter has not stopped the salt or sugar from passing through? Can they suggest an explanation?
Plenary	Ask: *Has the filter trapped the salt or sugar? Can you suggest why?* (When solids are dissolved they go into such small pieces that they can get through the holes in the filter paper like the water can.)
Outcomes	● Can recognise that a dissolved substance cannot be separated from water by filtering. ● Can suggest explanations based on previous experience and ideas.

ASSESSMENT

LESSON 18

OBJECTIVES
● To assess children's understanding of properties of materials.
● To assess their understanding of how to carry out a fair test.

RESOURCES

Assessment activities: 1. Two different types of boiled sweets, two transparent containers, water, a spoon. **2.** A copy of photocopiable page 109 for each child.

INTRODUCTION

These Assessment activities should be considered alongside the ongoing assessment opportunities indicated throughout the unit when making a judgement about the level the child is working at.

   If all the class are able to read and write independently or there is adult support for those who cannot, then you can carry out Assessment activity 1 with a group at a time while the rest of the class are doing Assessment activity 2.

ASSESSMENT ACTIVITY 1

Work with a group of up to six children at a time. Bring them slightly away from the rest of the class. Explain that you are going to do a test to try and see which sweet dissolves the best. You want the children to watch what you do and then answer some questions about whether or not it was a fair test.

   Set up a test as shown in the illustration. Put one sweet in at least 10 seconds before the other. Exaggerate the 'unfairness'.

Answers

Ask each child: *Is this a fair test?* (No.) Ask each child what they would do to make it a fair test, starting with the children who seemed less confident about their first answer. (Use the same amount of water; have the same-sized containers; stir them in the same way for the same amount of time; put the sweets in the water at the same time.)

Looking for levels

Children who are able to recognise that the test in Assessment activity 1 is not fair and make at least one suggestion for how to improve the test are working at NC Level 3/Scottish Level C. The majority of children should achieve this. If a child is able to suggest a comprehensive set of changes that will make the test completely fair, then they may be working at NC Level 4/Scottish Level C/D. If the child clearly does not understand what is meant by a fair test, but can describe differences, for example. 'that one has more water in', this indicates that they are working at Level 2/Scottish Level B.

ASSESSMENT ACTIVITY 2

Give each child a copy of photocopiable page 109. Ask them to do the test on their own. If you are unsure what a child means by their response to a question, then discuss it with them afterwards.

Answers
1a. 40°C
1b. 60°C
1c. 35°C
1d. 23°C (accept 22 and 24°C)
3. Water and peas: colander
Paper clips and plastic cubes: magnet
Flour and rice: sieve
Sand and water: filter paper.

Looking for levels

For Assessment activity 2, most children will be working at Level 3/Scottish Level C. This is indicated by their being able to read the first three temperatures, though they may not be able to read the last. They will make sensible suggestions about what to make the items out of and will be able to offer a reason, for example a winter hat out of wool because it keeps you warm, a saucepan out of metal because it won't burn on the cooker. They will have correctly linked the mixtures with how to separate them.

Lower attaining children may be indicated by being able to correctly read only the first two temperatures. They should be able to suggest appropriate materials for the items, but their reasons may be simple, for example a winter hat out of wool because it is warm, or they may not be able to suggest a reason. They may have correctly linked only some of the mixtures with how to separate them.

Some higher attaining children may correctly read all of the temperatures and offer more sophisticated explanations, for example a winter hat out of fur because it keeps the heat in well, a saucepan out of metal because it will get hot and heat the food, but won't melt.

PLENARY

With the whole class, identify the ways of making the test for dissolving sweets a fair test. Ask the children to think about the different skills they have learned in this unit (using a thermometer, planning a fair test, recording in different kinds of tables, making a bar chart, explaining ideas). Explain that they are scientists because this is what scientists do – carry out investigations to test their ideas and try to explain what they find.

Name

Measuring temperature

Use a thermometer to measure the temperature of these things.
Remember to write °C after the number to show that it is degrees
Celsius. Find some more things and measure their temperatures.

What I am measuring	Temperature
Inside my fist (gently!)	
The air	
Tap water in a container	
Warm water	
Icy water	

Name

Reading a thermometer

1.　　　　2.　　　　3.　　　　4.　　　　5.

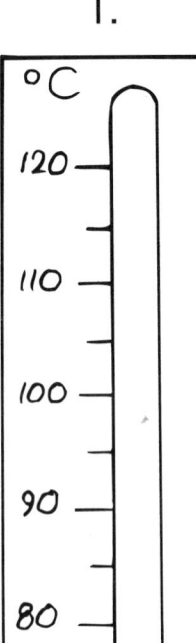
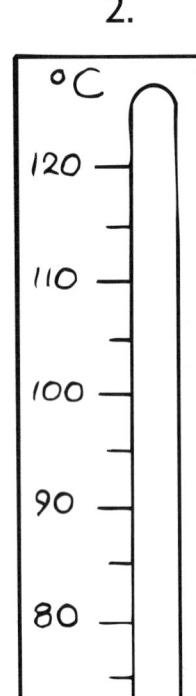
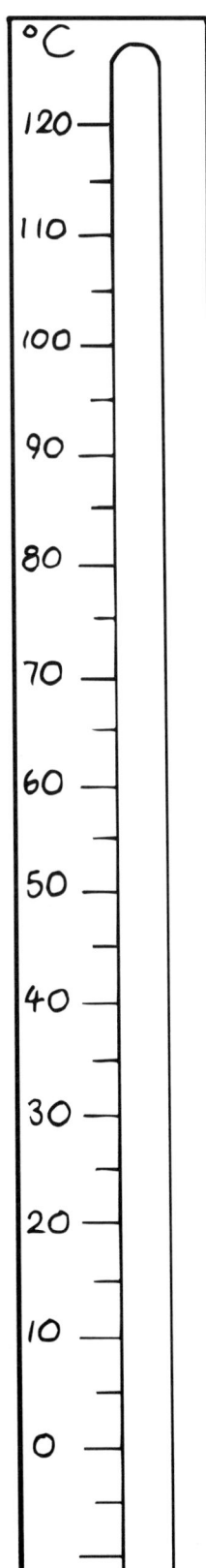
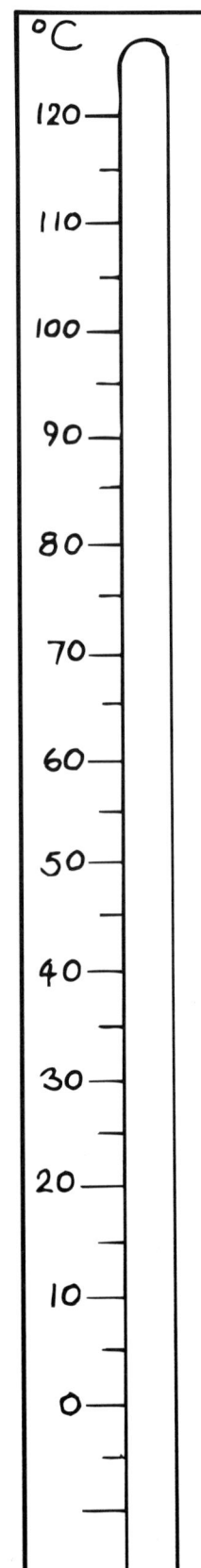
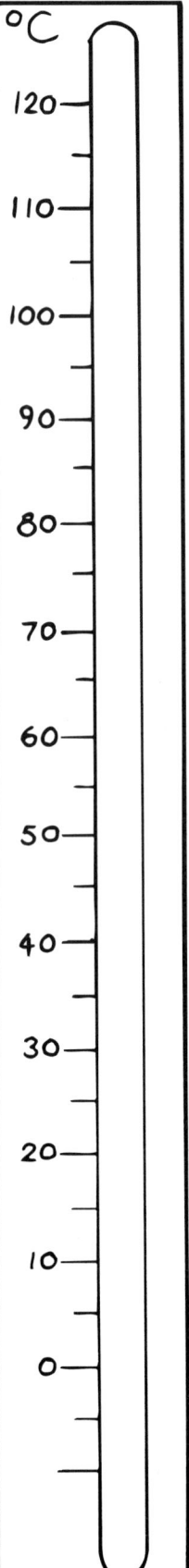

°C	°C	°C	°C	°C
120	120	120	120	120
110	110	110	110	110
100	100	100	100	100
90	90	90	90	90
80	80	80	80	80
70	70	70	70	70
60	60	60	60	60
50	50	50	50	50
40	40	40	40	40
30	30	30	30	30
20	20	20	20	20
10	10	10	10	10
0	0	0	0	0

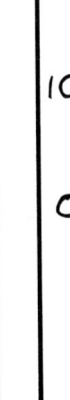

Name

Melting ice

Check the ice cube every ten minutes and put a tick in the box to show you have checked it.
When there is no ice left, put a cross in the box. Add any notes of your own below.

Time (minutes)	10	20	30	40	50	60	70	80	90	100	110	120	130	140	150	Total number of minutes
Cube 1																

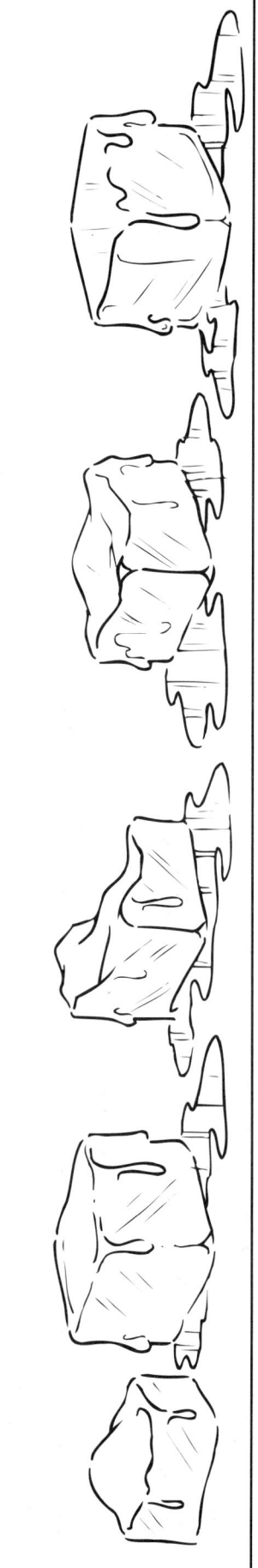

Name

Materials wordsearch

Can you find these materials in the grid?

cold	ice	measure	table
frozen	insulate	melt	temperature
hot	material	slow	thermometer

T	A	M	E	I	C	E	Z	E	S	Y	T
F	E	B	E	R	N	K	X	Q	L	J	A
A	G	M	N	A	L	S	D	C	O	W	B
R	M	S	P	M	S	C	U	J	W	B	L
G	T	A	F	E	Q	U	L	L	Y	P	E
D	A	F	T	P	R	K	R	C	A	I	X
L	B	R	O	E	M	A	H	E	I	T	V
O	S	O	D	M	R	L	T	T	R	I	E
C	Z	Z	E	F	N	I	I	U	M	G	L
T	T	E	M	E	L	T	A	P	R	J	H
U	O	N	W	R	S	U	Q	L	V	E	N
T	H	E	R	M	O	M	E	T	E	R	O

Slowing down the melting of the ice cube

A bar chart to show which material is the best at slowing down the melting of the ice cube.

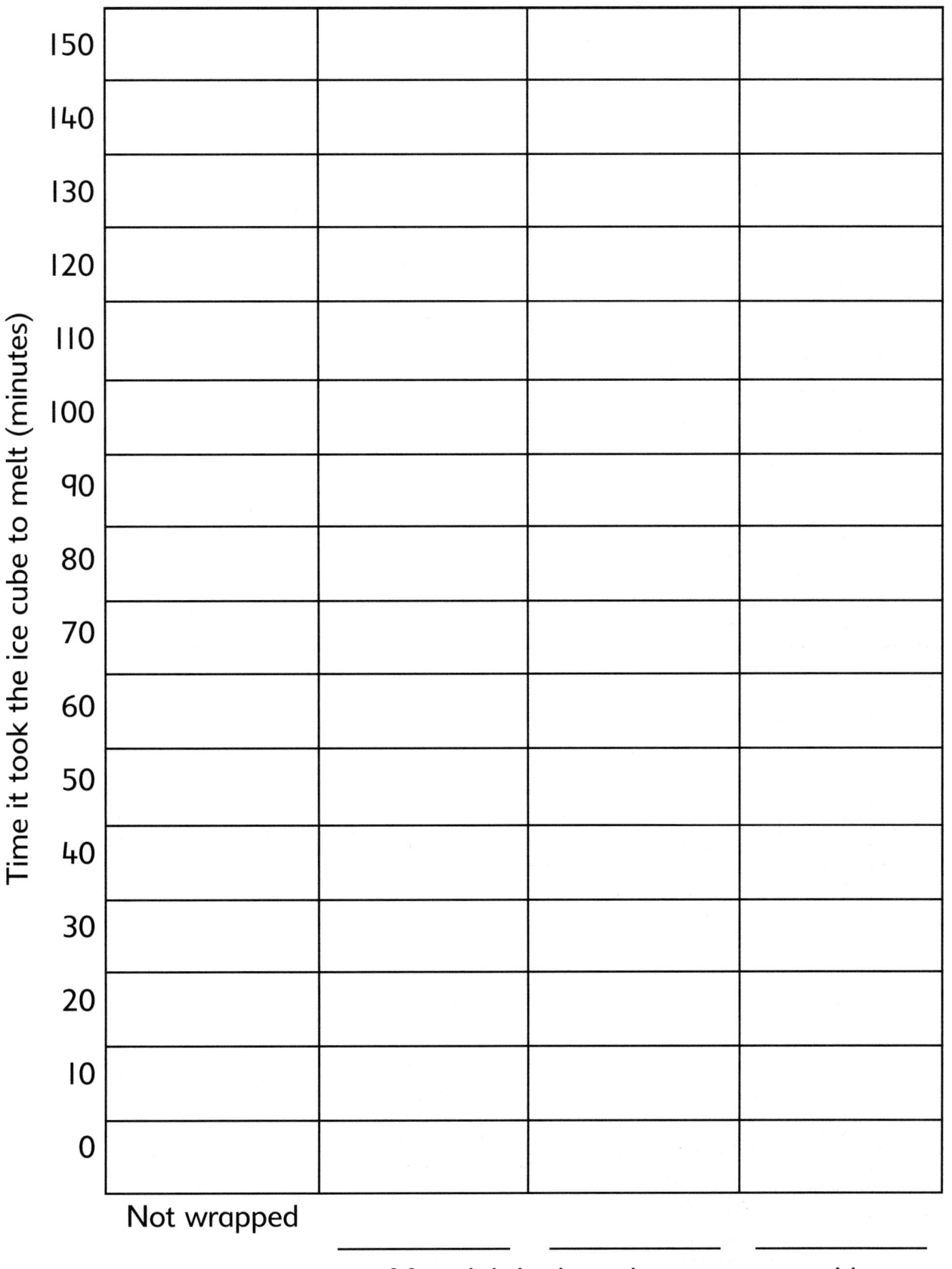

Time it took the ice cube to melt (minutes)

150
140
130
120
110
100
90
80
70
60
50
40
30
20
10
0

Not wrapped _____ _____ _____

Material the ice cube was wrapped in

Name

Warm liquids, cool solids

Some things are changed by heating or cooling them.
Sometimes they can go back to how they were before and we say the change is **reversible**. If they cannot go back, we say the change is **irreversible.**

Fill in the spaces in this chart.

How it is now	How it was before (do a drawing too)	How it changed	Is this change reversible? Yes/No
Water	Ice cube	It was heated so it melted.	
Charred wood			
Ice lolly			
Cake			
Hot milk			

Warm liquids, cool solids

1. Write down the temperature shown on the thermometers.

a)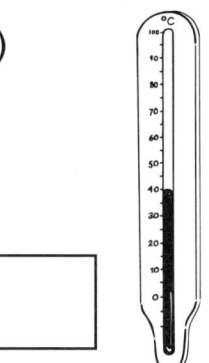

b)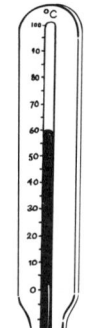

c)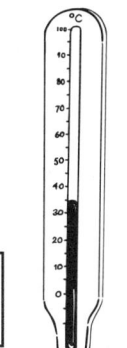

d)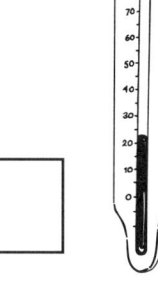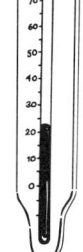

2. Finish these sentences by putting in your ideas.

I would make a winter hat out of _____

because _____.

I would make a saucepan out of _____

because _____.

3. Draw a line from the mixture to what you would use to separate it.

peas and water

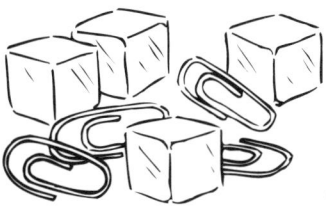

ice and paper clips

flour and rice

sand and water

magnet

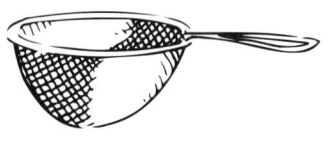

sieve

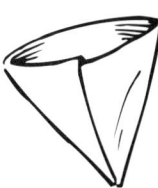

filter paper

colander

Choose one of these and draw or write to explain how it works.

Switches and conduction

ORGANISATION (11 LESSONS)

	OBJECTIVES	MAIN ACTIVITY	GROUP ACTIVITIES	PLENARY	OUTCOMES
LESSON 1	● To review work on electricity from Year 3, including the idea that a complete circuit is needed for a device to work. ● To elicit children's ideas about electricity. ● To know how to interpret drawings of electrical circuits and make circuits from them. ● To make and test predictions.	Eliciting children's existing ideas about electricity, reviewing circuit diagrams from previous year.	Predicting and testing whether different circuit diagrams will work in practice. Brainstorming 'What I know about electricity'.	Discussing the need to complete a circuit.	● Teacher is aware of children's existing ideas about electricity. ● Can interpret drawings of circuits and recognise those that will work. ● Can assemble a circuit from a drawing. ● Can make predictions and test them.
LESSON 2	● To know that circuits powered by batteries are safe to investigate, but mains electricity is too dangerous.	Listing items that are mains- or battery-powered. Exploring risks of mains electricity using secondary sources and writing 'cautionary tales'.		Sharing 'cautionary tales' to reinforce safety message.	● Can explain that circuits powered by batteries are safe to investigate, but mains electricity is too dangerous.
LESSON 3	● To know that mains electricity is a form of energy that has been converted from other forms of energy. ● To use secondary sources of information.	Where does electricity come from? Demonstration of waterwheel and windmill. Link to making electricity in power stations using secondary sources.		Review children's ideas about the sources of mains electricity.	● Can give examples of forms of energy that have been converted into electricity. ● Can use secondary sources of information.
LESSON 4	● To know that electricity flows through some materials and not others. ● To make predictions on the basis of previous experience. ● To design a circuit for testing the conductivity of materials. ● To make generalisations from results.	The question 'What can electricity travel through?' is discussed.	Children predict and test which materials can conduct electricity.	Generalising that metals are conductors and most non-metals are insulators.	● Can state that electricity flows through some materials and not others. ● Can make predictions. ● Can design a circuit for testing the conductivity of materials. ● Can make generalisations from results.
LESSON 5	● To know where conductors and insulators are used in mains and battery circuits. ● To know that more than one wire is in the cable for electrical appliances.	Considering how household electrical items use insulation for safety reasons.		Discussion reviewing safe use of electricity.	● Know where conductors and insulators are used in mains and battery circuits. ● Can recognise that more than one wire is in the cable for electrical appliances.
LESSON 6	● To know that switches can be designed in a variety of ways. ● To understand that a switch works by breaking a circuit.	Discussion and demonstration of making and breaking circuits.	Making a range of different switches and explaining how they work.	Discussing the roles of conductors and insulators in switches.	● Know that switches can be designed in a variety of ways. ● Can explain that a switch works by breaking a circuit. ● Can recognise air as an insulator.
LESSON 7	● To use appropriate designs of switches in model-making. ● To apply their understanding of switches in problem-solving.	Design and make a model using a switch.		Children present their models and explain how they work.	● Can use appropriate designs of switches in model-making. ● Can apply their understanding of switches in problem-solving.

ORGANISATION (11 LESSONS)

	OBJECTIVES	MAIN ACTIVITY	GROUP ACTIVITIES	PLENARY	OUTCOMES
LESSON 8	● To know that batteries may be connected together to provide greater electrical power. ● To follow children's own lines of enquiry. ● To develop skills of recording observations independently.	Observation of torch with two batteries. Question raised: 'What difference does the number of batteries make?'	Exploring circuits with different numbers of components and recording observations.	Feeding back observations. Considering the effect of adding a battery.	● Can assemble a circuit with two or three batteries. ● Can explain that batteries may be connected together to provide greater electrical power. ● Can follow their own lines of enquiry. ● Can record observations independently.
LESSON 9	● To investigate changing the number of bulbs in a circuit. ● To make and test predictions. ● To carry out a fair test by only changing one factor at a time.	Identifying different components that could be changed in a circuit. Focus on bulbs.	Investigate the effect of changing the number of bulbs.	Comparing how different groups have connected their bulbs (parallel and series).	● Can investigate changing the number of bulbs in a circuit. ● Can make and test predictions. ● Can carry out a fair test by only changing one factor at a time.
LESSON 10	● To consolidate and review work through drama. ● To communicate ideas about electricity learned through the unit.	Using drama to model an electric circuit.		Performing improvisations.	● Can communicate their understanding about electricity. ● Can relate the different aspects of the topic to each other.

	OBJECTIVES	ACTIVITY 1	ACTIVITY 2
ASSESSMENT 11	● To assess children's understanding of circuits, conductors and insulators. ● To assess the children's understanding of how switches work.	Practical challenge to make the 'clown's eyes' light up by making a complete circuit from a battery to bulbs using only one wire and a range of conducting materials.	Pencil and paper test on interpreting circuit diagrams, switches and safety with electricity.

LESSON 1

OBJECTIVES

● To review work on electricity from Year 3/Primary 4, including the idea that a complete circuit is needed for a device to work.
● To elicit children's ideas about electricity.
● To know how to interpret drawings of electrical circuits and make circuits from them.
● To make and test predictions.

RESOURCES

Main teaching activity: Flip chart and marker pens; enlarged circuit drawings as on photocopiable page 124 copied on to the flip chart.
Group activities: 1. Copies of photocopiable page 124, wires, batteries, bulbs, buzzers, screwdrivers. **2.** Writing and drawing materials.

PREPARATION

Copy the circuit drawings on photocopiable page 124 on to the flip chart. Put a selection of electrical equipment on each group's table. Have the children sitting on the carpet in front of the flip chart.

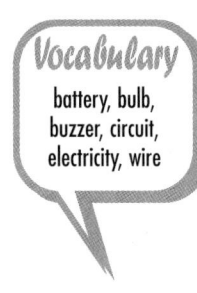

Vocabulary

battery, bulb, buzzer, circuit, electricity, wire

BACKGROUND

The initial whole-class discussion will enable you to find out children's existing ideas as a starting point for later work. Children tend to associate electricity with the mains rather than with batteries. This unit will consider both, and help children to see them both as sources of electricity.

There is a danger with this topic that children have similar experiences of making simple circuits as they go through school, with limited progression. This lesson recaps work on the need for a complete circuit to make it 'work' from Year 2/3/Primary 3/4 before moving on.

INTRODUCTION

Explain that the class is beginning a new topic on electricity that will develop the ideas they learned in previous years. Plug in and switch on a CD player and then sit playing on a 'Game Boy'. Besides getting the children's attention, this illustrates mains- and battery-powered equipment.

MAIN TEACHING ACTIVITY

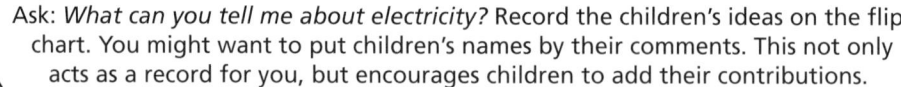

Ask: *What can you tell me about electricity?* Record the children's ideas on the flip chart. You might want to put children's names by their comments. This not only acts as a record for you, but encourages children to add their contributions.

Ask them to tell you about work they have done on electricity in previous years. Explain that you are going to give them some drawings of circuits. You want them to predict whether they think the circuit will work or not, and test it out by making the circuit.

GROUP ACTIVITIES

1. Give each pair of children a copy of photocopiable page 124. Ask them to record their prediction on the sheet then test it by making the circuit. Having the children working in pairs will support exchange of ideas, and help the children to draw on their previous learning. Circulate, asking children to explain the reasons for their predictions and the reasons why the circuit has or has not worked.

2. Ask the children to work in pairs but to record individually a brainstorm of 'My ideas about electricity'. This develops the discussion that was started as a whole class.

DIFFERENTIATION

Children who have physical difficulty in constructing the circuits may not complete them all. Make sure they do not become frustrated by supporting them. Others can be challenged by asking them to design and draw a circuit that they know does or does not work as a problem for other children to solve.

ASSESSMENT

Can the children make a prediction based on logical thinking? Can they construct circuits as in the diagrams? Can they explain that to work, there must be a complete circuit with no breaks? Note any children who are not secure with these ideas in order to give extra support in subsequent lessons.

PLENARY

Using the copies of the circuit drawings on the flip chart, consider each circuit in turn and ask the class: *Did this circuit work? Why? Why not?* Emphasise the idea of electricity travelling in a circuit by tracing the circuit round with your finger and coming to an abrupt halt if there is a break in the circuit. Encourage the children to do the same with their own circuit diagrams.

OUTCOMES

- Teacher is aware of children's existing ideas about electricity.
- Can interpret drawings of circuits and recognise those that will work.
- Can assemble a circuit from a drawing.
- Can make predictions and test them.

LINKS

PSHE: awareness of mains electricity supply.

LESSON 2

Objective	● To know that circuits powered by batteries are safe to investigate, but mains electricity is too dangerous.
Resources	A flip chart and marker pens; secondary sources on electricity and safety, such as *Electricity and Magnets* or *More about Electricity and Magnetism* (Nuffield Primary Science children's books); *Cats' Eyes: Electricity* and *Light and Sound* (BBC videos); *100 Literacy Hours: Year 4* (page 151 'Big Fears'; Scholastic).
Main activity	Ask the children to brainstorm appliances that run from batteries and appliances that run from mains electricity, listing them in two columns on the flip chart. Ask them to suggest reasons why, such as convenience, amount of power needed. Ask: *Is it OK for us to investigate electricity? Why? Why not?* Explore the children's existing ideas about the dangers of electricity. Use books or videos to explore the risks of mains electricity. Ask the children to write 'cautionary tales' about children who misused mains electricity: you may need to provide an example.
Differentiation	Choose secondary sources that different children can access. The 'cautionary tales' could be tape recorded or written in groups to support those with poorer literacy skills. Extend children by asking them to find out the voltage of mains electricity and compare it with that of batteries they use.
Assessment	Can the children explain why they must not explore mains electricity? Can they give some specific examples of dangerous behaviour with mains electricity? Can they explain why it is OK to investigate circuits with batteries?
Plenary	Share some of the stories. Return to the flip chart list and stress that it is safe to explore batteries and that everything you ask them to do in school is safe. Ask: *Why is it that mains electricity is dangerous and batteries are safe?* (Because mains electricity is much more powerful.)
Outcome	● Can explain that circuits powered by batteries are safe to investigate, but mains electricity is too dangerous.

LESSON 3

Objectives	● To know that mains electricity is a form of energy that has been converted from other forms of energy. ● To use secondary sources of information.
Resources	A paper windmill; waterwheel bath toy; flip chart and marker pens; secondary sources on generation of electricity, for example *More about Electricity and Magnetism* (Nuffield Primary Science books); *Energy from Nature* (Channel 4 video) and/or a visit to a power station.

Main activity	Ask: *Where do you think mains electricity comes from?* Write down the children's ideas on the flip chart.
	    Show children the toy windmill. Blow on it so that it turns and ask: *How am I making it move? Where is the energy to make it move coming from?* (From you; from the wind.) Demonstrate a toy waterwheel. Explain that windmills and waterwheels used to be a source of energy to grind corn. Now we use the energy of the turning wheel and change the energy into electricity. Explain that there are other ways to make wheels (turbines) turn to make electricity, and that's what happens in power stations. Ask: *How could we find out more?*
	    Use secondary sources (perhaps during non-fiction work, for example, in a Literacy Hour) or a visit to a power station to explore this further.
	    Ask: *Where does mains electricity come from?* Ask children to present their ideas as an annotated drawing in response to the question. (See more on this in *100 Science Lessons: Year 5/Primary 6*.)

Differentiation	Support children in their use of secondary sources, by helping them to apply research skills as learned during the Literacy Hour. Expect some accounts to show a good understanding of the different stages in power generation and others to indicate a lower level of understanding.
Assessment	There is likely to be a wide variation in the children's understanding of power generation. Use the annotated drawings to judge the level of understanding. Can they give examples of sources of energy that are used? (For example, wind or coal.) Are they aware that the turbines are an important part of the process? Can they describe how electrical cable, pylons and underground cables bring electricity to our homes?
Plenary	Revisit the flip chart showing children's ideas about where electricity comes from. Ask the children if any of their ideas have changed, if any were on the right lines, and what they would add to the list now.
Outcomes	● Can give examples of forms of energy that have been converted into electricity. ● Can use secondary sources of information.

LESSON 4

OBJECTIVES
- To know that electricity flows through some materials and not others.
- To make predictions on the basis of previous experience.
- To design a circuit for testing the conductivity of materials.
- To make generalisations from results.

RESOURCES

Group activities: 1. Batteries, wires, bulbs; collections of materials that do and do not conduct electricity such as a paper clip, card, silver foil, plastic, scissors with plastic handles, a penny, a pencil, a container of water. **2.** Writing and drawing materials.

PREPARATION

Put the collections of materials out on the tables. Have the electrical equipment divided into sets for each table, but keep these to one side. Have the flip chart showing the circuit drawings from Lesson 1 available.

Vocabulary

conduct, conductor, insulator, material

It is not essential that the children use the correct terminology at this stage, but the words 'conductor' and 'insulator' are introduced in the Plenary session, once the children have a good understanding of the concepts they represent.

BACKGROUND

Materials can be classified as electrical conductors or electrical insulators depending on how well electricity can flow through them. Metals are particularly good conductors and plastics are particularly good insulators. Graphite (pencil lead) is the most well-known example of a non-metal conductor. Remember that air is also an insulator, which is why a break in a circuit stops the electricity from flowing. However, at very high voltages, electricity will flow through almost anything! The children can explore the materials provided, but will probably have suggestions of their own of things to test and should have the opportunity to try these out.

Materials can be inserted into a simple circuit, as illustrated, to test them. However, rather than simply giving them this method, it is better to allow children to devise their own circuit for this, only providing suggestions if needed.

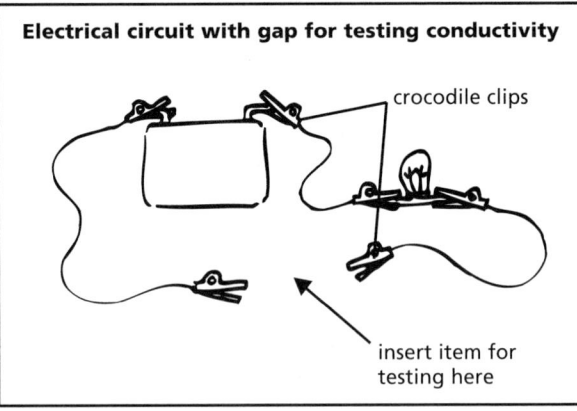

Electrical circuit with gap for testing conductivity

crocodile clips

insert item for testing here

INTRODUCTION

Show the class the drawings of circuits from Lesson 1 on the flip chart. Ask: *Can you explain why some of the circuits we made worked and some of them didn't?* (Some of them had breaks in the circuit so the electricity could not go all the way around.)

MAIN TEACHING ACTIVITY

Ask: *In our circuits, what is the electricity travelling through?* (It is travelling through the wires, bulbs and batteries.) *Do you think electricity can travel through anything?* Listen to the children's responses to this, they will have a variety of ideas and explanations which should be acknowledged. Note any ideas that need challenging and target those children for questions in the Group activities. Explain that you want the children to explore a collection and predict whether electricity will flow through the different items or not.

GROUP ACTIVITIES

1. Ask the groups to sort the collection into those materials they think electricity will and will not go through and record those predictions in their own way: as lists, Venn diagrams, tables and so on. Give out the electrical equipment and ask the children to devise a way of finding out if their predictions were right. Give them some time to tackle the problem themselves, but intervene if any group is becoming frustrated. Ask them to do a drawing showing how they carried out the test and to record the results in their own way.

2. If there are insufficient batteries and bulbs for all the groups to test their predictions at once, then as a 'holding' activity ask some groups to look around the classroom and note the materials that different battery and mains items are made from. An item, for example a listening centre and headphones, could be recorded as an annotated drawing. This is good preparation for Lesson 5.

Safety: Remind children not to plug items into the mains electricity, nor to take them apart.

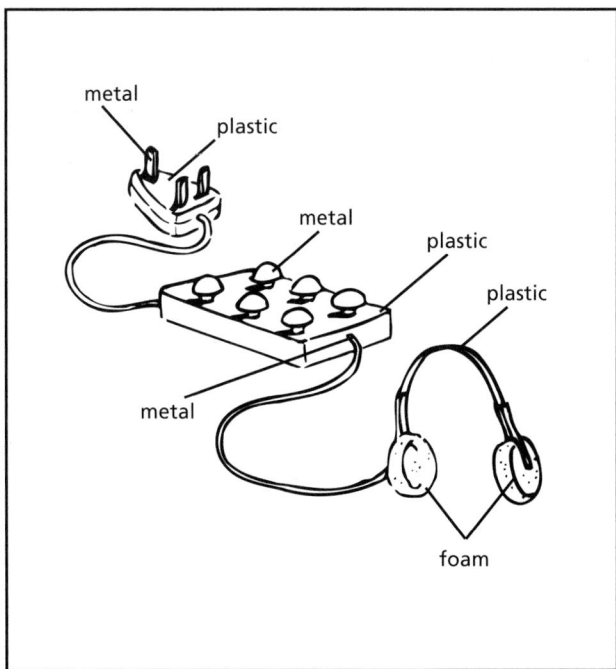

DIFFERENTIATION

If children cannot find their own way of testing the materials, show them how to put them into a gap in a circuit. Ask children who are higher achievers in science to give a reason for their prediction.

Expect some children to list which materials do and do not let electricity go through them, but challenge other children to make a generalisation by asking: *What have all those materials got in common? Can you tell me what sorts of materials conduct electricity and which don't?* Ask them to suggest other materials that would or would not conduct electricity, and to test those too to support their idea.

Provide a word bank of the names of the materials to support those with poorer writing skills, and if necessary scribe their predictions so that they can move onto the testing quickly.

ASSESSMENT

Can the children give examples of materials that electricity can flow through and materials that it cannot flow through? Can they make predictions? Are they able to design a circuit to test the materials independently? Can they make generalisations from their results (for example, that metals are good at conducting electricity)?

PLENARY

Draw two columns on the board or flip chart and write 'Conductors – do let electricity through' and 'Insulators – do not let electricity through', to head the columns. Explain that there are special scientific words for the two groups that they have found: 'conductors' and 'insulators'. Ask different children to provide examples of a conductor or an insulator and write them in the relevant column.

Ask: *Is there anything the conductors have in common?* (Most are metals.) *Is there anything the insulators have in common?* (Various possible responses; focus on the idea that they are 'non-metals'.)

OUTCOMES

- Can state that electricity flows through some materials and not others.
- Can make predictions.
- Can design a circuit for testing the conductivity of materials.
- Can make generalisations from results.

LINKS

Unit 4 Materials: use of the words 'conductor' and 'insulator' in the context of heat.

LESSON 5

Objectives	● To know where conductors and insulators are used in mains and battery circuits. ● To know that there is more than one wire in the cable for electrical appliances.
Resources	A collection of electrical cables cut to show the different parts inside; electrical leads; 3-pin plugs with the backs removed; simple torches that can be disassembled. **Safety:** Never offer plugs wired to short lengths of cable, as the live cable is potentially lethal if the plug is put into a wall socket.
Main activity	Recap the previous lesson on conductors and insulators, making sure the children are aware that metals are conductors and plastics are insulators. Ask the children to explore the collection, looking carefully to see which parts are metal and which are plastic. Ask each group or pair to take one item and make a large drawing of it, showing the different parts clearly and labelling them 'conductor' or 'insulator' to make a poster. Give clear instructions that the children are not to try to plug in any of the items, as that could kill them. Remind them of Lesson 2.
Differentiation	It will be more appropriate for some children to use the labels 'metal' and 'plastic'.
Assessment	Can the children identify the different parts as conductors and insulators? Can they suggest reasons for the choice of materials? Are they aware that there is more than one wire inside an electric cable?
Plenary	Ask each group to show their poster to the whole class. Invite them to think about the reasons for using the different materials in certain places by asking questions, such as: *Why do you think that part is made of plastic?* Relate this back to the work on safety in Lesson 2. Draw the children's attention to the fact that there is more than one wire inside the cables, so there is a circuit, even though it does not look like that from the outside. Reinforce the safety message that this is not something to try at home and never to tamper with appliances that are plugged in.
Outcomes	● Know where conductors and insulators are used in mains and battery circuits. ● Can recognise that there is more than one wire in the cable for electrical appliances.

LESSON 6

OBJECTIVES

● To know that switches can be designed in a variety of ways.
● To understand that a switch works by breaking a circuit.

RESOURCES

Main teaching activity: A simple circuit of bulb, battery and two connecting wires.
Group activities: 1. Batteries, wires, wire cutters, bulbs, buzzers, paper fasteners, paper clips, drawing pins, aluminium foil, clothes pegs, balsa wood, card, plastic bottles, cardboard tubes, copies of photocopiable page 125. **2.** 'Bought' switches for use in simple circuits that can be disassembled (TTS [see page 8] and other educational resource companies supply these), and household switches which are also interesting. **2.** Writing and drawing materials.

PREPARATION

Copy photocopiable page 125 so that there are enough copies for one between two. These could be laminated for future use. Put a selection of resources on the tables and have others on one side. Make up the circuit for the Main teaching activity. Have the children sitting in a circle on the carpet.

Vocabulary

conductor, insulator, switch

BACKGROUND

Switches work by breaking and making circuits. This relates to the previous lessons as the circuit is completed when a conductor is put across the break, and broken when an insulator, often air, is across the break. Although switches can be bought for use in model-making, by making their own switches, children are developing their understanding of circuits and of conductors and insulators.

  Buzzers need to be put into a circuit the right way round. If a circuit is not working, try connecting the buzzer the other way.

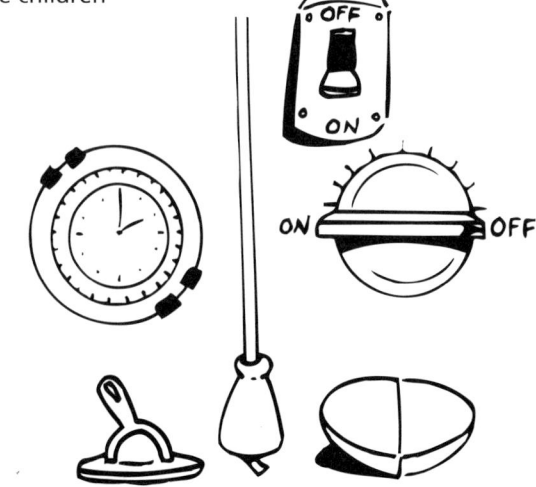

INTRODUCTION

Remind the children of what they have done in previous lessons on circuits, conductors and insulators, and explain that they will need to use those ideas to help them in this lesson on switches. Ask: *Where do we have switches in our homes?* (For lights, on the TV, on the computer, and so on.)

MAIN TEACHING ACTIVITY

Put the ready-made circuit on the floor in the centre of the circle, fully connected so that the bulb is on. Ask: *How could we switch the bulb off?* Invite a child to show you by breaking the circuit. Ask them to explain what they have done. Remake the circuit and ask: *Can anyone find a different way of switching the bulb off?* Repeat the process of inviting children to show and explain how they have broken the circuit.

Explain that we can switch the light on and off just by making and breaking the circuit. That is all a switch does, but as it would be a bit fiddly trying to join up bits of wire, switches are designed specially to make this easier.

GROUP ACTIVITIES

1. Give the children copies of photocopiable page 125. Ask them to try making some different switches and trying them out in simple circuits. Circulate, asking children to explain how their switches work, focusing on children who are quiet in whole-class discussions.
2. Children could also take apart 'bought' switches to see how they have been made and make annotated drawings to explain how they work.

DIFFERENTIATION

Some children will make several designs and some children only one. Extend children by asking them to design their own switches.

ASSESSMENT

Can the children explain that a switch works by breaking a circuit? Can they use their understanding of conductors and insulators to explain that air is an insulator in many switches?

PLENARY

Ask some children to demonstrate their switches to the class, including particularly any that the children have designed themselves. Ask: *Which part of your switch is a conductor/insulator?* Where air is the insulator, ask: *What is in that gap?* (Air is in the gap.) *Can electricity get through air?* (No, not in these circumstances, though the children may raise the idea that lightning travels through air.) Explain that in the next lesson they will be using what they have learned in making some models.

OUTCOMES

● Know that switches can be designed in a variety of ways.
● Can explain that a switch works by breaking a circuit.
● Can recognise air as an insulator.

LINKS

Design and technology: incorporating electrical circuits into models.

LESSON 7

Objectives	● To use appropriate designs of switches in model-making. ● To apply their understanding of switches in problem-solving.
Resources	Batteries, wires, bulbs, buzzers, wire cutters, paper fasteners, paper clips, drawing pins, aluminium foil, clothes pegs, balsa wood, card, plastic bottles, junk materials, other modelling materials, scissors, glue.
Main activity	Ask the children to design and make a model that uses a switch. Ideally the model should be related to other work going on, such as a history topic or a story. Let the children know how much time is available so that they can plan accordingly and are not overambitious. You may want to make suggestions of models or leave it completely up to the children, depending on how experienced they are with design and technology activities. Possible models include: a light for reading in bed (with a pressure switch in the bed); a model of the Iron Man with eyes that light up; a 'wolf alert' buzzer in one of the houses of the Three Little Pigs; or, more challenging, a set of quiz-show lights to show which contestants want to answer.
Differentiation	Children can support each other in pairs or groups. The circuits can be very simple on/off switches through to more complex designs involving more than one bulb. Encourage children to challenge themselves, but ensure that plans are achievable in the time available.
Assessment	Have the children chosen an appropriate switch for the task? Have they persevered in solving problems with the circuits, for example checking for breaks in the circuit if it didn't work?
Plenary	Children can demonstrate their designs, showing how they work.
Outcomes	● Can use appropriate designs of switches in model-making. ● Can apply their understanding of switches in problem-solving.

LESSON 8

OBJECTIVES

● To know that batteries may be connected together to provide greater electrical power.
● For children to follow their own lines of enquiry.
● To develop skills of recording observations independently.

RESOURCES

Main teaching activity: A range of types and sizes of batteries; a torch that needs two batteries and can be opened to show the space for them; a flip chart and marker pens.
Group activities: 1. A range of types and sizes of batteries; connecting wires; bulbs; buzzers; motors; writing equipment.
2. Copies of photocopiable page 126, writing and drawing materials.

PREPARATION

Put out a selection of electrical equipment on each table, keeping the rest in reserve.

Vocabulary

battery, circuit, power

BACKGROUND

Different batteries have different voltages, which means they have different amounts of 'push' to move electrons around a circuit. You could use the analogy that some things need more 'push' to make them move than others. Avoid saying they have different amounts of electricity in them as this is misleading. Batteries can be joined together in series or in parallel (see diagram). Children do not need to know these terms, but you could draw their attention to the fact that the batteries are connected in a different way.

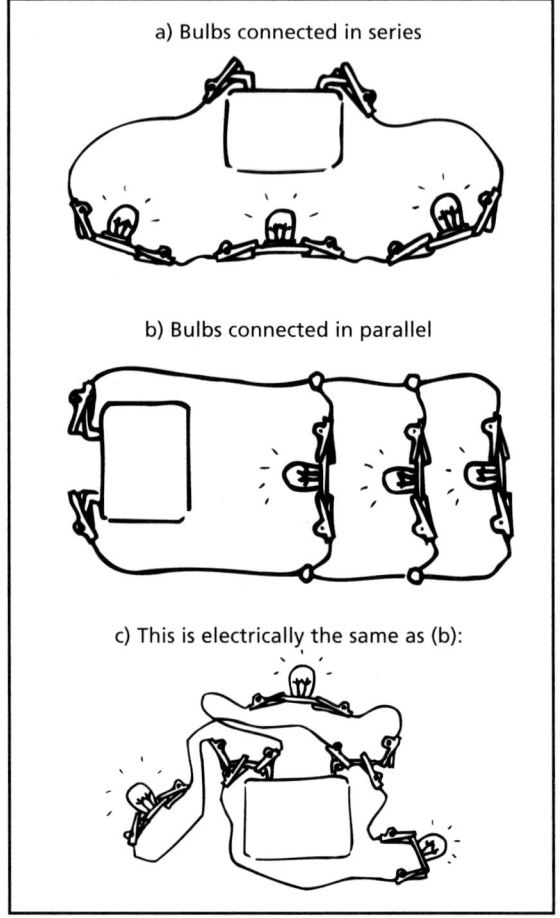

a) Bulbs connected in series

b) Bulbs connected in parallel

c) This is electrically the same as (b):

This activity can become costly on bulbs if too many are 'blown' as large voltages are applied to them. Be prepared for this to happen and raise the question of why with the children, but do keep control of the supply of bulbs so you don't lose too many. Limiting the number of batteries available can also help with this. Also beware of batteries becoming too hot.

INTRODUCTION

Ask: *What can you say about this collection of batteries?* (They are different sizes and different 'strengths'; they go into different appliances; they have different numbers on the sides.) Ask: *Why do you think we have different sorts of batteries?* (Some things need lots of power, some only need a bit, some are too small for a big battery.) Ask the children to pick out examples of any batteries they know would fit into certain toys or appliances they have at home.

MAIN TEACHING ACTIVITY

Show the children the cavity of a torch that needs two batteries. Ask: *Which battery from our collection do you think would fit in there?* Try out any suggestions. When someone suggests that two batteries are needed, ask why that might be. (To make it light; to make it bright; to fit in so all the connections are made.) Ask: *How could we find out what difference it makes having more than one battery?* Listen to suggestions. Ask the children to try out some of their own ideas, explaining that you want them to keep a record of the process as they go along. Model this on the flip chart, such as 'First I am going to connect the batteries like this and see if the motor goes.' Draw on the chart. 'I found that it went quite fast. Now I am going to try _____.'

Explain that if they notice any of the batteries getting hot, they should tell you. Also explain that you will keep the spare bulbs and they should come to you if they need more.

GROUP ACTIVITIES

1. The children can work in pairs to explore their own ideas, recording them as they go. Encourage them to explore using a range of types of battery and different buzzers and motors. Circulate, suggesting that children explore different ways of connecting the batteries (in series and parallel).

2. Give the children a copy of photocopiable page 126. Ask them to fill in their responses.

DIFFERENTIATION

Children will differentiate themselves as they explore their own ideas. Intervene with questions to encourage thought at higher levels, such as: *Can you show me with your finger where you think the electricity is flowing? Can you explain why you think that is happening?*

ASSESSMENT

Are the children able to make suggestions of things to try out in their exploration? Can they make observations and record them? Can they suggest explanations for what they notice?

PLENARY

Ask different groups to report back to the class one interesting thing they found out. Ask: *What do you think happens when more than one battery is connected together?*

OUTCOMES

- Can assemble a circuit with two or three batteries.
- Can explain that batteries may be connected together to provide greater electrical power.
- Can follow their own lines of enquiry.
- Can record observations independently.

LINKS

Design and technology: incorporating simple electrical circuits into models.

LESSON 9

OBJECTIVES

● To investigate changing the number of bulbs in a circuit.
● To make and test predictions.
● To carry out a fair test by only changing one factor at a time.

RESOURCES

Main teaching activity: A battery, bulb and two connecting wires made into a simple circuit; spare connecting wires and bulbs to hand; Post-it notes and planning board (optional).
Group activities: 1. Batteries, bulbs, connecting wires, writing materials. **2.** Copies of photocopiable page 127 copied onto card; scissors; writing and drawing materials.

PREPARATION

Copy photocopiable page 127 onto card, enough for one per pair or group of three children. Have the resources for the Main teaching activity to hand. Put out resources for the Group activities on the tables. Have the children sitting on the carpet in a circle.

Vocabulary

bulb, connection, fair test, investigate

BACKGROUND

Bulbs can be arranged in series or in parallel (see diagram on page 116). The way that they are connected will affect how bright they are. If the bulbs are in series, the more bulbs that are added, the less current flows through the circuit and the bulbs glow less brightly. However, if the bulbs are connected in parallel, each bulb would be as bright as if it were connected to a separate battery, but, the battery would run down more quickly. The children do not need to know the terms 'in series' or 'in parallel' at this stage, but you will need to be aware of this to explain differences in results depending on how the children have chosen to connect their bulbs.

Different bulbs have different voltages written on the side, though they may look the same in other respects. Make sure that the bulbs the children are using for this investigation are all the same or they will have different brightnesses that will confuse the results.

In this lesson, children will develop their investigation skills, building on the less-structured enquiry of the previous lesson.

INTRODUCTION

Remind the children of how in the previous lesson they had changed the batteries and other components of circuits. Ask: *What do you know about circuits now?* Help the children to review their learning so far. Praise them for their efforts.

MAIN TEACHING ACTIVITY

Show the children the simple circuit and ask: *What could we change about this circuit?* List the ideas on the board or use Post-it Notes on a planning board: number of batteries, type of battery, type of wires, number of bulbs, type of bulb. Explain that you want them to investigate what happens when the number of bulbs is changed. Ask: *Can we turn that into a question?* ('When I change the number of bulbs what happens?') Write this question on the board. Ask: *What happens to what? What might we see when we change the number of bulbs?* (They may not light; they may be brighter; they may be less bright.) Change the question so that it reads: 'When I change the number of bulbs what happens to the brightness of the bulbs?'

Explain that you want the children to plan their test before they begin.

GROUP ACTIVITIES

1. Ask the children to plan and carry out their tests using the following frame:
Our question:
Our prediction:
Drawing of our test:
What I will change:
What I will keep the same:
What I found out:
Initially, leave children to make their own plans, but if it becomes clear that they have not controlled the variables, for example they have planned to add more batteries at the same time as adding more bulbs, then intervene and discuss with the child if it is possible to compare the two circuits.
2. Give each pair or group of three children a copy on card of photocopiable page 127. Ask them to look at the pictures and think about how bright the light needs to be. Ask a child in each pair or group to cut the out the twelve cards. Ask the children to put the cards in order from the one

they think needs to be the brightest to the one they think could be least bright. Ask them to draw some ideas of their own on the blank cards and include these in the order. Stress the importance of discussing their ideas over finding 'right answers'.

DIFFERENTIATION

The writing frame can be provided as headings on a worksheet, or to encourage independence it could be presented as a list of prompt headings. Support children with limited writing skills by scribing for them or providing more writing on the frame, for example under the heading 'Our prediction', write: 'I think that when I add more bulbs...' Challenge children by asking them to try to give a reason for their prediction or an explanation for their findings.

ASSESSMENT

Have the children made a prediction about what will happen? Have they given a reason for their prediction? Are the children able to control the variables independently or have they needed support with this?

PLENARY

Choose one group who have connected their bulbs in series and one who have connected their bulbs in parallel and ask them to report their findings to the rest of the class, showing the circuits they have made. As the group who have connected their bulbs in parallel will have found no difference in the brightness and the ones who connected in series will have found a difference, ask the class if they can see any reason why the groups got different results. Discuss their ideas, reaching the conclusion that it depends on how the bulbs are connected.

OUTCOMES

- Can investigate changing the number of bulbs in a circuit.
- Can make and test predictions.
- Can carry out a fair test by only changing one factor at a time.

LINKS

Design and technology: incorporating simple electrical circuits into models.

LESSON 10

Objectives	● To consolidate and review work through drama. ● To communicate ideas about electricity learned through the unit.
Resources	Enough balls or beanbags for at least one each; other resources such as hoops, card, sticky tape and felt-tipped pens may be useful for the improvisations.

Main activity	Have the whole class in a circle. Explain that they are going to model an electric circuit with your bodies. Say that you will be the battery that will 'push around' the electric current and they will be the wires. Give each child a ball and tell them all to start together passing balls around the 'circuit' to represent electricity flowing along the wires. Ask different children to act out being different components: a buzzer, a motor or a bulb, for example. Ask a child to be a switch by stepping in and out of the circle to create a gap.
	    Divide the class into six groups and ask each group to take one of the following aspects of the unit: safety, making electricity, conductivity of different materials, switches, varying the number of bulbs, varying the number of batteries.
	    Ask each group to devise a short improvisation in which they present what they have learned about their aspect of the topic. These presentations and role-plays could be presented to another class or used in an assembly.

Differentiation	The easier areas to improvise around are safety and switches. The more difficult are making electricity and varying the number of batteries. These could be allocated to different groups accordingly.
Assessment	Is there evidence that the children are expressing understanding of the topic through their improvisations?
Plenary	Present the improvisations, either to the rest of the class or invite another class as the audience.
Outcomes	● Can communicate their understanding about electricity. ● Can relate the different aspects of the topic to each other.

ASSESSMENT

LESSON 11

OBJECTIVES

● To assess children's understanding of circuits, conductors and insulators.
● To assess children's understanding of how switches work.

RESOURCES

Assessment activities: 1. Copies of photocopiable page 128 on card for each pair of children; a box to include one 4.5V battery, two bulbs in bulb holders, two short connecting wires with clips on the ends (make sure the circuit cannot be completed using only these); a variety of conducting materials such as paper clips, coins, aluminium foil, metal strips, and a variety of non-conductors such as plastics, string, rubber (be aware of kitchen foils and some paper clips having plastic coatings); sticky tape. **2.** A copy of photocopiable page 129 for each child.

INTRODUCTION

These Assessment activities should be considered alongside the ongoing assessment opportunities indicated throughout the unit when making a judgement about the level the child is working at. If you are unsure what a child means by their response to a question, then discuss it with them afterwards.

ASSESSMENT ACTIVITY 1

Give the children the card picture of the clown. Explain that the challenge is to make the clown's eyes light up using only the materials in the box. As there is not enough connecting wire, the children will have to make a complete circuit using different conducting materials touching each other. They will also have to make a complete circuit. They make the circuit simply with materials touching each other, but provide sticky tape to hold connections in place if needed.

If you are able to observe a group, make notes about how the children approach the problem and how independent they are in solving it. If the whole class is doing the task, then ask the children to write and draw an account of how they solved the problem and focus observations on children about whose level of achievement you are particularly concerned.

Looking for levels
Children who are working at NC Level 3/Scottish Level C will be able to solve the problem fairly quickly and give a simple explanation of why they chose certain materials. Their solution will demonstrate the use of a complete circuit. Children working at Level 2/Scottish Level B may need

help in solving the problem, but will then be able to describe what they have done to make the bulb light up. Children working at Level 4/Scottish Level C/D will be able to provide more advanced explanations, relating the conductivity of the materials to the reason for their inclusion in the circuit, and will be able to explain that a complete circuit is needed.

ASSESSMENT ACTIVITY 2

Give each child a copy of photocopiable page 129. You may wish to read the questions to a group of children with poor reading skills, or read each question to the whole class to explain how to fill in the sheet.

Answers
1a. The bulb will light up. 1b. The motor will turn. 1c. The bulbs will go off. 1d. The bulb will go off and the buzzer will buzz. 2. The switch can make either the buzzer circuit or the bulb circuit complete, but not both, so when one is switched off, the other is switched on and vice versa. 3. The child might get an electric shock/might die! Advice might include: never put anything metal in the toaster, switch off at the plug, unplug it first, stop!

Looking for levels
Most children working at NC Level 3/Scottish Level C should be able to answer 1a, b and c on the photocopiable sheet correctly. Correct answers to question 1d suggest the child may be working at Level 4/Scottish Level C/D. In the answers to question 2, look for the quality of explanation. Children working at NC Level 2/Scottish Level B may have a simple description: 'It switches it on'. At NC Level 3/Scottish Level C, children should be able to provide some explanation of switching between the two components and children working at Level 4/Scottish Level C/D should be explaining how it works in terms of completing circuits, possibly with reference to conductors and insulators.

PLENARY

Ask the children to share some of their solutions to making the clown's eyes light up. Ask the children what learning *they* think they have demonstrated in this activity. (A need for complete circuits and materials that do and do not conduct electricity.) Go through the answers to the test, asking the children to explain their answers and providing explanations where needed. Ask them to turn to a partner and decide two things that they have learned during this unit. Listen to what the pairs of children have to say.

Name

Will the bulb light up?

Make a prediction, then test it!

1.

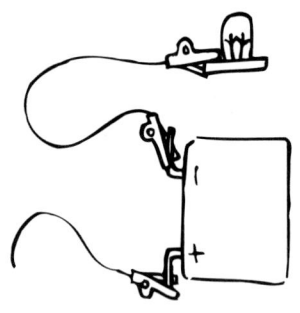

Prediction

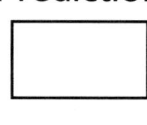

Test

2.

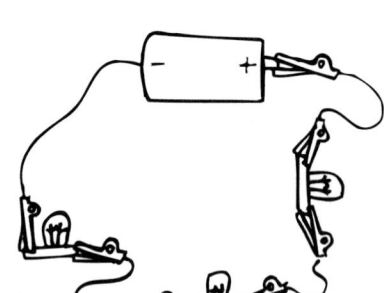

Prediction

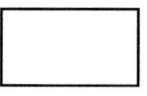

Test

3.

Prediction

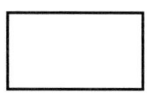

Test

4.

Prediction

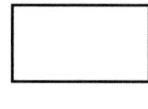

Test

5.

Prediction

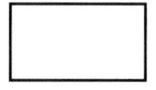

Test

6.

Prediction

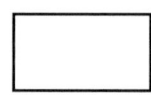

Test

7.

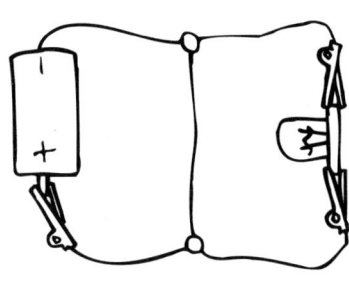

Prediction

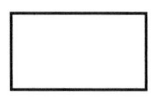

Test

8. Now draw a circuit of your own to test.

Switches to make

1.

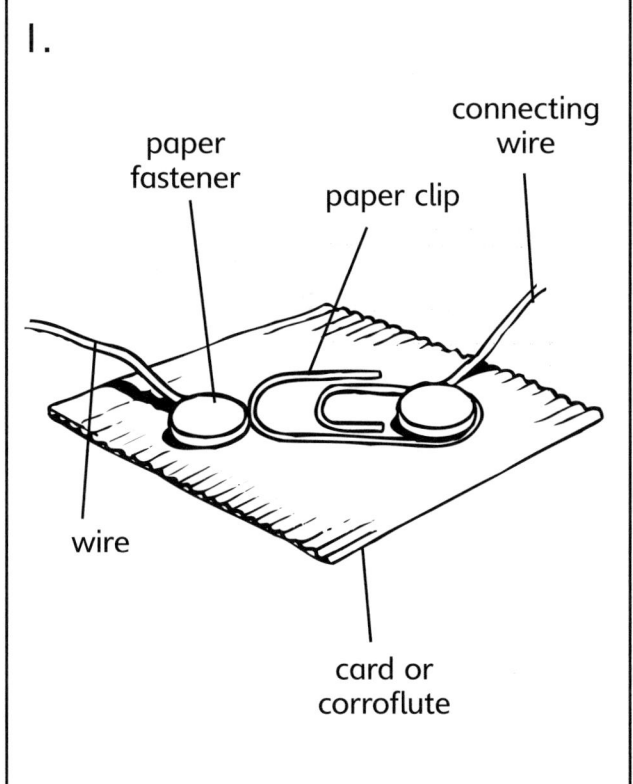

paper
fastener

paper clip

connecting
wire

wire

card or
corroflute

2.

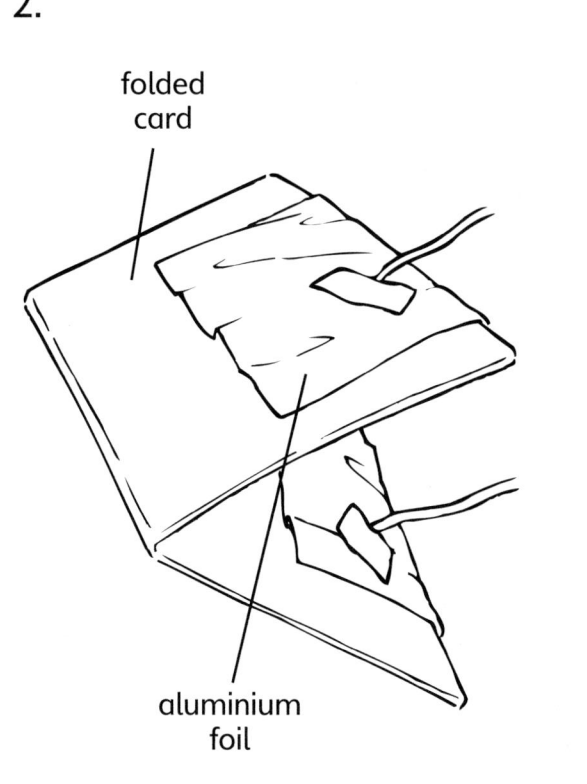

folded
card

aluminium
foil

3.

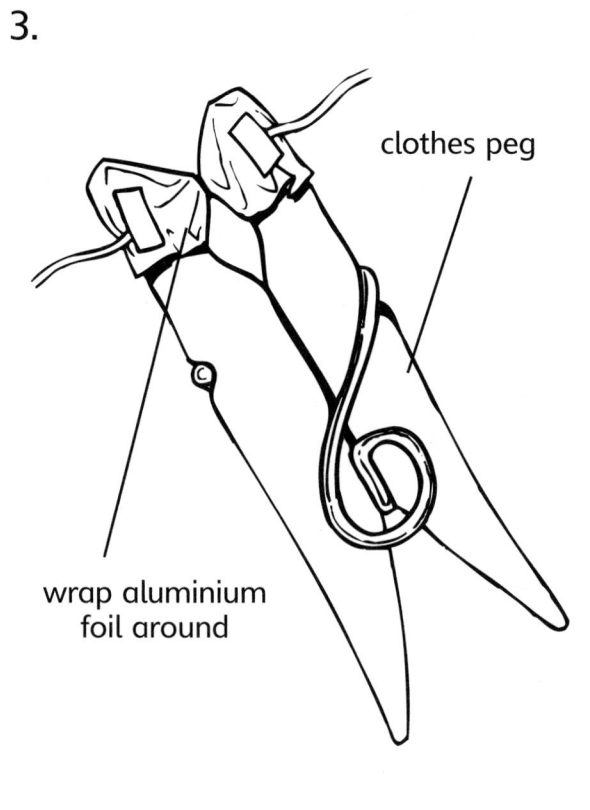

clothes peg

wrap aluminium
foil around

4.

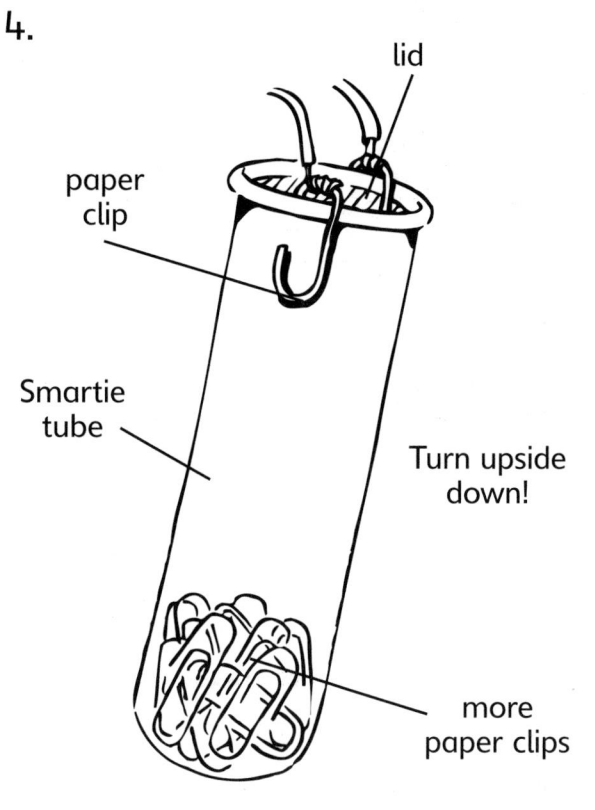

lid

paper
clip

Smartie
tube

Turn upside
down!

more
paper clips

Try these switches, then make up your own ideas!

Buzzers and motors

Motors

These machines use a motor to turn parts around. Which parts turn?
Label them with an arrow.

bus

helicopter

big wheel

washing machine

electric fan

roundabout

Buzzers

Lots of things use electricity to make a sound. Write and draw all the
ones you can think of.

radio

fire alarm

How bright is the light?

Cut the cards out along the dotted lines.

Which light needs to be the brightest? Put them in order starting with the brightest. You might not agree!

Use the blank cards to add ideas of your own.

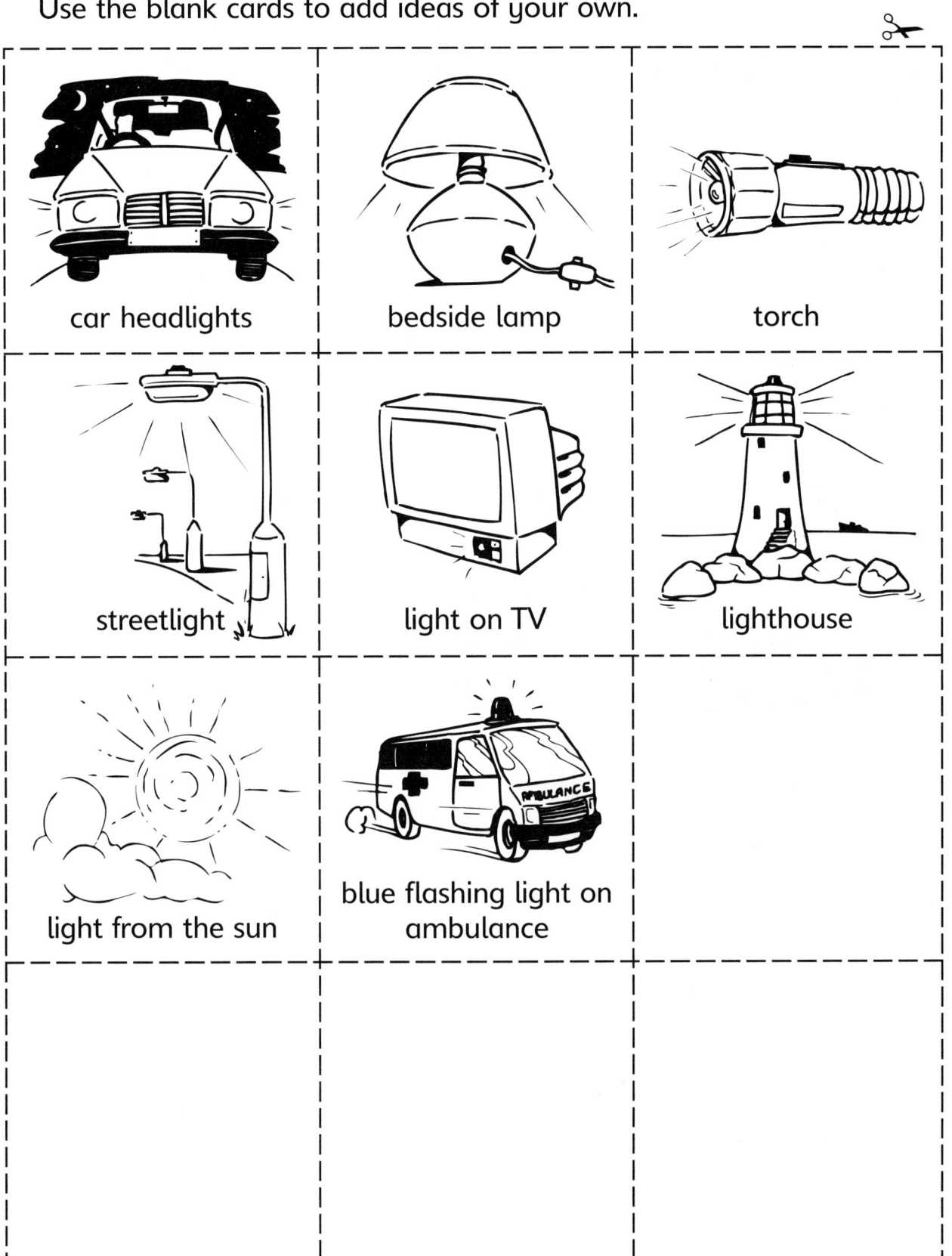

car headlights	bedside lamp	torch
streetlight	light on TV	lighthouse
light from the sun	blue flashing light on ambulance	

Switches and conduction

hole for bulb

space for battery

Switches and conduction

1. Look carefully at each of these circuits. Write down what you think will happen when you operate the switch.

a)

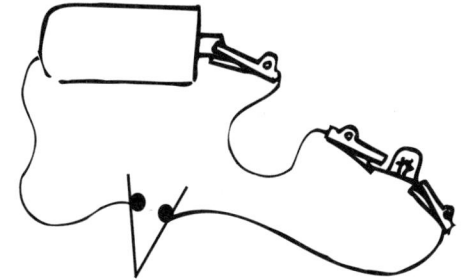

b)

motor

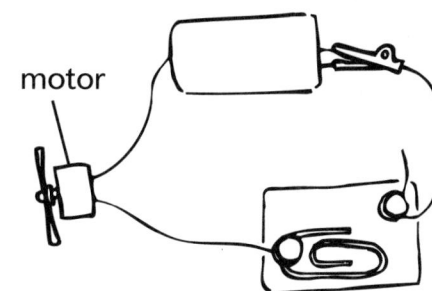

c)

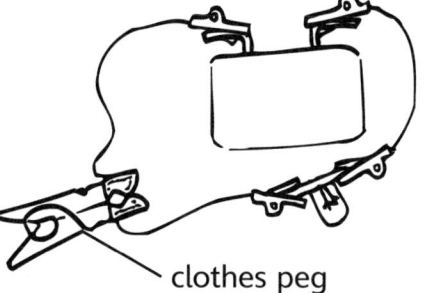

clothes peg

d)

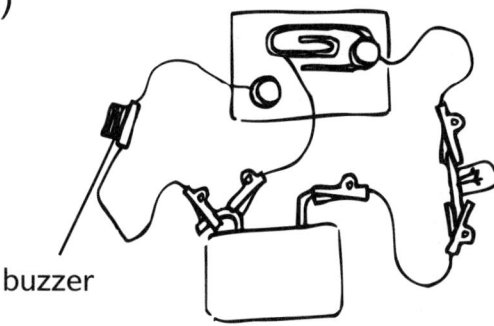

buzzer

2. Explain how the switch in drawing d) works.

_____

_____

3.

a) What might happen to this child?

_____

_____

b) What could you say to the child to help him?

_____

_____

UNIT 6

Friction

ORGANISATION (13 LESSONS)

	OBJECTIVES	MAIN ACTIVITY	GROUP ACTIVITIES	PLENARY	OUTCOMES
LESSON 1	● To revise previous work on forces and to elicit children's current understanding. ● To reinforce the idea that forces are exerted by magnets and springs. ● To know that forces act in a particular direction and this can be represented by an arrow.	Introducing how to use an arrow to represent the direction of a force on a drawing.	Exploring a collection of magnets and springs. Describing observations in terms of pushes, pulls and twists.	Clarifying the difference between a force and the resulting movement.	● Can describe the forces exerted by magnets and the direction in which the forces act. ● Can describe the forces exerted by springs and the direction in which the forces act. ● Can represent their ideas as drawings. ● Can use arrows to indicate the direction of a force.
LESSON 2	● To revise that forces can change the shape of objects. ● To use drama to express ideas about forces.	Using a collection of materials to stimulate drama work in which children use their bodies and voices to represent stretching, squashing and so on.		Performing drama work to the class.	● Can recognise that forces can change the shape of objects. ● Can express scientific ideas through drama.
LESSON 3	● To know that forces can be measured using a force meter. ● To be able to use a force meter.	Demonstrating how to use newton meters, including how to read the scale.	Practising using a newton meter to measure different forces.	Relating large and small forces to their measurement in newtons.	● Can use a force meter. ● Can read the scale on a force meter to an appropriate degree of accuracy. ● Have a 'feel' for a force of 1N and 10N.
LESSON 4	● To elicit children's ideas about friction. ● For children to question a 'taken for granted' situation.	Observing a toy car and questioning what makes it stop moving when it has been pushed.		Considering how the car could be made to travel further by increasing the push or changing the surface.	● Improved teacher understanding of children's existing ideas about friction. ● Children can consider a 'taken for granted' situation in a new way.
LESSON 5	● To make predictions and test them. ● To compare results with predictions. ● To apply skills of measuring with a force meter. ● To know that friction is a force. ● To know that a force meter can be used to investigate friction. ● To know that friction depends on the surfaces in contact.	Demonstration of how to measure the force needed to move a brick on different surfaces	Groups predict and test which surfaces need more force to move the brick.	Discussion on how friction is a force.	● Can make predictions and test them. ● Can apply measurement skills with a newton meter to an investigation. ● Understand that the frictional force depends on the nature of the surface.
LESSON 6	● To know that the force of friction can be investigated using slopes. ● To know that the force of friction depends on the surfaces in contact. ● To carry out a fair test. ● To know that measurements can be repeated for greater accuracy.	Explanation of how a ramp can be used to test the grip of a shoe on different surfaces. Discussion on the need to repeat measurements.	Children investigate the 'grippiness' of different shoes and take rubbings of the soles.	Groups feed back their findings, discuss possible reasons for variation in results.	● Can understand how repeating measurements can improve accuracy. ● Know that slopes can be used to investigate friction. ● Know that different materials and surfaces have different frictional properties. ● Can make independent decisions about fair testing.

ORGANISATION (13 LESSONS)

	OBJECTIVES	MAIN ACTIVITY	GROUP ACTIVITIES	PLENARY	OUTCOMES
LESSON 7	● To know that frictional forces occur in many places.	Hunting for examples of friction around the classroom and school.		Discussing where friction is helpful and where it is not.	● Can recognise where frictional forces occur. ● Can describe instances where friction is useful and can describe instances where friction is not useful.
LESSON 8	● To know that water resistance slows down the speed of an object and is related to the object's shape. ● To measure short time spans.	Demonstration of dropping balls of Plasticine in air, water and wallpaper paste. Introduction of the term 'resistance'.	Making different shapes in Plasticine and observing how they fall in water.	Discussion of streamlining.	● Can describe how water resistance slows down the speed of an object.
LESSON 9	● To know that air resistance can slow down the movement of objects. ● To design and carry out an investigation as independently as possible.	Investigating independently how changing the shape of the front of a toy car with card affects its movement.		Reporting back findings and relating them to streamlining in water.	● Can recognise where frictional forces occur. ● Can carry out an investigation with increased independence and confidence. ● Can understand that streamlining can affect the movement of objects in air as well as in water.
LESSON 10	● To explore and compare how different objects fall. ● To introduce the term 'gravity' as the force which pulls things down.	Observing how different materials fall.		Demonstration and discussion of how A4 paper falls when flat and crumpled.	● Can explore and compare how different objects fall. ● Can use the term 'gravity' appropriately.
LESSON 11	● To know that air resistance can slow down the movement of objects. ● To identify and control variables in an investigation. ● To carry out an investigation with an awareness of safety.	Considering the variables in finding the best design of a paper spinner.	Investigating how changing one variable, such as size, affects how the paper spinner falls.	Presenting findings to the class.	● Can change one variable and keep others constant. ● Can carry out an investigation safely.
LESSON 12	● To present data in the form of a bar chart. ● To understand the value of graphs. ● To suggest explanations for their findings.	Explaining how to draw a graph from the data collected in Lesson 11.	Drawing graphs from the results of Lesson 11.	Showing graphs and discussing the value of graphs in interpreting results.	● Can present their own data as a graph. ● Can understand the value of presenting data as a graph. ● Can suggest explanations for their own results.

	OBJECTIVES		ACTIVITY 1		ACTIVITY 2
ASSESSMENT 13	● To assess the children's knowledge and understanding about how forces can affect the shape and movement of objects. ● To assess the children's ability to plan a test, predict and suggest explanations.		Test to assess children's understanding of forces with a focus on air resistance.		Assessment of children's skills in designing a test and suggesting explanations.

LESSON 1

OBJECTIVES

● To revise previous work on forces and to elicit children's current understanding.
● To reinforce the idea that forces are exerted by magnets and springs.
● To know that forces act in a particular direction and this can be represented by an arrow.

RESOURCES

Main teaching activity: Flip chart and pens.
Group activities: 1. A collection of various magnets; paper clips, paper fasteners, 1p and 2p coins (to explore the magnets), elastic bands and springs for each group (TTS, see page 8, supply bags of assorted springs), writing materials **2.** Photocopiable page 147, writing materials.

PREPARATION

Put out a collection of resources for the Group activities on each table. Have the flip chart situated where all the children can easily see it when sitting on the carpet.

Vocabulary
force, magnet, pull, push, spring, twist

BACKGROUND

The children may have explored magnets and springs, and carried out simple investigations previously (see Unit 6 of *100 Science Lessons: Year 3/Primary 4*). This lesson aims to elicit the children's understanding of forces, concentrating on those exerted by magnets and springs. Forces are pushes, pulls and twists. Forces can be different sizes. Forces are always exerted in a particular direction, and this can be indicated by the direction of an arrow on a drawing or diagram.

INTRODUCTION

Have the children sitting in front of you on the carpet. Write the words 'push', 'pull' and 'twist' on the flip chart. Ask: *Can anyone come to the front and show us what we mean by a push?* When a child has demonstrated in their own way, perhaps by pushing an object or person (gently!), repeat this for a pull and a twist. Say to the children: *I want you to think about what you did when you got up and got ready for school this morning. Can you think of some pushes, pulls and twists that you did? For example, the first thing I did this morning was push the button on my alarm clock.* Invite different children to give their suggestions until everyone has had a go. (I pushed back the duvet; I pulled on my socks; I twisted the tap.) Remind the children that pushes, pulls and twists are forces and write the word 'force' on the flip chart.

Remind the children that they have investigated magnets and springs before. Write the words 'magnet' and 'spring' on the flip chart. Explain that they have 10 minutes to explore their collection of magnets and springs and that you want them to think about pushes, pulls and twists while they are doing that. Encourage the children to handle different items, manipulate them and see how they can make them move and change their shape. Tell them that you will ask some children to talk to the others about what they notice.

GROUP ACTIVITIES

1. Allow 10 minutes to explore the collection. Circulate, encouraging children to explain what is happening using the words 'push', 'pull' and 'twist'. Ask questions: *What happens when you pull that? What can you tell me about those magnets?*

2. Give each child a copy of photocopiable page 147. Ask them to describe what is happening in each picture, writing in as much detail as possible, including the words 'push', 'pull' or 'twist'. (For example: 'The person is pulling hard on the spring and it has stretched'.)

MAIN TEACHING ACTIVITY

Bring the children back to the carpet. Ask several of the children to tell the others what they noticed. Extend their descriptions by asking questions about direction, such as: *In what direction were you pulling? Which way did the magnet move?*

Choose one example and explain that you are going to represent what happened as a drawing. On the flip chart do a simple drawing and label it (see diagram, opposite).

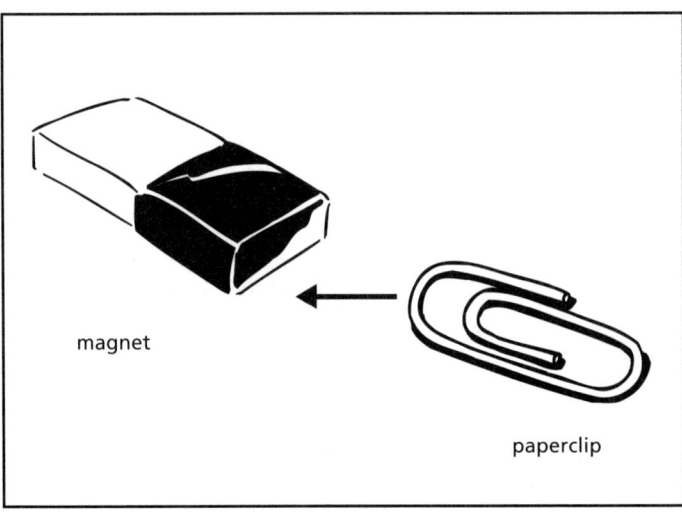

magnet

paperclip

Ask the children: *In which direction is the push/pull?* Represent this with an arrow and write 'push', 'pull' or 'twist' on the arrow. Write a sentence underneath to describe what is happening, for example 'The magnet is pulling the paper clip towards it.' Explain that you would like the children to do their own annotated drawings using arrows in the same way to show what they have found out about the collection.

The children go back to their tables and do their own annotated drawings.

DIFFERENTIATION

In the initial exploration, focus your time on those who are less likely to contribute orally in a large group setting and on those who tend to have a weaker scientific vocabulary, helping them to express their ideas verbally.

When the children are doing their own annotated drawings, expect a greater number of drawings from the higher attainers. Support those with weaker literacy skills by scribing for them or by providing a bank of useful words.

Some children may find it difficult to use arrows to indicate the force rather than the resulting movement. Asking them to use two different coloured pencils, showing the movement in one colour and the push or pull in another colour can support these children.

ASSESSMENT

Can the children describe what is happening in terms of pushes, pulls and twists? Have they distinguished between the force and its effect? Look at the children's drawings to see whether they are representing the direction of the *force* using arrows.

PLENARY

Ask some children to share their work. If there has been confusion about representing the force and the effect/movement then clarify the difference for the class. Finish by asking the children to think of other examples of forces in their everyday lives, for example pushing their chair in, pushing and pulling a knife to cut through bread, twisting the lid from a jam jar.

OUTCOMES

- Can describe the forces exerted by magnets and the direction in which the forces act.
- Can describe the forces exerted by springs and the direction in which the forces act.
- Can represent their ideas as drawings.
- Can use arrows to indicate the direction of a force.

LINKS

Design and technology: mechanisms.

LESSON 2

Objectives	• To revise that forces can change the shape of objects. • To use drama to express ideas about forces.
Resources	Plasticine, sponges, elastic bands, pipe cleaners, space for drama/movement work.
Main activity	Give the children time to manipulate the materials. As a class, brainstorm words that are suggested by this ('push', 'pull', 'stretch', 'squash', 'bend', 'bounce'). Explain that this relates to their science work on forces because they are using forces (pushes, pulls and twists) to change the shape of the materials. Ask: *Did you use a push, a pull or a twist to make that shape? What could you do to make it longer, shorter, bend it?* Ask the children to work in pairs, using their bodies to represent one of the materials being manipulated and changing shape. Now ask the children to work in groups of four, again using their bodies, but also their voices, with intonation that fits the movement and the word (such as s-t-r-e-t-c-h!) as they mime an elastic band being pulled. Ask: *What have these performances got to do with forces?* (We have been acting out changing shapes by using forces.)
Differentiation	Work alongside children who find it difficult to get started with their own ideas.
Assessment	Are the children associating words with the relevant movements? Do their movements represent the materials?
Plenary	Each group performs its work for the rest of the class.
Outcomes	• Can recognise that forces can change the shape of objects. • Can express scientific ideas through drama.

LESSON 3

OBJECTIVES

● To know that forces can be measured using a force meter.
● To be able to use a force meter.

RESOURCES

Main teaching activity: Flip chart with scales drawn on (see below); marker pens, newton meters, a large spring; a copy of the story 'The Enormous Turnip'.
Group activities: Writing equipment. **1.** Flip chart as above; three newton meters with different scales. **2.** A collection of seven objects that can be suspended from a newton meter such as: a large stone, a toy car, a teddy bear, a pencil, a doll, half a brick, a pair of scissors. (you could use elastic bands or string tied like a parcel on objects to allow them to be 'hooked') **3.** Yoghurt pots with elastic bands around the rim to attach string handles so they are like small buckets; marbles; sensitive newton meters. **4.** Various newton meters.

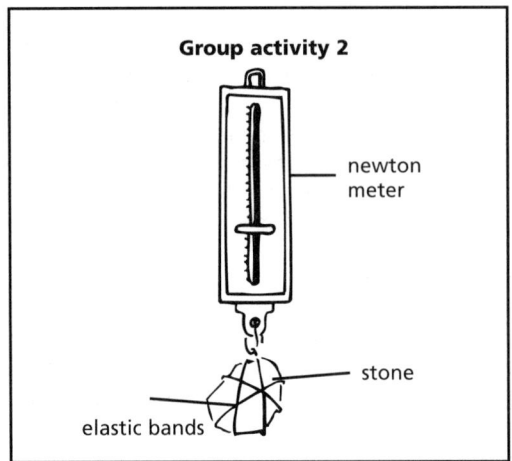

Group activity 2

newton meter

stone

elastic bands

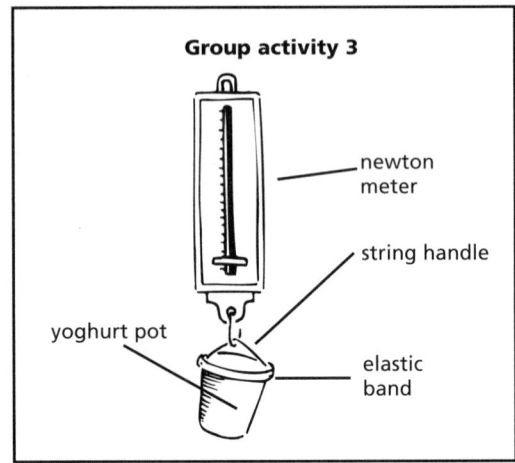

Group activity 3

newton meter

string handle

yoghurt pot

elastic band

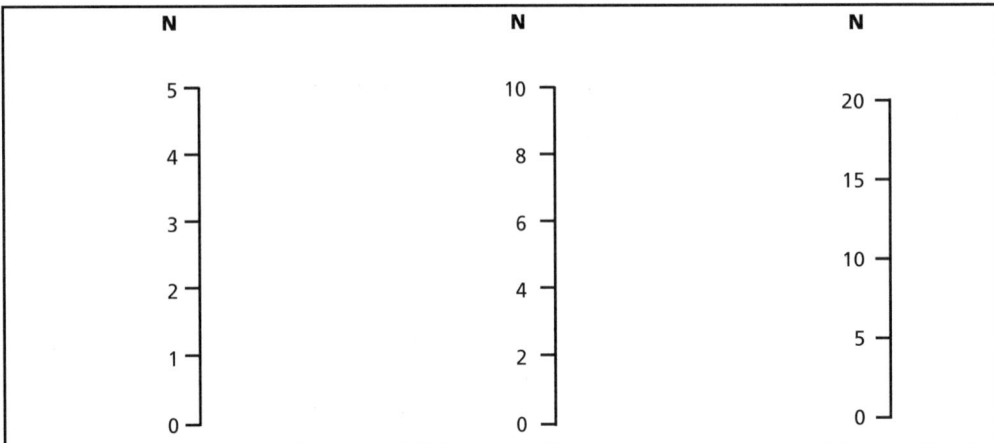

PREPARATION

Draw the newton meter scales on the flip chart (see left), using a new page for each one. Set up three tables for Group activities 2, 3 and 4 and have equipment for Group activity 1 and the Main teaching activity near the flip chart.

Vocabulary

force, force meter/ newton meter, newton

BACKGROUND

Forces are measured in units called 'newtons' (N) and can be measured using a newton meter (or force meter). These work by having a spring inside that stretches when it is pulled. It can sometimes be confusing because the scale on a newton meter may be given in grams as well as in newtons. Make sure that the children are using the correct scale. Scales can be difficult to interpret, as they require some mathematical skills. The activities in this lesson will help to address some of these skills. Different force meters have different scales – some have very strong springs and are good for measuring large forces, others have weaker springs and are good for measuring smaller forces. They are usually sold in different colours to make it easier to distinguish them, and children will need to try out a range of meters to get a feel for which will be the most appropriate for what they are measuring.

INTRODUCTION

Read the children the story of 'The Enormous Turnip', acting it out, with more and more children joining on the line to add their 'pull'. Explain that this may be a story they think is for younger children, but it includes some very important science. Ask the children: *Why did they need lots of people to help pull up the Enormous Turnip?* (To make the pull/force bigger.)

MAIN TEACHING ACTIVITY

Explain that we can measure a force – how big the pull is – by using a force meter, and show them one. Hold up a large spring and explain that the force meter has a spring inside it. Ask: *What do you think will happen to the spring if I give it a small pull?* If necessary, refer to the previous lesson's work. (It will stretch a bit.) Demonstrate this. Ask: *And what do you think will happen if I give it a big pull?* (It will stretch a lot.) Demonstrate this. Explain that this is how a force meter works. Pass around different force meters so that the children can try pulling on them and watching the slider move up and down the scale. Ask: *What do you think the numbers on the force meter are for?* (To tell you how big the force is.) Explain that the unit of force is a newton, and that the numbers on the scale are telling you how many newtons the pull is. The bigger the pull, the more newtons it measures.

Show the children the first drawing of a scale on the flip chart. Tell them to use the scale marked in newtons not in grams. Show them on the flip chart and on the newton meter how to read whole newtons.

GROUP ACTIVITIES

Allow the children to circulate around the tables, spending about 10 minutes on each activity.
1. Work with this group. Show the children a variety of newton meters and how the scales are different. On the flip chart look at different scales with the children – counting up in ones, fives and tens as appropriate. Show the children how to measure to an appropriate degree of accuracy. (See Differentiation below for further details.)
2. Ask the children to hang different objects from the collection of newton meters and look at the readings. The group needs to put the objects in order from the biggest pull to the smallest pull and record this.
3. Ask the children to find out how many marbles they need to put in a yoghurt pot container hanging on a newton meter in order to make it read exactly 1N, 2N… The children should record this.
4. Allow the children to decide for themselves what forces they would like to measure around the classroom, for example pulling a desk, opening a door. They measure and record the force using a simple table.

DIFFERENTIATION

Use groups based on mathematical ability. Have the highest attaining group working with you first, as they can then apply this accuracy of measurement to the remaining Group activities. The other groups will benefit from extending their practical experience before this input. Teach lower maths attainers to measure to the nearest marked interval; middle maths attainers to approximate to the nearest marked interval and work out what the half-way points between marked intervals represent. Teach higher maths attainers how to calculate and approximate measurements between the marked intervals.

ASSESSMENT

Can the children tell you that forces are measured using a force meter and that the unit is the newton? Are the children able to read the newton meter with an appropriate degree of accuracy? Do they understand that the more newtons recorded the bigger the force?

PLENARY

Ask the children: *Can you think of an example of a very small force?* (Blowing a feather; pushing your hair off your face and so on.) *Can you think of an example of a very big force?* (Pushing a heavy shopping trolley; lifting the box in PE and so on.) Ask the children to share some of the measurements they chose to make. Write up some of the examples from Group activity 4 on the board or flip chart to help them get a feel for the size of force represented by 1N and 10N. Ask them: *How many newtons do you think it took to pull up the Enormous Turnip?*

OUTCOMES
- Can use a force meter.
- Can read the scale on a force meter to an appropriate degree of accuracy.
- Have a 'feel' for a force of 1N and 10N.

LINKS
Maths: measurement in standard units, using scales.

LESSON 4

Objectives	● To elicit children's ideas about friction. ● For children to question a 'taken for granted' situation.
Resources	A toy car.
Main activity	Have the children sitting in a circle on the carpet. Roll the toy car several times and ask: *What do you notice about how the car moves?* (Accept all answers.) Then ask: *How am I making the car start moving?* Listen to the children's responses; some may say 'by pushing it', which is correct, but there may be other ideas expressed such as 'by giving it energy'. Some children may use the word 'force' instead of 'push'. 　Ask: *How does the car stop? Why doesn't it just go on for ever?* (It stops because of the friction between the wheels and the floor surface.) Children may suggest that it 'runs out of push', or 'it runs out of energy'. However, some may suggest that 'the wheels are catching on the carpet'. 　Ask: *How does the car keep going?* (The answer is that the push has not yet been overcome by friction acting in the opposite direction, but do not expect children to articulate this!) They may say 'it just goes', or 'the wheels make it move'. 　Ask each child to do an annotated drawing in response to the following three questions: ● How does the car start moving? ● How does it keep going? ● How does it stop?
Differentiation	There may be some children who are still at a stage of development in which they make suggestions such as 'the car runs out of petrol' or 'it puts the brakes on'. Intervene by looking at the toy car with the child and asking: *Do you think real petrol goes in here? Is there a person to press the brakes? What else might be making this toy car slow down and stop?* 　Children with poor writing skills can express their ideas mainly through the drawing, with the teacher scribing the annotations to the drawing. 　Extend children who have completed this by asking: *How could we make the car stop quicker?*
Assessment	In their annotated drawings, are the children using the term 'force', showing that they are applying what they have learned in previous lessons? Do they mention the surface when explaining how the car stops? If so, are they using the word 'grip', or even 'friction'?
Plenary	Ask: *How could we make the car go further before it stops?* (Push it harder, give it a bigger force, or put it on a smoother surface.) If necessary introduce the idea of a surface by asking: *What might happen if we pushed it on the floor rather than the carpet?* Test this out briefly. 　Explain that there seem to be two things – the push and the surface – that affect how the car moves, and that the next lessons will help the children to explore these ideas.
Outcomes	● Improved teacher understanding of children's existing ideas about friction. ● Children can consider a 'taken for granted' situation in a new way.

LESSON 5

OBJECTIVES

- To make predictions and test them.
- To compare results with predictions.
- To apply skills of measuring with a force meter.
- To know that friction is a force.
- To know that a force meter can be used to investigate friction.
- To know that friction depends on the surfaces in contact.

RESOURCES

Main teaching activity: Several samples of different surfaces from the groups' collections as listed below.
Group activities: 1. Each group needs a collection of surfaces such as carpet (both sides), hardboard (both sides), corrugated cardboard, fur fabric, plain woven fabric and bubble wrap; bricks with string tied around like a parcel so they can be 'hooked'; newton meters. **2.** Sugar paper and felt-tipped pens.

PREPARATION

Put out the resources for the Group activities on the tables, but reserve some surfaces for the Main teaching activity.

Vocabulary

friction, force, grip, surface

BACKGROUND

Friction is a force that acts between two surfaces. It acts in the opposite direction to pushes and pulls, resisting the movement. We tend to take friction for granted in our everyday lives unless it – or lack of it – becomes a problem, for example taking the lid off a jam jar or driving on ice. Because we take it for granted, it is not obvious that it is a force. The children's responses in Lesson 4 may have shown a lack of awareness of the role of friction in slowing things down. If there was no friction then the toy car, when pushed, would have rolled on forever! This is what would happen up in space where there is nothing, not even air, to exert a frictional force in the opposite direction. In our everyday experience, things just stop 'naturally' if we stop pushing or pulling them, and we need to help children become aware of the role of friction in these situations.

This lesson helps children to explore the different frictional forces exerted by different surfaces. By making friction more obvious, it will help children to be more aware of it as a force.

INTRODUCTION

Review the children's ideas about the toy car from the previous lesson. Can the children suggest reasons why the surface on which the car rolls makes a difference?

MAIN TEACHING ACTIVITY

Show the class the range of surfaces and how to hook the newton meter to the string around the brick to measure the amount of pull that is needed. Explain that the brick is representing a car full with people.

GROUP ACTIVITIES

1. Ask groups to choose three surfaces to work with. Ask them to predict which surface would need more force put on the 'car' to pull it along and to record their prediction. They can then test their prediction by measuring and recording their results in a table. Ask them to compare their results with their predictions. Can they suggest reasons why some surfaces needed more force to pull the 'car' over them than others? (They may use the word 'grip', or suggest that wool gets stuck on the brick.) Allow children to express their ideas in their own words.
2. Give each group a piece of sugar paper and some felt-tipped pens. Ask them to fold the sheet in half to form two columns and write 'smooth/slippery surfaces' and 'rough/grippy surfaces' as headings. Ask them to write or draw as many examples as they can in each column. They could move around the classroom to find examples as well as using previous experience.

DIFFERENTIATION

Work in mathematical ability groups so that the children apply the degree of accuracy of measurement they learned in the previous lesson. A ready-made table could be used to support those children with weaker recording skills.

ASSESSMENT

Are the children able to make predictions and test them? Do they use the force meter to measure with an appropriate degree of accuracy? Do they recognise that it takes more pull to move the brick on some surfaces than others? Can they suggest possible reasons for this? Do they relate the roughness/smoothness of the surface to the speed of an object travelling over it?

PLENARY

Ask groups to report back which surface took the most and least force to pull the brick. Do all the groups agree?

Introduce the term 'friction' as the 'grip' or 'pull' that the surfaces had on the brick. Explain that friction is a force. Ask: *Which surfaces had the most friction? Which surfaces had the least?*

OUTCOMES

- Can make predictions and test them.
- Can apply measurement skills with a newton meter to an investigation.
- Understand that the frictional force depends on the nature of the surface.

LINKS

Maths: measurement.

LESSON 6

OBJECTIVES

● To know that the force of friction can be investigated using slopes.
● To know that the force of friction depends on the surfaces in contact.
● To carry out a fair test.
● To know that measurements can be repeated for greater accuracy.

RESOURCES

Main teaching activity: A copy of the story of 'Sam's Slippery Surfaces' from photocopiable page 148, a ramp, a shoe, a ruler, a flip chart and marker pens.
Group activities: 1. Rulers; ramps (these could be any suitable rigid materials available such as sheets of thick card); collections of materials and surfaces as in Lesson 5. **2.** footwear; wax crayons; newsprint paper for taking rubbings.

PREPARATION

Draw up a table for the results (see diagram) on the flip chart ready. Put out the resources for the Group activities.

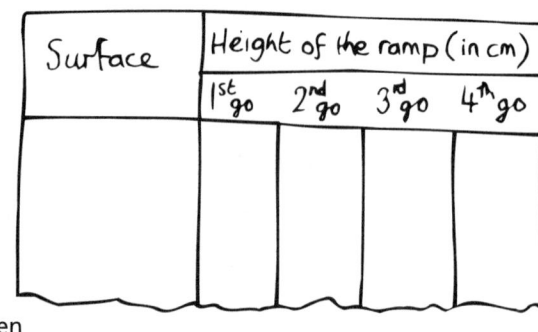

Surface	Height of the ramp (in cm)			
	1st go	2nd go	3rd go	4th go

Vocabulary

friction, rough, slope, smooth, surface

BACKGROUND

Friction is the force of resistance when two surfaces move across each other. It pushes in the opposite direction to the movement. Children experience friction as grip or slipperiness and can relate this to their own lives. Friction can be measured directly with a newton meter as in Lesson 3 (on page 134, or seeing how much a ramp needs to be tilted before an object starts moving and making comparisons between surfaces.

Friction can be helpful – for example we need a certain amount of friction between our feet and the ground when we walk, which is why walking on ice is so difficult. Friction can also be unhelpful, which is why we oil the moving parts of machinery to reduce it.

INTRODUCTION

Read together the story of 'Sam's Slippery Surfaces' (on photocopiable page 148). Ask the children: *Which surfaces had the most friction? Which surfaces had the least friction? How can you be sure? Is carpet usually slippery? What about the kitchen floor?*

MAIN TEACHING ACTIVITY

Have two different surfaces; move a shoe on each surface by pushing and pulling. Ask: *Is this a fair test?* (No, because we don't know if we are giving the same push or pull on each surface.) Explain that the children could compare different surfaces by using a ramp. Demonstrate putting a shoe on the ramp and lifting the ramp until the shoe starts to slip. Ask the children: *How could we compare this surface with other surfaces?* (Put different surfaces on the ramp and repeat.) Ask: *How could we measure the difference?* (Measure how high the ramp is lifted.) Demonstrate this with a child's help and record it on the table on the flip chart.

Start the test again and ask the children how high the ramp will need to be to get the shoe to move. They will probably suggest the same measurement as before. Repeat the test and measurement four times, showing that there is a small variation, recording the measurements on the table. Do not calculate the mean (average), but together decide on a number that best represents the measurements to put in the last column of the table. This could be the middle number, for example, or a number that occurred twice.

GROUP ACTIVITIES

1. Ask each group to carry out a test to find out which surface has the most friction using the approach you have demonstrated. Ask the children to record their results in a table drawn on sugar paper so they can feed back to the class.

Circulate, questioning how the test has been made fair, intervening to help the children improve the test when necessary. Ask: *Which surface do you predict will have the most friction? Why? Why is it better to repeat the measurements more than once?*
2. Ask the children to take rubbings of the soles of the shoes/trainers of the children in their group. Tell them to cut out the shoe shapes to form part of a display on friction. Ask: *What similarities/differences do you notice about the soles of the shoes? Can you explain why some soles grip better than others?* Ask the children to write captions to go alongside the shoe shapes to communicate their ideas to the rest of the class.

DIFFERENTIATION

Work in mixed-ability groups so that the children support each other.

ASSESSMENT

Do the children carry out the test in a fair way, such as using the same shoe, measuring in the same way each time? Can they suggest reasons why the different surfaces have different frictional properties? Can they explain why it is better to repeat the measurements?

PLENARY

Each group feeds back their findings to the whole class. If different groups had different results this may be because they used different types of shoe. Can the children suggest why using different shoes would make a difference? Ask the children to relate this to Lesson 3. Did they get the same results with this different way of testing friction?

Ask the children to think of the story and whether they can think of any examples of how different surfaces are used for safety, for example bath mats, rough tiles around swimming pools.

OUTCOMES

- Can understand how repeating measurements can improve accuracy.
- Know that slopes can be used to investigate friction.
- Know that different materials and surfaces have different frictional properties.
- Can make independent decisions about fair testing.

LINKS

Unit 4 Materials: properties of materials.

LESSON 7

Objective	● To know that frictional forces occur in many places.
Resources	Writing materials.
Main activity	Review the examples of friction that the children are aware of so far – outdoor surfaces, floor surfaces, shoes. However, explain to the children that there will be friction wherever two surfaces touch each other. 　Ask them to work in pairs to collect examples of friction around the classroom and school. For example; wiping feet on a doormat, pushing chairs across the floor, moving a pencil across paper. This could be extended for homework, for example riding a bike on grass, washing up and so on.
Differentiation	Ask higher-attaining children to classify their examples as high or low friction.
Assessment	Are the children able to identify examples of friction in their surroundings? Can they distinguish between higher and lower friction? Can they suggest examples of when friction is useful and when it is not?
Plenary	Collate all the examples together as a class. Each pair could write two examples on card and these could be put together as a short-term wall display. Ask the children to pick out an example of where friction is useful and where it is not.
Outcomes	● Can recognise where frictional forces occur. ● Can describe instances where friction is useful and can describe instances where friction is not useful.

LESSON 8

OBJECTIVES

● To know that water resistance slows down the speed of an object and is related to the object's shape.
● To measure short time spans.

RESOURCES

Main teaching activity: Photographs of boats and fish taken from different angles (*Junior Education* magazine is a good source of photographs); models of fish and boats (or real fish would be even better); Blu-Tack; Plasticine; three tall transparent containers such as plastic lemonade bottles; water; non-allergenic wallpaper paste prepared according to the instructions on the packet.
Group activity: Plasticine; a tank of water; copies of photocopiable page 149; writing materials.

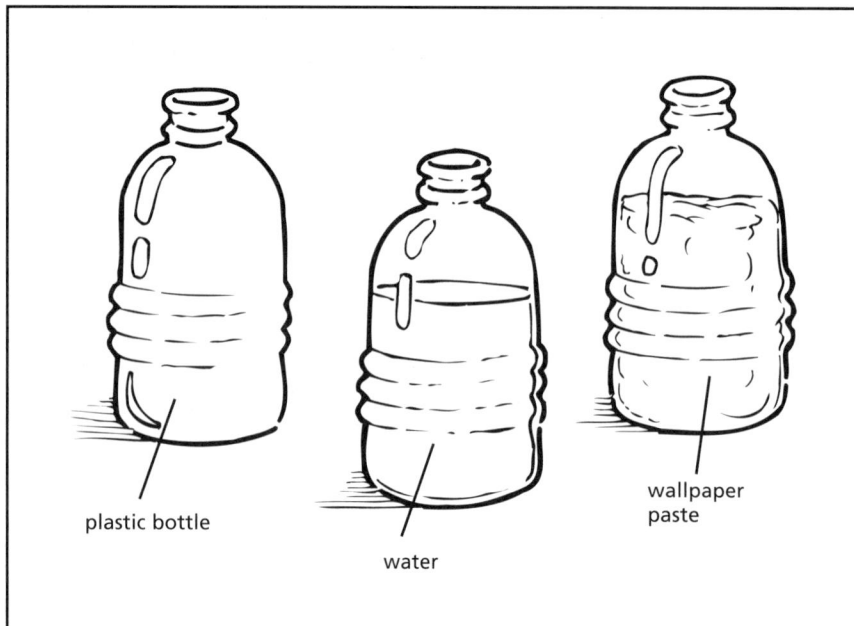

plastic bottle

water

wallpaper paste

PREPARATION

Have a flip chart to Blu-Tack the photographs onto. Set up the three transparent containers: leave one empty, put water in the second and wallpaper paste in the third (see opposite). Divide the Plasticine into a lump for each group, fill the water tanks and put a set out on each group's table.

Vocabulary

resistance, streamlined

BACKGROUND

Water and air resistance are forms of friction – both are forces that oppose the movement of objects through them. Children will have some experience of water resistance from swimming. By comparing the movement of objects in water with objects in air and the more viscous wallpaper paste, children will gain an understanding of the effects of water resistance and be prepared for ideas about air resistance that will be developed in subsequent lessons.

Air resistance acts in a very similar way to water resistance, but as it cannot be seen, its effects are less obvious. Often, the way objects fall is put down to how heavy they are, but in fact a heavy object and a light object dropped at the same time will hit the ground at the same time. However, in our everyday experience, many light objects are shaped so that they have more surface area for the air to push up on. Imagine dropping a feather and how it catches the air and 'floats' down.

So a key idea to the next series of lessons is how the shape of an object affects its movement – the idea of 'streamlining' is introduced.

INTRODUCTION

Show the children the photographs or models of boats and fish and ask them to describe their shapes. Ask: *Why do you think the fish and boats have pointed fronts?* Ask the children to describe their own experiences of moving through water. *What does it feel like? Is it easy to walk in water? Are there any forces involved?* (It feels like the water is pushing you back; you can't go as fast as on land.)

MAIN TEACHING ACTIVITY

Make three round balls of Plasticine about the size of a marble and drop one into the container of air. Ask the children to predict what will happen when you drop it into the container of water. Drop it. Ask for their reactions: *Was it slower or faster than you expected?* Show them the wallpaper paste and explain that the third container is full of it. Ask the children to predict what will happen to the Plasticine in this container. Drop it. Ask for their responses and ideas: *Would anyone like to say anything about this?* Introduce the term 'resistance'.

If the children do not suggest changing the shape of the Plasticine, then you can ask: *How could we change how fast the Plasticine falls?* Ask: *How can we make this a fair test?* (Use the same-sized balls of Plasticine.)

GROUP ACTIVITY

Ask each group to make some Plasticine shapes they think will fall quickly and some that they think will fall slowly. Most children can quantify the time it takes to reach the bottom of their tank of water by counting. They can record their predictions and the results of their test on photocopiable page 149. Ask them to write what they found out on the photocopiable sheet, thinking about the shapes of the Plasticine and what difference it made to how they fell.

Ask the children to record what happened in the Main teaching activity. Some children may like to have a go with the three containers from the Main teaching activity.

DIFFERENTIATION

Children who are less able mathematically can record their results qualitatively (it was fast, slow, very fast, it wobbled as it went down). Children with more advanced investigative skills can be extended by suggesting that they repeat the measurements.

ASSESSMENT

In their writing and drawing, do the children show an understanding that streamlined shapes fall faster? Are they able to use a stopclock with a reasonable degree of precision?

PLENARY

Each group shows the rest of the class which of their shapes dropped the fastest and slowest. Ask: *What do all the slow shapes have in common? What do all the fast shapes have in common?* Introduce the term 'streamlined'. Ask the children when it would be good to have a streamlined shape and when it might be an advantage not to be streamlined.

OUTCOMES

● Can describe a streamlined shape and its usefulness.
● Can describe how water resistance slows down the speed of an object.

LINKS

Design and technology: evaluating designs.

LESSON 9

Objectives	● To know that air resistance can slow down the movement of objects. ● To design and carry out an investigation as independently as possible.
Resources	Ramps, toy cars, rulers, stopclocks, card, sticky tape, Blu-Tack, sugar paper and felt-tipped pens for presenting work.
Main activity	Remind the children about the streamlined shapes of Plasticine in water and wallpaper paste in Lesson 6. Explain that you want them to investigate how changing the shape of the front of a car by sticking card onto it affects its speed. Demonstrate with one example. Explain that the group is to make its own decisions about how to do the test and that each group will present their findings to the rest of the class. Circulate, asking the groups questions such as: *Are you going to take any measurements? How have you made sure this is a fair test? What will you keep the same and what will you change each time? How are you going to record your results?*
Differentiation	Have mixed-ability groups for peer support. Accurate timing with stopclocks can be quite challenging. If this is too advanced, then groups could measure the distance the car travels before stopping instead. Give additional teacher support where groups are struggling.
Assessment	This is a good opportunity to assess how the children are applying the investigative skills focused on and developed in previous lessons. Have they made predictions? Have they planned fair tests? Have they made appropriate measurements? Have they designed a table to record results? Are they able to suggest explanations for what they have found?
Plenary	Each group reports their findings to the class. Develop ideas about the area of the card and the shapes. The children should find that the more pointed shapes travel faster or further, and that flatter shapes travel more slowly or stop sooner. Relate this back to ideas about streamlining in water.
Outcomes	● Can carry out an investigation with increased independence and confidence. ● Understand that streamlining can affect the movement of objects in air as well as in water.

LESSON 10

Objectives	● To explore and compare how different objects fall. ● To introduce the term 'gravity' as the force which pulls things down.
Resources	A collection of objects to drop for each group, such as a feather, a piece of card, tissue paper, Plasticine, a plastic cube, a cork, a paper clip, two pieces of A4 paper.
Main activity	Demonstrate dropping a piece of Plasticine, linking this to the previous lesson. Ask: *What is making it fall?* It is likely that a child will use the term 'gravity'. If not, introduce the idea that gravity is a force that pulls things down. 　Ask the children to explore dropping the different objects in their collection and to make annotated drawings about what happens in each case. Circulate, asking the children: *Can you describe how that falls? What differences have you noticed between how the objects fall? Why do you think the Plasticine fell faster than the tissue paper?* Ask the children to make notes about any comparisons they make, for example 'I have noticed that the paper clip fell faster than the feather.' Ask: *Why are the objects falling downwards?* (Because of the force of gravity.)
Differentiation	Support children with poorer writing skills by providing a word bank with the names of the items, and words such as 'fall', 'fast', 'slowly', 'air', 'move', 'force', 'heavy', 'light'.
Assessment	Have the children noted differences in how different objects fall? Have they made comparisons? Can they use the term 'gravity' appropriately? 　Do not be surprised if some children are not convinced that the two pieces of paper are the same mass. Their ideas will continue to be developed in the next lessons.
Plenary	Ask the children to feed back any of their observations. Hold up the feather and the paper clip. Ask: *Which of these do you predict will land first?* (The paper clip.) Try it. Ask: *Why do you think that the paper clip landed first?* It is likely that some children will say that it is because it is heavier. Hold up a piece of A4 paper and drop it. Ask: *What did you notice about how it fell?* (It went from side to side, like the feather.) Take another piece of A4 paper and fold it up. Hold up both pieces and ask: *Which do you think will hit the ground first?* (The folded piece.) Ask: *Is this piece of paper heavier than the other?* (No.) So why did it hit the ground first? (It is a more 'streamlined' shape.) Link this to the lessons on resistance in liquids.
Outcomes	● Can explore and compare how different objects fall. ● Can use the term 'gravity' appropriately.

LESSON 11

OBJECTIVES

● To know that air resistance can slow down the movement of objects.
● To identify and control variables in an investigation.
● To carry out an investigation with an awareness of safety.

RESOURCES

Main teaching activity: A paper spinner (photocopiable page 150) ready to cut out and make up with a paper clip, scissors.
Group activities: Stopclocks, metre rulers, rulers, paper clips, templates of different sizes of paper spinners (photocopiable page 150), various types of paper and card, photocopiable page 151 (recording sheet).

PREPARATION

Set up the resources for the Group activity on each table. Have the resources for the Main teaching activity to hand.

Vocabulary

paper spinner

BACKGROUND

'Spinners' are used to explore air resistance from Key Stage 2 to Key Stage 4/Primary 4 to school leaving. This lesson focuses on the process skill of developing an awareness of variables – the different things that can be changed in a test. To have a controlled, fair test, only one variable can be changed while the rest are held constant. Children often find this a difficult concept to grasp and try to change more than one thing at a time. Test planning boards are given in *Making Sense of Primary Science Investigations* by Anne Goldsworthy and Rosemary Feasey (published by ASE, 1994) and would provide useful support for this lesson.
Safety: Make sure you set clear boundaries about what may or may not be stood on safely to reach heights for releasing the spinners.

INTRODUCTION

Show the children how to make the paper spinner. Drop the spinner and ask the children to observe carefully. Drop it again. Ask the children to describe anything they notice about it: how fast it falls, whether it turns, whether it falls differently at the start.

MAIN TEACHING ACTIVITY

Explain that we want to try and make the best possible paper spinner. As a class, brainstorm the different things that could be changed about the spinner – size, type of paper, number of paper clips, length of the wings – recording this on the flip chart.

Decide as a class what you are going to observe/measure – the time it takes to drop is the most straightforward.

Explain that each group can take one thing to change, and that they need to make sure that they keep all the other things the same. Explain that if you changed two things at once, you wouldn't know which had made the difference. Negotiate which groups will take which variable. (See Differentiation.)

Ask the children if they can think of any safety risks that they need to consider, such as falling off chairs/tables. Set appropriate behaviour boundaries.

GROUP ACTIVITY

Each group should investigate changing one variable. Circulate, and assist with making the spinners if necessary.

Provide tables for recording (photocopiable page 151), but expect the children to put the data in the correct place. This photocopiable page includes space for repeated measurement, but an approximate average, not a calculation of the mean, is all that is needed for Year 4/Primary 5.

DIFFERENTIATION

Work in attainment groups according to investigative skills. When negotiating which group takes which variable, give the lower attainers a qualitative variable such as type of paper or small, medium and large spinners; the middle attainers can look at a discrete quantitative variable such as number of paper clips, and the high attainers a continuous quantitative variable such as length of wing. Three different spinners are enough for the lower attainers, while higher attainers could make up to five.

The accuracy of measurement can also be differentiated, with lower attainers counting, most children timing to the nearest second and very high attainers recording time to one decimal place.

Support lower-attaining groups with more teacher time. Intervene if children are changing more than one aspect of the spinner.

ASSESSMENT

Observe the children working. Are the children changing only one variable while keeping the others the same? Are they working safely?

PLENARY

Ask each group to report any problems they had and how they overcame them. Explain that in the next lesson they will make graphs of their data and consider what they have found out.

OUTCOMES

- Can change one variable and keep others constant.
- Can carry out an investigation safely.

LINKS

PSHE: safety.

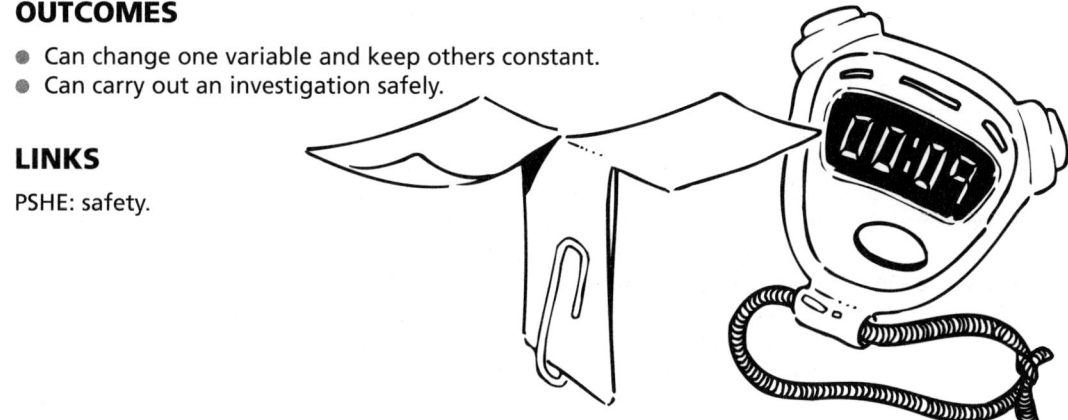

LESSON 12

OBJECTIVES

● To present data in the form of a bar chart.
● To understand the value of graphs.
● To suggest explanations for their findings.

RESOURCES

Main teaching activity: Prepared data (see below) on a sheet of sugar paper, a grid drawn on a flip chart or large squared paper, marker pens.
Group activities: Squared paper, pencils, rulers, coloured pencils.

What we changed Number of paper clips.	1st drop time (in counts)	2nd drop time (in counts)	3rd drop time (in counts)	Overall drop time (in counts)
1	4	4	3	4
2	3	3	4	3
3	1	2	1	1

PREPARATION

Draw the table of data as shown opposite on the flip chart or sugar paper. Have the resources for the Main teaching activity ready where they will be clearly visible. Put out the resources for the Group activity on the tables.

Vocabulary

bar chart, line graph, table

BACKGROUND

The class may have learned about making graphs from tables of data in maths, and may be ready to apply this skill. However, many children find this difficult, particularly choosing scales, and using real data can be problematic. It is a good idea to model this process for the children.

Getting to Grips with Graphs by Goldsworthy, Watson and Wood-Robinson (ASE 1999), has some useful ideas for developing these skills, including computer-based activities.

INTRODUCTION

Remind the children of their investigations into paper spinners. Explain that you want them to present their results as graphs (perhaps for a display or assembly) to help other people understand what they have done.

MAIN TEACHING ACTIVITY

Using the chart of prepared data, model how to draw a graph. Show the children that the variable they changed goes along the bottom (x-axis), and what they measured goes up the side (y-axis). In this activity the scale on the y-axis is most likely to cause problems, but one square can represent one second or one 'count'. Show them how to set out the numbers on the y-axis on the lines, not in the spaces of the squares. Label the axes. Ask different children to come up and show where the bars should go for each part of the data from the table. Make sure they understand which number they are plotting.

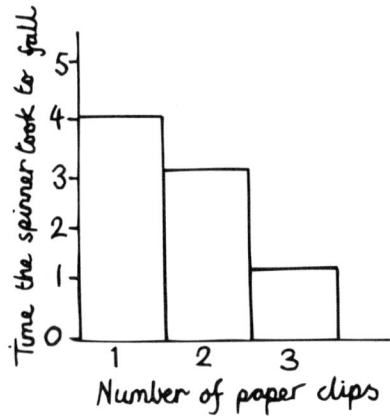

Ask the children questions about the graph: *How long did it take the spinner with 1/2/3 paper clips to fall? Which spinner fell the fastest? How many paper clips were on the spinner that took longest to reach the ground? How long did the spinner with one paper clip take to fall? Why do you think that spinner stayed up the longest?*

Explain that you want the children to draw their own graphs and to think and write about what they found out.

GROUP ACTIVITY

Each group draws a graph of their results from the previous lesson on squared paper. Ask them to write a few sentences about what the graph is telling them. Ask them to try and explain *why* it happened.

DIFFERENTIATION

Support the lower-attaining groups in setting up their graphs.

If, in Lesson 8, higher-attaining children used quantitative data then they will be able to draw a line graph, but for most Year 4/Primary 5 children a bar chart is appropriate. They may need extra teacher input to do this.

ASSESSMENT

Are the children able to construct a graph that represents their data accurately? Can they comment on what the graph is showing?

PLENARY

Each group shows one other group their graph and tells them what they found out about their paper spinners. Ask the whole class if they find it easier to understand each other's results with a graph to look at. Ask if drawing the graph helped them to think about their own results.

OUTCOMES

- Can present their own data as a graph.
- Can understand the value of presenting data as a graph.
- Can suggest explanations for their own results.

LINKS

Maths: data-handling.

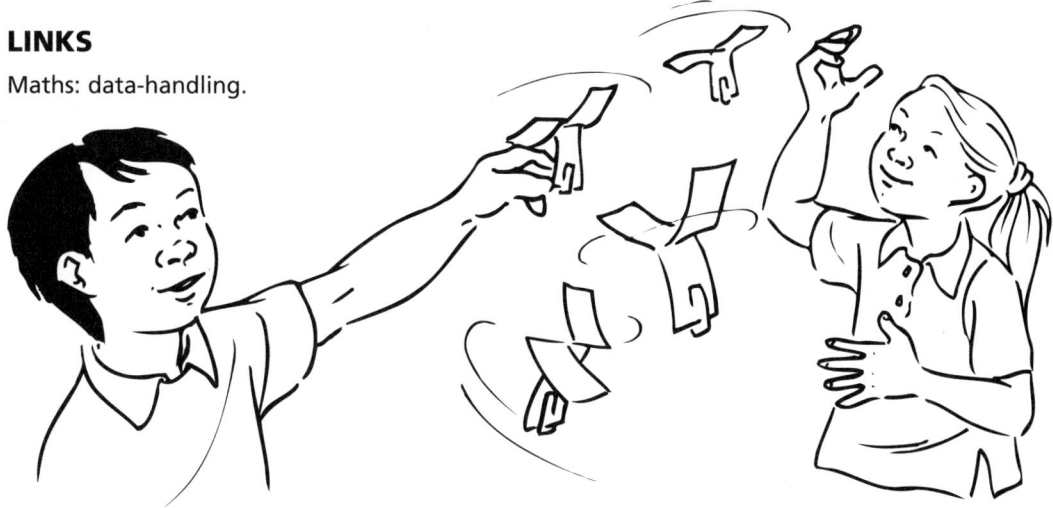

ASSESSMENT

LESSON 13

OBJECTIVES
- To assess the children's knowledge and understanding about how forces can affect the shape and movement of objects.
- To assess the children's ability to plan a test, predict and suggest explanations.

RESOURCES

Assessment activities: 1. A school shoe, a trainer, a Wellington boot, photocopiable page 152. **2.** Photocopiable page 153.

INTRODUCTION

These Assessment activities should be considered alongside the ongoing assessment opportunities indicated throughout the unit when making a judgement about the level the child is working at. If you are unsure what a child means by their response to a question, then discuss it with them afterwards.

ASSESSMENT ACTIVITY 1

Hand out copies of photocopiable page 152. Explain that the children should try to write their ideas down, but that they could do a drawing to help them explain. Let them know that it is not a writing test and you will help to write down their ideas.

Looking for levels

For question 1 on photocopiable page 152, look for words such as 'push', 'pull', 'squeeze', and 'bend'. Most of the class should answer this securely. If they use the word 'force' they have a more sophisticated use of scientific vocabulary. For question 2 accept 'force meter' or 'newton meter'. A child with a weaker vocabulary may show that they know what the equipment is by drawing it. Most of the class should know what the equipment is. In question 3 most children should be able to explain that the parachute slows the soldier down. Accept this, or answers that show an understanding of this. More able children may give an explanation involving the shape of the parachute, or how it 'catches the air', indicating a greater understanding of air resistance.

ASSESSMENT ACTIVITY 2

Hand out copies of photocopiable page 153. Show the children the three shoes and explain the task. For those children with limited writing skills, scribe for them to annotate their drawing.

Looking for levels

For photocopiable page 153, most children will be able to suggest a test that could be carried out with some elements of measurement or control, for example using a ramp or force meter. Others may suggest trying out the shoes on an icy day, which indicates the type of response typical of a lower level of understanding. Explaining how the test can be made fair would indicate aspects of a higher level of attainment.

Most children in the class will be able to make a prediction (Wellington or trainer). An explanation related to past experience such as 'because my trainers have got good grip' is a response typical of NC Level 2/Scottish Level B. Referring to the nature of the surface ('it's got bumps', 'it's made of rubber') is indicative of NC Level 3/Scottish Level C.

PLENARY

Ask the children to share their responses and discuss their answers. Reinforce the use of the words 'force' and 'newton meter'. Ask them what they have learned from the unit and whether any of their ideas have changed. Discuss with the children their responses to Assessment activity 2 and relate it to the practical work they carried out in the unit. Ask them to list the new process skills they have learned during the unit, for example predicting, explaining, measuring with a newton meter, and record these on the board or flip chart.

Name

Magnets and springs

Describe what is happening in each picture.
Include the words 'push', 'pull' or 'twist'.

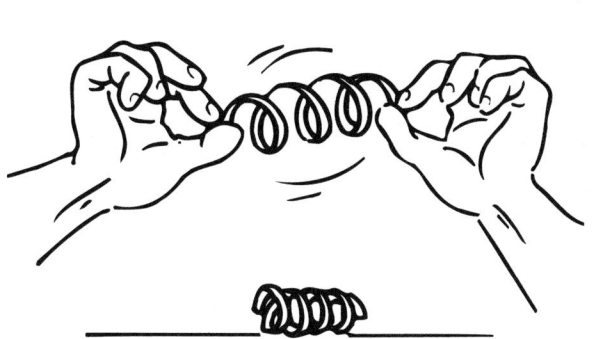

_____

_____

_____

_____

_____

_____

_____

_____

_____

_____

_____

_____

Now make up some of your own.

Sam's Slippery Surfaces

Sam looked out of the window. It was a beautiful frosty morning and, best of all, it was Saturday! Sam put on her tracksuit and some warm woolly socks and ran down the hall. She was going so fast that she slipped on the carpet. Her heart seemed to miss a beat as she skidded towards the front door, only just keeping her balance by grabbing on to the banisters.

'Steady on Sam – you'll do yourself an injury!' said her Dad. 'It's a lovely day. Why don't you go out in the garden before breakfast?'

Sam slipped on her shoes and rushed out, 'Whee!' The path was all icy and she did some great skids along it. Sam tried skidding on the grass, but that didn't seem to work so well, so she went back to the path. Sam's little brother, Nick, came out to join in. He had a go at skidding, but he didn't go very far at all. Sam laughed at him.

'Idiot – you've got your trainers on – no wonder you aren't slipping!' Nick wasn't too happy at having his big sister make fun of him. He stomped back inside and stood in the kitchen leaving frosty puddles on the floor.

'Come on Sam, time for breakfast!' called her Dad. Sam zoomed up the path and in the back door. She did the biggest skid of all along the kitchen floor, landing on her bottom with a graceless thump!

As Sam fought to hold back the tears, Nick just smirked.

Name

Water resistance

Our own test:

Plasticine shape (drawing)	What I predict will happen	How long it took this shape to drop

What we found out:
These pictures show the containers that the Plasticine was dropped into.
Write and draw about what happened in each case.

In air: _____

_____

In water: _____

_____

In wallpaper paste: _____

_____

Name

Paper spinners

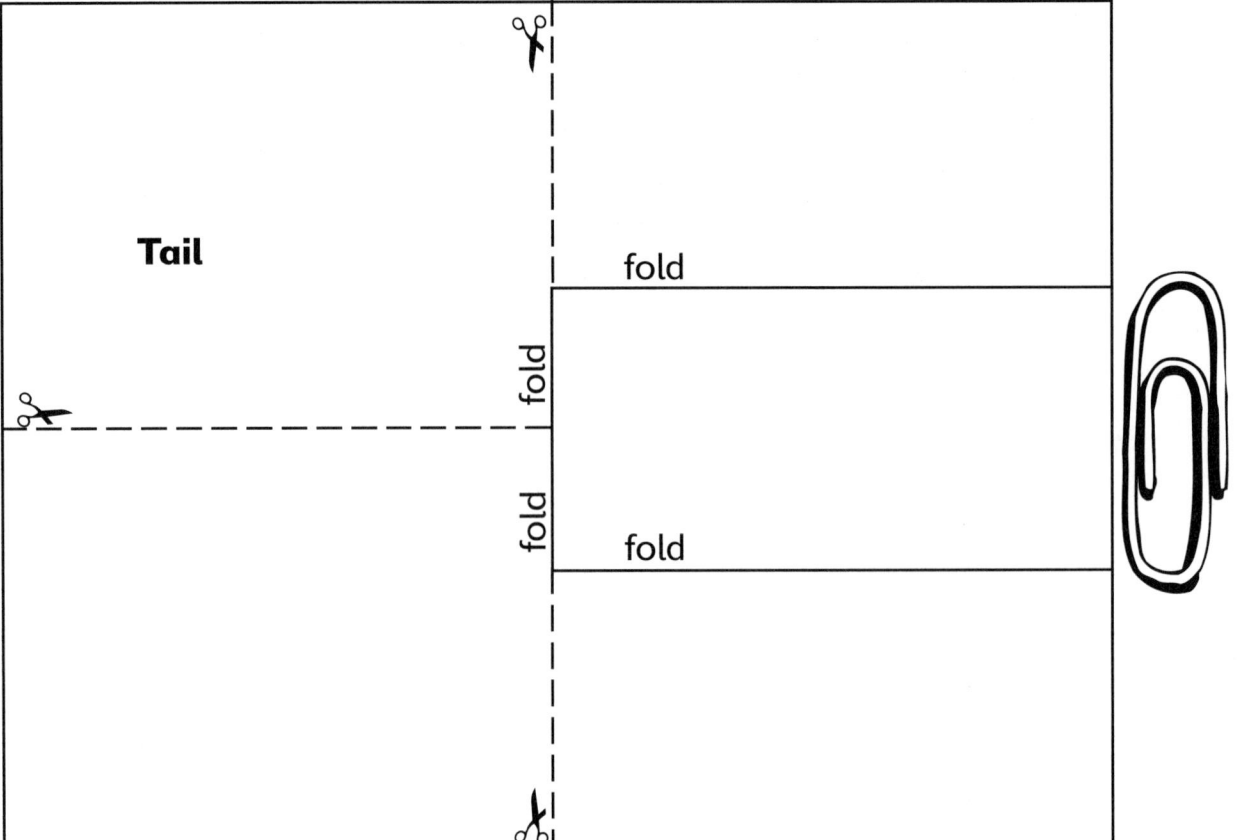

Tail

fold

fold

fold

fold

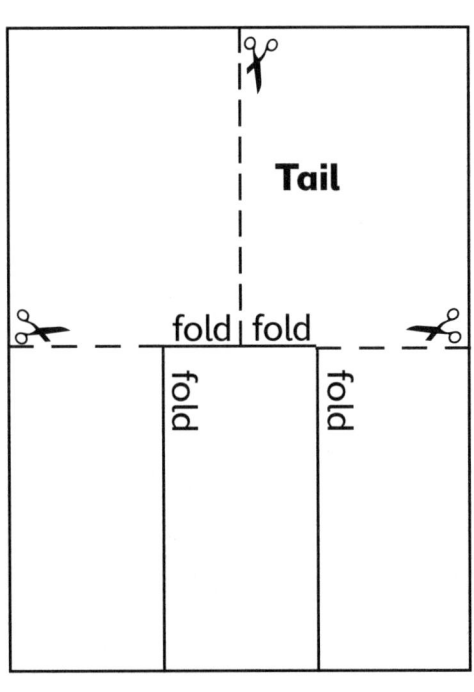

Tail

fold | fold

fold

fold

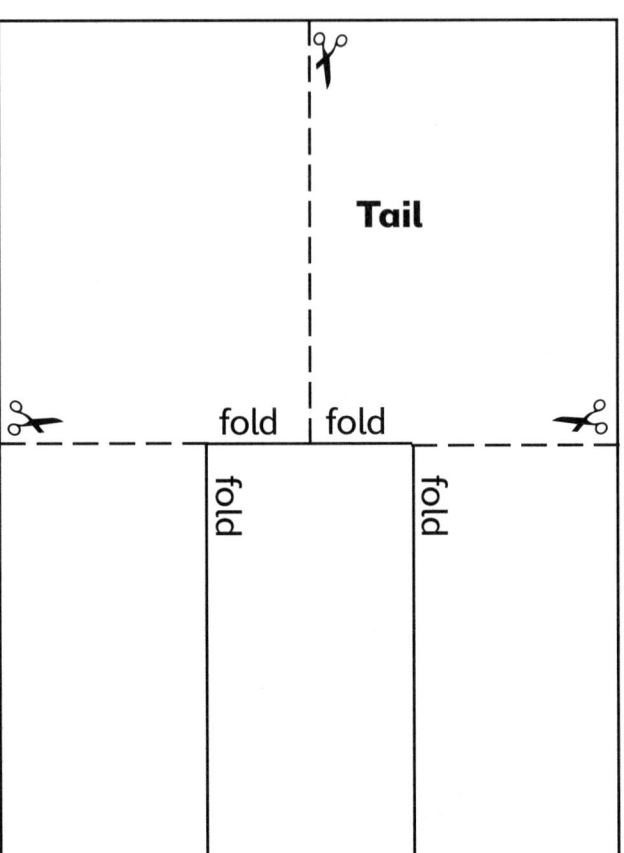

Tail

fold | fold

fold

fold

Hold the two sides of the tail together with a paper clip.

Our spinner test

What we changed	First drop time	Second drop time	Third drop time	Overall drop time

Name

Friction

1. What could Luke do to the Plasticine to change its shape?

_____

_____

_____

_____

_____

2. Nasreen wants to know how much force it will take to pull the door closed. What equipment could she use to find out?

_____

_____

_____

_____

_____

3. How will the parachute help the soldier?

_____

_____

_____

_____

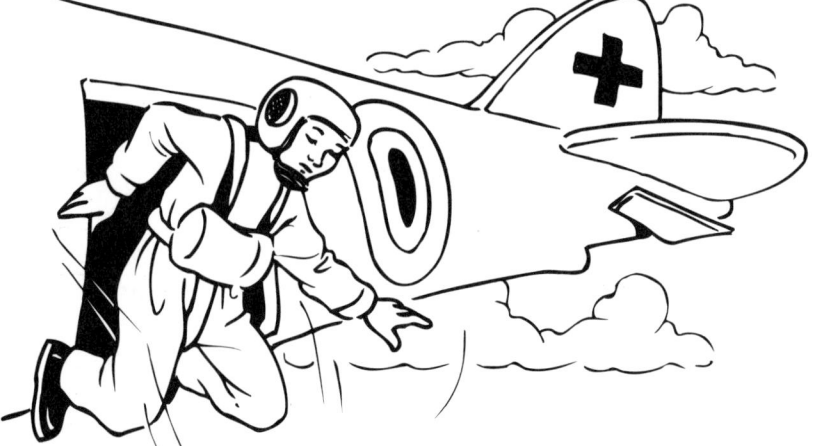

Friction

Sam and her brother Nick want to find out which shoes have the best grip. They looked at Sam's school shoes, Nick's trainers and their Dad's wellies.

What could Sam and Nick do to find out which shoes had the best grip? Draw and write your ideas.

Which do you think will have the best grip? Explain why you think that one will be the best.

_____

_____

Travelling and reflecting

ORGANISATION (15 LESSONS)

	OBJECTIVES	MAIN ACTIVITY	GROUP ACTIVITIES	PLENARY	OUTCOMES
LESSON 1	● To elicit children's existing ideas about light. ● To encourage children to question their own ideas.	Observing shadows in the playground.	Annotated drawings to explain what a shadow is.	Discuss the range of ideas held.	● The teacher has a greater awareness of children's existing understanding. ● The children are more aware of their own ideas and are ready to question them.
LESSON 2	● To begin to recognise that light travels from a source in straight lines. ● To explore and make notes about relevant observations.	Discuss how a mirror can be used to see behind you.	Activities using mirrors, torches and ray boxes to explore how light travels in straight lines.	Introducing the idea that light travels in straight lines.	● Can begin to recognise that light travels in straight lines. ● Can recognise that the sharp edge to a shadow is due to light travelling in straight lines.
LESSON 3	● To understand that the position of a shadow is dependent on the direction of the light source. ● To make and test predictions.	Predicting the position of a shadow cast by a torch shining on a Plasticine figure.	Predicting and testing the position of shadows when the position of the torch is changed.	Relating the position of the shadows to how light travels in straight lines.	● Can make and test a prediction. ● Can understand how the position of the light source affects the position of the shadow.
LESSON 4	● To know that materials can be grouped as opaque, translucent or transparent according to how light behaves when it is shone onto them. ● To carry out a test. ● To use light meters. ● To interpret results and draw conclusions.	Demonstrating how to compare the amount of light that can pass through different materials.	Carrying out tests on how much light passes through a range of materials.	Grouping materials as transparent, translucent and opaque.	● Can distinguish between opaque, translucent and transparent materials. ● Can use a light meter/data-logger. ● Can interpret own data to draw conclusions.
LESSON 5	● To know that translucent and opaque materials form shadows and transparent ones do not. ● To make predictions and suggest explanations based on previous knowledge.	Investigating the shadows cast by transparent, translucent and opaque materials.		Suggesting reasons for results of investigations.	● Can recognise that opaque and translucent materials form shadows and that transparent materials do not.
LESSON 6	● To know that rays are reflected from surfaces. ● To know that flat and curved mirrors reflect light in different ways. ● To observe closely.	Exploring reflections in flat and curved mirrors.		Discussing observations.	● Can recognise that light reflected from a smooth surface produces an image, but light reflected from a rough surface does not. ● Can recognise that curved mirrors change the image of the reflection.

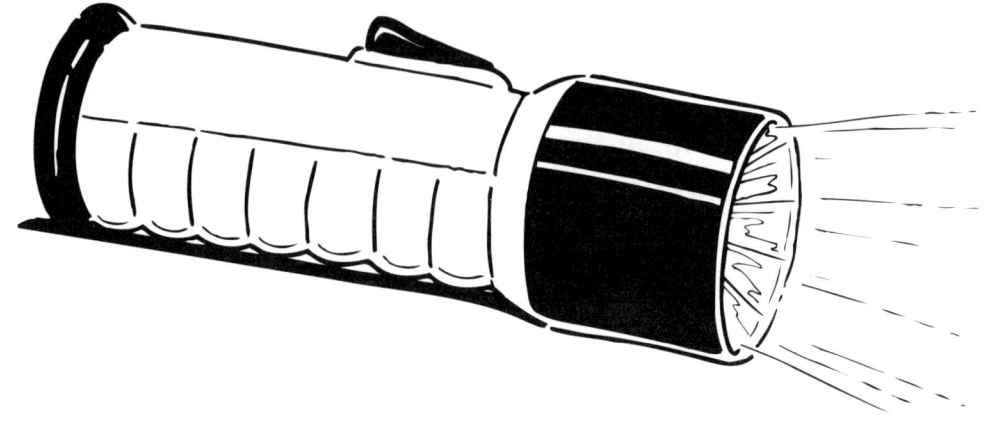

ORGANISATION (15 LESSONS)

	OBJECTIVES	MAIN ACTIVITY	GROUP ACTIVITIES	PLENARY	OUTCOMES
LESSON 7	● To find out children's existing ideas about sound. ● To help children make connections with previous work on sound and stimulate curiosity. ● To introduce the idea of vibration.	Discussion of how a chime bar makes a sound that we hear.	Annotating drawings of children's ideas on how the chime bar makes a sound.	Demonstration of how stopping the vibration of the chime bar stops the sound.	● Teacher is aware of children's existing ideas about sound. ● Ideas about sound and interest in further exploration have been stimulated. ● Can recognise vibration of the chime bar.
LESSON 8	● To understand what is meant by 'vibrate'/'vibration'. ● To recognise that sound is the result of vibration. ● To recognise that different things vibrate differently and this makes different sounds. ● To observe carefully using hearing, sight and touch. ● To make connections between different experiences and ideas.	Using the word 'vibration' to describe observations.	Circus of activities exploring vibration.	Discussing children's observations of how different things vibrated.	● Can recognise that sound is the result of a movement called a vibration. ● Can recognise that different things vibrate differently and so make different sounds. ● Can observe carefully using hearing, sight and touch, and link ideas to observations.
LESSON 9	● To recognise high and low pitch. ● To recognise that the pitch of a sound is related to the size of the vibrating part of an object. ● To notice patterns in their observations and to make generalisations.	Introducing '-er' statements (generalisations) to relate pitch to length of chime bar.	Looking for patterns in the sounds made by collections of objects and musical instruments.	Sharing '-er' statements to make generalisations about patterns in the collections.	● Can recognise high and low pitch. ● Can recognise that the pitch of a sound is related to the size of the vibrating part of an object. ● Can notice patterns in their observations and make generalisations in the form of '-er' sentences.
LESSON 10	● To consolidate recognition of high and low pitch. ● To know that the pitch of a sound is related to the size of the vibrating part in a range of instruments.	Exploring how changing the length of a ruler 'twanged' on a table changes the pitch and express this as an '-er' statement.		Discussing findings.	● Can recognise high and low pitch in a variety of contexts. ● Understand that pitch is related to the size of the vibrating part of a musical instrument.
LESSON 11	● To know that a larger vibrating body makes a louder sound. ● To make generalisations from the results of their own investigations.	Comparing volume of a tuning fork placed on different-sized tins.	Planning and carrying out tests into how the size of an 'ear trumpet' affects the sound.	Discussing findings.	● Can recognise that a large vibrating body makes a louder sound. ● Can make generalisations from the results of their own investigations.
LESSON 12	● To apply knowledge and understanding of sound gained in previous lessons. ● To apply scientific understanding in a design and technology context.	Designing and making a musical instrument from junk materials.		Demonstrating how the instruments make sounds.	● Can apply knowledge and understanding of sound in a design and technology context.
LESSON 13	● To know that sound can be reflected. ● To introduce 'echoes'.	Discussing experiences of echoes.	Modelling echoes using ropes.	Modelling echoes using a 'slinky'.	● Can recognise that sound can be reflected. ● Can explain an echo in terms of reflected sound.
LESSON 14	● To know that sound travels at a certain speed through air and that this is slower than the speed of light.	Taking advantage of a thunderstorm to compare when we observe the thunder and lightning.		Discussing the speed of light and sound.	● Can recognise that sound travels slower than light. ● Can recognise that sound travels at a certain speed.

	OBJECTIVE	ACTIVITY 1		ACTIVITY 2
ASSESSMENT 15	● To assess children's understanding of light and sound.	Concept map on light and sound.		Test focusing on reflection, transparency and pitch.

LESSON 1

OBJECTIVES
● To elicit children's existing ideas about light.
● To encourage children to question their own ideas.

RESOURCES
Main teaching activity: 'Shadow' from *Star Poems* by Michael Rosen (ASE Publications, 2000).
Group activity: Writing materials.

PREPARATION
Take advantage of a sunny ten minutes to do the 'shadow walk', in case the Sun isn't shining on the day of the lesson.

Vocabulary
light, shadow

BACKGROUND
This activity will enable you to find out what ideas the children have about light and shadows so that this can be built on and challenged if necessary. It is quite common for children to confuse shadows and reflections, and their drawings may show this. Other children may not have grasped from their work in Year 3/Primary 4 that a shadow is an absence of light; that light has been blocked. Light travels in straight lines and this can be used to explain why shadows have sharp edges.

When working outside, it is important that the children are told not to look directly at the Sun as this could damage their eyes.

INTRODUCTION
Read the poem 'Shadow' by Michael Rosen to the children and discuss it using the suggested questions below. If you do not have a copy of the poem to stimulate interest in shadows, then engage children in thinking about shadows by asking them: *Have you ever noticed your shadow? Can you describe it to me? When do you notice that you have got a shadow?* (On a sunny day.) *What else can you tell me about shadows? Is your shadow always the same?* This will help to focus the children's observations during the 'shadow walk'.

MAIN TEACHING ACTIVITY
Go for a ten-minute 'shadow walk'. Ask the children to look out for any shadows and to think about how they are made. This could be replaced by five minutes of observation within the classroom if there are shadows cast by lights and windows.

Back in the classroom, ask the children to briefly describe what they saw and explain that you are interested in finding out *their* ideas about light and shadows.

GROUP ACTIVITY
Ask the children to work individually and do an annotated drawing of themselves with a shadow on a sunny day. Explain that you want the picture and writing to show as much as possible about what they understand about light and how a shadow is made.

Circulate, asking questions to assess understanding, for example: *Do you ever get a coloured shadow? Why have you shown the shadow there – could it be on the other side?*

DIFFERENTIATION

You may need to scribe for children with limited writing skills. Questions will depend on the children's responses.

ASSESSMENT

Analyse the annotated drawings – are shadows represented by solid blocks or are they like reflections? Are the shadows drawn starting at their feet? Are they in the correct place with respect to the light source? Is there evidence of understanding that the light has been blocked?

PLENARY

Choose several children who have represented their shadows differently to show their work to the class. Point out that there are some different ideas here and that the class needs to do some investigations to check out their thoughts. Explain that scientists are always trying to understand things better and this means they change their ideas when they find new evidence.

OUTCOMES

● The teacher has a greater awareness of children's existing understanding.
● The children are more aware of their own ideas and are ready to question them.

LINKS

Unit 8 Earth and beyond: Lesson 4.

LESSON 2

OBJECTIVES

● To begin to recognise that light travels from a source in straight lines.
● To explore and make notes about relevant observations.

RESOURCES

Main teaching activity: A flat mirror.
Group activities: 1. A flat mirror.
2. Torches, cards with holes in the centre, a wall or other surface to shine the torch onto. **3.** Ray boxes (home-made ones can be made using a simple bulb and battery circuit in a container such as a short Pringles tube that has a slit cut into the bottom edge).
Plenary: A torch and object.

PREPARATION

Have the resources for the Main teaching activity to hand. Set up the Group activities on the tables. Have the children sitting on the carpet in front of you.

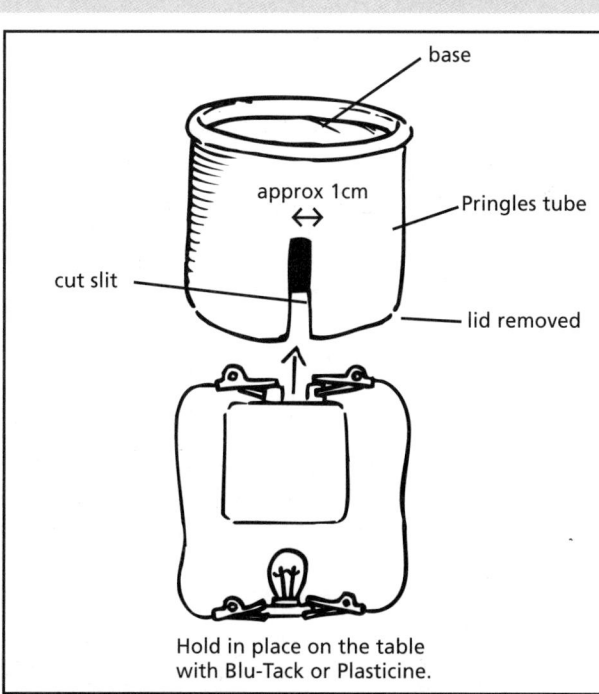

Hold in place on the table with Blu-Tack or Plasticine.

Vocabulary
light, mirror, ray box, reflection

BACKGROUND

The three Group activities will help children to get a 'feel' for light travelling in straight lines, but the Plenary is important to pull these experiences together and articulate a clear idea: light always travels in straight lines, so leave plenty of time for discussion. This is a start point for the development of this concept. It can be more helpful to think of it in terms of what light does not do – go around things.

INTRODUCTION

Ask two children to come out to the front and stand one in front of the other. Give the child in front a mirror. Tell the child behind to pull a silly face and ask the child in front to see if they can copy the face by using the mirror. Ask the children: *How can Pete see what Kelly is doing?*

MAIN TEACHING ACTIVITY

On a board or flip chart, model an annotated drawing that expresses the children's explanations of how Pete can see Kelly.

GROUP ACTIVITIES

Explain that in the Group activities the children will need to record their ideas by drawing and writing. Explain that there are three different activities and they will each get a chance to do each one in turn.

1. As in the Introduction, ask the children to stand or sit in pairs and take turns to use a mirror to copy the silly faces pulled by the child behind. Children record their ideas as an annotated drawing.

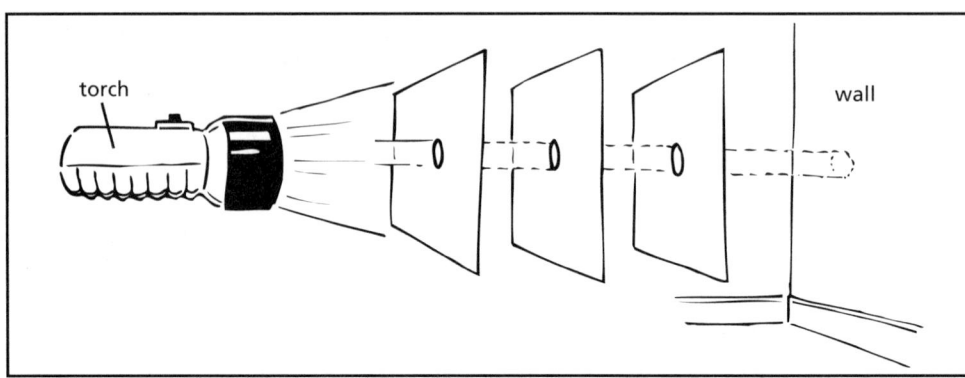

2. Working in pairs, shine a torch onto a card with a hole in it and look at the spot of light it makes on a wall. Take another card with a hole in it and place it so that there is still a spot of light. Can you do it with three cards? Children record their ideas as an annotated drawing.

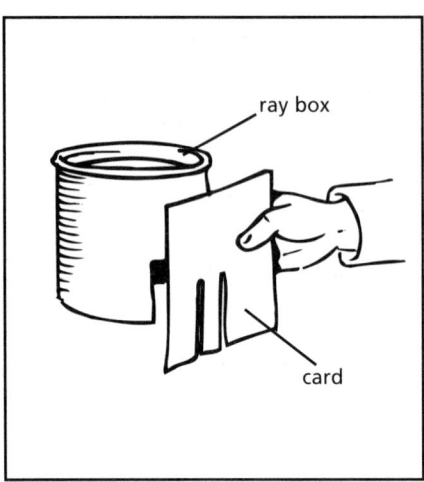

3. Look at the light coming out of a ray box. Explore putting different pieces of card with slits in front of the light and observe what happens. Cut your own design of slit in card and see what happens. (These are often provided with commercially produced ray boxes.)

DIFFERENTIATION

Scribe or provide a key word bank for children with weaker literacy skills. Extend the exploration by encouraging children to add extra mirrors or extra children in Group activity 1; using extra cards or different sizes of hole for Group activity 2, or moving and combining the card slits for Group activity 3.

ASSESSMENT

Is light indicated by straight lines in the children's drawings? Do the children realise that light cannot go around corners unless a mirror is 'helping'?

PLENARY

Ask the children to feed back any interesting observations they have made, and any things they tried out in their exploration. Ask: *Can light go around things?* (No.) *How do you know that?* (There are examples from Group activities 2 and 3.)

Introduce the idea that light always travels in straight lines. Use a torch to cast a shadow on an object. Explain that because light travels in straight lines, when it is blocked it cannot get around the corner to fill up the gap, so there is a sharp edge to the shadow.

OUTCOMES

● Can begin to recognise that light travels in straight lines.
● Can recognise that the sharp edge to a shadow is due to light travelling in straight lines.

LINKS

Unit 8 Earth and beyond: Lesson 4 Sun and shadows.

LESSON 3

OBJECTIVES
● To understand that the position of a shadow is dependent on the direction of the light source.
● To make and test predictions.

RESOURCES

Main teaching activity: A Plasticine figure or toy play person, a torch, a large sheet of white paper, two different-coloured felt-tipped pens, rulers.
Group activities: 1. Plasticine, a torch, white paper and felt-tipped pens for each group.
2. Copies of photocopiable page 173, rough paper, writing equipment.

PREPARATION

Put the resources for the Group activities out on the tables. Have the children sitting in a circle on the carpet with the white paper and Plasticine figure in the centre.

Vocabulary
beam, light, ray, shadow

BACKGROUND

This lesson aims to develop children's ability to make and test predictions, and to understand how their predictions relate to their experience and understanding. It will further develop children's understanding that light travels in straight lines and how shadows are formed when that light is blocked.

INTRODUCTION

Remind the children of the drawings they did of their shadows. Ask them what they have learned about light from Lesson 2. (Light travels in straight lines/cannot go around corners.)

MAIN TEACHING ACTIVITY

Put the Plasticine figure or toy play person on a sheet of white paper in the centre of the circle. Point a torch at the figure, but don't switch it on. Ask: *Where do you think the shadow is going to be?* Ask several children to point to where they predict the shadow will fall. Make sure that they understand the word 'predict'. Show how their predictions can be drawn onto the paper with a felt-tipped pen. Switch on the torch and ask a child to draw around the shadow in a different coloured pen. Explain that they are going to do a similar activity in their groups – making predictions and testing them.

GROUP ACTIVITIES

1. Each group carries out ten predictions and tests, with children taking turns to hold the torch and draw the predictions and outcomes.
2. If resources limit the number of groups who can work on this, give some groups photocopiable page 173 and ask them to devise an acrostic for the word 'shadow'. Suggest they work on rough paper for their first drafts.

DIFFERENTIATION

Have mixed-attainment groups to allow cross-fertilisation of ideas. Extend individuals by asking them to explain the reasons for their predictions in terms of light travelling in straight lines.

ASSESSMENT

Are the children able to make and test predictions? Do their predictions show an understanding of how the position of the shadow is related to the position of the torch? Can they use the idea that light travels in straight lines to explain this?

PLENARY

Bring the class back to sit in the circle and repeat pointing the torch and asking a child to predict where the shadow would be. Ask: *Can you explain why you think the shadow will be there?* Help the children to visualise the ray of light by using a ruler to show its straight line path.

OUTCOMES

● Can make and test a prediction.
● Can understand how the position of the light source affects the position of the shadow.

LINKS

Unit 8 Earth and beyond: Lesson 4.

LESSON 4

OBJECTIVES

● To know that materials can be grouped as opaque, translucent or transparent according to how light behaves when it is shone onto them.
● To carry out a test.
● To use light meters.
● To interpret results and draw conclusions.

RESOURCES

Main teaching activity: A selection of materials from the collection below.
Group activities: 1. A collection for each group of materials that are opaque such as card, aluminium foil and wallpaper; that are transparent such as cellophane and clingfilm; and that are translucent such as tracing paper; light meters (or data-logging equipment if available); torches. **2.** Copies of photocopiable page 174.

PREPARATION

Put one collection on each group's table. Keep the torches out of sight in case the children request them. Have data-logging equipment or light meters set up ready at the side.

Vocabulary

light meter, opaque, translucent, transparent

BACKGROUND

Opaque materials do not let any light through and so they make dense shadows. Transparent materials let light through and so they don't form shadows. Translucent materials such as bathroom windows let some light through, but scatter it, so the shadows are not as dark. The terminology is not as important as the ideas, but the children may enjoy using the scientific vocabulary. Avoid using the word 'see-through' as this encourages the idea that rays are coming out of the eyes, rather than the correct idea that light is going into them.

Light meters and data-logging equipment can be used by children to measure how much light is coming through, rather than trying to judge it by eye. However, if these are not available to you, the children can develop their own index instead with 0 meaning 'no light comes through' and 5 meaning 'all the light comes through', with the numbers in between representing degrees of translucence.

INTRODUCTION

Give each group a collection of materials to sort in as many different ways as they can.

MAIN TEACHING ACTIVITY

Explain that some materials let more light come through than others. Ask the children to pick out items from their collection that they think let no light through, and lots of light through. Ask: *How could we test how much light each material lets through?* Suggestions will probably include holding them up and shining a torch on them. Ask: *How will we know how much light is coming through?* Explain that there are devices that can measure how much light there is, and demonstrate how to use the light meters or data-loggers. It is important to point out that the normal daylight will be measured too, so they are looking for a change in the reading on the meter.

As part of the demonstration, exaggerate putting the light meter very close to the torch, then much further away and ask the children: *Is that fair?* (No.) *Why not?* (Because when it is nearer it might get more light.) *How can I make it fair?* (Keep it the same distance away.)

Material	How much light comes through

GROUP ACTIVITIES

1. Ask each group to plan and carry out a test to find out how much light comes through some of the materials in their collection. The group is to make decisions on how many materials to test and how to carry out the test. Ask them to record their results in a table as shown on the left. Circulate and ask children to explain their test design. Ask each child to write down two or three sentences about what they found out.

2. Give each child a copy of photocopiable page 174 and ask them to look at the graph and interpret it by answering the questions.

DIFFERENTIATION

Have the children working in mixed-attainment groups to support each other. Target questions about the test according to the child, for example: *Why did you choose those materials? Which one do you think will let most/least light through? Why? Are you doing anything to make the test fair? Can you tell me what you have found out so far?* Scaffold the data interpretation by providing phrases such as: 'We found that the _____ let the most light through. The _____ and _____ didn't let any light through. This is a list of objects in order of how much light went through.'

ASSESSMENT

Can the children use the light meter effectively? Have they carried out a test? Can they give examples of materials in their collection that let a lot/a little/no light through?

PLENARY

Bring the class to sit in a circle on the carpet. Ask each group to give a piece of the material that let all the light through. Put these in a group with the label 'transparent'. Ask each group for a material that lets no light through. Put these materials together and label them 'opaque'. Ask: *Were there any materials that let a bit of light through but you can't see things clearly?* Put these in a group labelled 'translucent'.

Bring out some new samples of materials and ask the children which group they think they would belong to and why. Put them with the relevant group.

OUTCOMES

- Can distinguish between opaque, translucent and transparent materials.
- Can use a light meter/data-logger.
- Can interpret own data to draw conclusions.

LINKS

Maths: measurement, interpretation of measurement.
Unit 4 Materials: properties of materials.

LESSON 5

Objectives	● To know that translucent and opaque materials form shadows and transparent ones do not. ● To make predictions and suggest explanations based on previous knowledge.
Resources	A collection of materials as for Lesson 3; an overhead projector; a screen or wall area for projection.
Main activity	Explain that you want the children to use what they learned in the previous lesson to help them with a new investigation. Hold up an opaque material. Ask: *Do you think this would make a shadow if I put it in the way of the light? Why?* Ask the children to work in pairs to choose five materials and discuss what they think the shadow would be like. Ask them to record their predictions in a table (see below). The children carry out the test and record their findings. Remind them to think back to the previous lesson to help explain why they got the results.

Material	What I predict will happen	What did happen	Why I think this happened

Differentiation	Provide a key word bank ('light', 'travel', 'through', names of the materials), and include phrases such as *'I think... because'* to support children with weaker literacy skills or who are finding it hard to draw on their previous experience. Ask others to extend their thinking by drawing a diagram of what they think is happening in each case, using arrows to represent the light.
Assessment	Can the children make predictions? Are they drawing on the previous lesson in their suggested explanations? Can they explain why shadows are formed by some materials and not others?
Plenary	Ask the children for some of their explanations, then clarify them. Hold up a new material, ask the children to make a prediction about what the shadow will be like and to explain their reason.
Outcome	● Can recognise that opaque and translucent materials form shadows and that transparent materials do not.

LESSON 6

Objectives	● To know that rays are reflected from surfaces. ● To know that flat and curved mirrors reflect light in different ways. ● To observe closely.
Resources	Ray boxes, flat mirrors, curved mirrors, shiny spoons, make-up mirrors.
Main activity	The children use the ray boxes to make single and parallel rays, observing the reflection of those rays and making annotated drawings as they go. They work through the following sequence of activities: reflections of rough/shiny materials; reflections in a flat mirror; reflections in curved mirrors; set a flat mirror at an angle to the ray and look at the angle of the reflected ray. Circulate and ask the children to describe their observations.
Differentiation	Expect lower attainers in science to do the first two activities; most children to do the first three activities, and high attainers to do all 4. (This is revisited and extended in *100 Science Lessons: Year 6/Primary 7* to explain what is observed and the associated laws. At this stage, therefore, you may prefer to keep to just discussing the children's observations.)
Assessment	Are the children's observations careful and accurate? Can they describe differences between the way different surfaces and mirrors reflect the light rays?
Plenary	Ask the children to describe what they observed in each activity and to suggest explanations for it. Discuss how the reflection is the light 'bouncing off', and that this works best on shiny surfaces.
Outcomes	● Can recognise that light reflected from a smooth surface produces an image, but light reflected from a rough surface does not. ● Can recognise that curved mirrors change the image of the reflection.

LESSON 7

OBJECTIVES
● To find out children's existing ideas about sound.
● To help children make connections with previous work on sound and stimulate curiosity.
● To introduce the idea of vibration.

RESOURCES

Main teaching activity: A chime bar and beater.
Group activity: Chime bars and beaters (one per pair or group), sticky tape, Blu-Tack, writing materials.

PREPARATION

Have the children sitting in a circle. Put out resources for the Group activity on the tables. Have the chime bar and beater to hand.

Vocabulary

chime bar, ear, sound, vibration

BACKGROUND

The children will have explored ideas about loud and quiet sounds and high and low sounds previously, and these lessons aim to help the children to make connections with that and to elicit their current ideas about sound. Children may well associate sound with a movement, for example hitting a drum, plucking a string, stamping feet, but may not be aware that sounds are about vibrations. They may have some ideas about sound travelling to the ear, but may not have thought about what it travels through to get there.

Ideas about volume and pitch are often confused as the language we use to talk about them is similar: we 'turn the sound up' (volume), but also make a sound 'higher' (pitch).

INTRODUCTION

Ask the children to close their eyes and listen for one minute to any sounds they can hear. When the time is up ask them to open their eyes and describe the sounds they heard. Ask: *Was it loud or quiet? How do you think the sound was made? Did it sound high or low?*

MAIN TEACHING ACTIVITY

Bring out the chime bar. Ask: *How can I make a sound with this chime bar?* Try out the children's suggestions. Ask: *How do you think the sound is made?* Listen to a selection of children's ideas, valuing their suggestions, but not agreeing or disagreeing with them at this stage. They may make suggestions about what different parts of the chime bar are for. Ask: *How do you think we hear the sound?* The children are likely to talk about the role of the ear. You may need to extend this by asking: *How does the sound get from the chime bar to our ears?*

Now ask: *How could we change the sound?* Again there is likely to be a wide range of suggestions, for example covering up the hole, hitting it harder/more gently, hitting it with something different.

GROUP ACTIVITY

Write these three questions on the board:
● How do you think the sound is made?
● How do you think we hear it?
● How can we change the sound?
Ask the children to explore the chime bars on their tables, then do annotated drawings in response to the three questions. Circulate, focusing particularly on questioning children who did not contribute in the whole-class session. Encourage children to feel the vibration of the bar by touching it gently.

DIFFERENTIATION

You may need to scribe for children with weaker writing skills. Expect lower attainers in science to produce descriptions of what happens and higher attainers in science to be forming explanations.

Be aware of any children with hearing difficulties and encourage them to take part by feeling and looking carefully.

ASSESSMENT

Assessment is formative as the children's ideas will form the basis for differentiation and adjustment of subsequent lessons. Note where children have ideas that are not in line with scientific ideas and need to be challenged, and where ideas can be extended.

PLENARY

Bring the children back to sit in a circle. Ask: *What else did you notice about the chime bar and how sounds were made?* If necessary, introduce the idea of the chime bar moving up and down very fast and explain that this is called a vibration, writing the word on the board or a card. Demonstrate how hitting the chime bar in the centre makes a different sound from when it is hit near the end. Ask: *Why do you think this happens?* (Because the fixed ends cannot vibrate as much.) Demonstrate how you can stop the note by touching the bar firmly with a finger. Ask: *Why do you think this happens?* (Because you are stopping the chime bar from vibrating up and down.) Explain that you will all think about this more in the next lesson.

OUTCOMES

● Teacher is aware of children's existing ideas about sound.
● Ideas about sound and interest in further exploration have been stimulated.
● Can recognise vibration of the chime bar.

LINKS

Music: exploring sounds made by musical instruments.

LESSON 8

OBJECTIVES

● To understand what is meant by 'vibrate'/'vibration'.
● To recognise that sound is the result of vibration.
● To recognise that different things vibrate differently and this makes different sounds.
● To observe carefully using hearing, sight and touch.
● To make connections between different experiences and ideas.

RESOURCES

Main teaching activity: A guitar, a tuning fork.
Group activity: A guitar, ping-pong balls threaded on to thick thread; a bowl of water, two tuning forks, a drum, rice, a tank of water, pebbles, a slinky (three would be ideal), a cymbal and soft beater, photocopiable page 175, card.

PREPARATION

Copy photocopiable page 175 on to card, enlarged to A3 if possible. Cut the page into individual cards. Set up the Group activities on tables around the room with their appropriate instructions.

Vocabulary

hear, see, sound, touch, vibration

BACKGROUND

When things are made to vibrate, perhaps by being struck, they vibrate in different ways according to what they are made of and their size and shape. The vibrations move the air next to the object, which moves the air a bit further away and so on. This is what is called a sound wave; every time the vibration pushes the nearby air it sets off a 'ripple'. This moves out in all directions, like when a pebble is dropped in a pond. The ripple may reach the air near our ears; the ears are really vibration detectors and our brains construct the idea of a 'sound'.

INTRODUCTION

Ask the children to put their hands gently on their throats (on their voice box) and make a humming noise. Ask: *What does it feel like?* (A 'buzzing'; a vibration.) Some children may find it easier to feel on a partner. Demonstrate playing a chime bar and ask some children to feel the bar, reminding them of the previous lesson. Ask: *What do we call that 'buzzing', that tiny up and down movement?* (A vibration.) Write the word 'vibration' on the board or hold up the card with the word written on it.

This lesson is structured with a short Main teaching activity to help the children focus their attention on the Group activities, but has a longer Plenary in which important ideas are clarified.

MAIN TEACHING ACTIVITY

Explain that the children are going to experience all sorts of vibrations using their senses of hearing, sight and touch. Explain that you will demonstrate some first, but that they will all be able to experience them for themselves in their groups.

Ask a child to gently touch the body of the guitar. Pluck a string of the guitar and ask the child to describe what they see, hear and feel. Now ask: *Can you use the word 'vibration' to explain what you have noticed?*

Demonstrate how to use a tuning fork, holding it by the unforked end and striking a prong on a hard surface. Show how it makes a note by holding the unforked end onto a surface. Ask: *What do you think will happen if I touch the end of the fork on some water?* Show interest in the children's suggestions and then try them! Don't get involved in explanations at this stage.

Briefly outline the Group activity, reminding the children to use their senses and to think about vibrations. Explain that they will have 5 minutes on each activity and you will discuss their ideas in the Plenary.

GROUP ACTIVITY

The children need to be in groups of about four, though these can be larger if equipment is scarce. The activities are set up as a circus. Tell the groups to try each activity for five minutes, then move on to the next activity.

Circulate, asking questions, for example: *What have you noticed? What did that feel like?* Help the children to use the equipment effectively if necessary.

DIFFERENTIATION

Target questions differently, asking some children to focus on description and others to try to form explanations. Use this opportunity to address any individual issues raised by Lesson 1.

ASSESSMENT

Do the children understand what is meant by the term 'vibration'? Can they describe different examples of vibration? Are they making links between vibration and sound?

PLENARY

Gather the children together. Invite different children to comment briefly on each activity, bringing the equipment to the circle. Ask: *Did all the things make the same sound?* (No.) *What differences did you notice in how the things vibrated?* (This one was difficult to feel; this one vibrated a lot and so on.) Ask: *What do we mean by a vibration?* (Something moving backwards and forwards very fast.) *What have vibrations got to do with sound?* Listen to the children's ideas and draw on them in your explanation. Explain that our ears are 'vibration detectors' so when something vibrates they notice and our brain calls it a sound. Ask: *How do our ears up here* [indicating up] *pick up a vibration down there* [point to an object]? Listen to the children's ideas. Explain that the sound travels through the air, a bit like a ripple travels through water or along a slinky and gets to our ears.

OUTCOMES

- Can recognise that sound is the result of a movement called a vibration.
- Can recognise that different things vibrate differently and so make different sounds.
- Can observe carefully using hearing, sight and touch, and link ideas to observations.

LINKS

Music: musical instruments have a vibrating part.

LESSON 9

OBJECTIVES

- To recognise high and low pitch.
- To recognise that the pitch of a sound is related to the size of the vibrating part of an object.
- To notice patterns in their observations and to make generalisations.

RESOURCES

Main teaching activity: A xylophone or a glockenspiel and beater, a flip chart, marker pens.
Group activity: Sugar paper and felt-tipped pens. Six different sets of equipment: 1. A collection of bottles with different amounts of water in them (not in order) and a beater. 2. A collection of different chime bars. 3. A collection of elastic bands and different boxes to stretch them around. 4. A collection of recorders or whistles of different sizes, for example descant, treble, tenor. 5. A collection of different-sized tins and a beater. 6. A collection of different-sized drums (or saucepans!) and beaters.

PREPARATION

Set up the equipment for the Group activities on tables around the room.

Vocabulary

high, low, pattern, pitch

BACKGROUND

Pitch is to do with the frequency of vibration. Short or small things vibrate quickly, and so have a high pitch. Large or long objects vibrate more slowly and so have a lower pitch.

Children often find it difficult to distinguish between a sound getting louder and a sound getting higher in pitch. By discussing the words used to describe different sounds this can be clarified for them. This lesson also helps children learn how to express a relationship between two variables as a generalisation, such as 'the larger the object, the lower the pitch of the note.'

INTRODUCTION

Ask the children to hum the same note as you. Now hum a lower note, then a higher note and indicate that they should join in. Develop this by asking the children to raise and lower their hands as the humming gets higher and lower. They could stand up and move their whole bodies up and down in line with the pitch of the hum. Ask: *How are we making that humming noise?* (Something in our throats – our vocal chords in our voice box – is vibrating.) Ask: *What were we changing about the sound we made?* (It went up and down; higher and lower.)

If some children are confusing pitch and volume, then explain that people often get muddled between them and demonstrate the difference by hitting one note on the xylophone loudly then softly, then hitting different notes to change the pitch.

MAIN TEACHING ACTIVITY

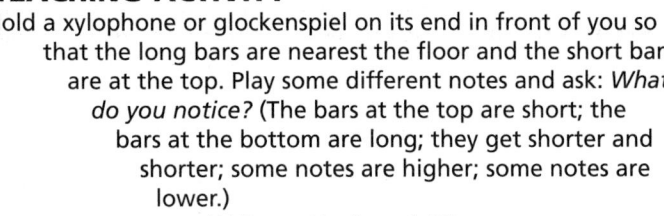
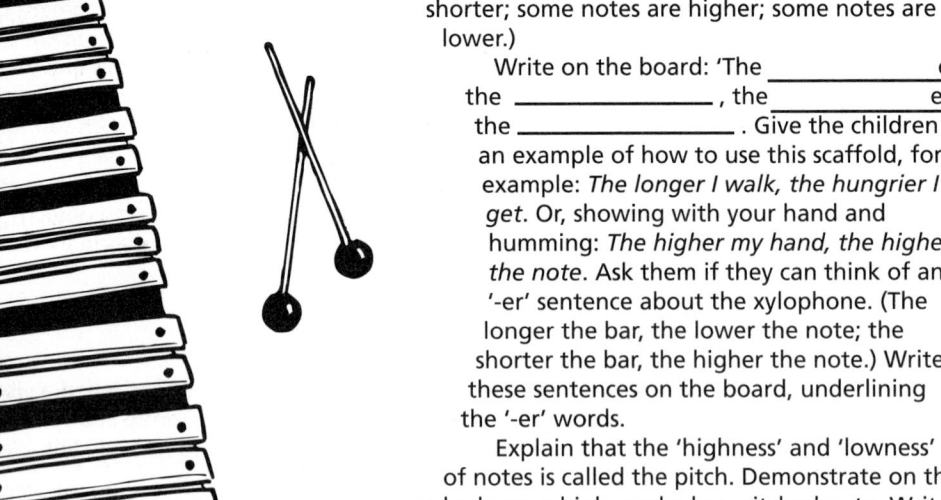

Hold a xylophone or glockenspiel on its end in front of you so that the long bars are nearest the floor and the short bars are at the top. Play some different notes and ask: *What do you notice?* (The bars at the top are short; the bars at the bottom are long; they get shorter and shorter; some notes are higher; some notes are lower.)

Write on the board: 'The _____ er the _____ , the_____ er the _____ . Give the children an example of how to use this scaffold, for example: *The longer I walk, the hungrier I get*. Or, showing with your hand and humming: *The higher my hand, the higher the note*. Ask them if they can think of an '-er' sentence about the xylophone. (The longer the bar, the lower the note; the shorter the bar, the higher the note.) Write these sentences on the board, underlining the '-er' words.

Explain that the 'highness' and 'lowness' of notes is called the pitch. Demonstrate on the xylophone a high- and a low-pitched note. Write the word 'pitch' on the board.

Explain that in the Group activities, you want the children to think about the pitch of the sound and try to write some '-er' sentences. Explain that they need to be ready to tell the class what they have found out.

GROUP ACTIVITY

Each group is to explore their collection of equipment and look for patterns. Ask them to write down some '-er' sentences on sugar paper. The group will feed back what they have found to the rest of the class. Circulate, supporting the groups.

DIFFERENTIATION

Support children by writing the first or second half of the '-er' sentence for them, for example: 'The more water, the_____er'. Extend others by challenging them to add 'I think this is because _____', so they are providing explanations too.

The water and elastic band collections are the most challenging, and the chime bars are easiest because they are most similar to the example provided.

ASSESSMENT

Can the children put the collection in order relating to the pitch of the sound? Can they make an '-er' sentence to generalise their findings. Are they correctly relating the pitch to the size of the object?

PLENARY

Ask each group to show the rest of the class their findings, demonstrating the change in pitch of their collection and reading out their '-er' sentences. Ask: *Do you notice anything about what we all found?* (There is a common relationship between the pitch and the size of the objects.)

OUTCOMES

● Can recognise high and low pitch.
● Can recognise that the pitch of a sound is related to the size of the vibrating part of an object.
● Can notice patterns in their observations and make generalisations in the form of '-er' sentences.

LINKS

Music: the size of musical instruments is related to the pitch of the notes produced.

LESSON 10

Objectives	● To consolidate recognition of high and low pitch. ● To know that the pitch of a sound is related to the size of the vibrating part in a range of instruments.
Resources	Rulers, writing and drawing materials.
Main activity	Show the children how a ruler 'twanged' on a table can make different sounds depending on how much of the ruler is sticking out. Ask: *Which part of the ruler is vibrating?* (The part sticking out.) Ask: *Can someone give me an '-er' sentence about this?* (The shorter the part of the ruler sticking out, the higher the sound.) Ask the children to observe closely and look at how fast the ruler is vibrating. This produces other '-er' sentences: 'The longer, and the slower, the lower the sound', 'The shorter, and the faster, the higher the sound.' Ask the children to try out the pitch of different ruler lengths for themselves. Ask them to record their findings as an annotated drawing and an '-er' statement. Some children could be encouraged to change the length of the ruler systematically, such as 2cm at a time.
Differentiation	Children with musical skills and talent will have the opportunity to contribute to this lesson directly.
Assessment	Can the children apply their knowledge and ideas from previous lessons to explain how the instruments make different sounds?
Plenary	Ask: *What have you learned so far about sound?* (Sound is the result of a vibration; the pitch of a note can be changed; the pitch is related to the size of the vibrating part of the object.)
Outcomes	● Can recognise high and low pitch in a variety of contexts. ● Understand that pitch is related to the size of the vibrating part of a musical instrument.

LESSON 11

OBJECTIVES

● To know that a larger vibrating body makes a louder sound.
● To make generalisations from the results of their own investigations.

RESOURCES

Main teaching activity: A tuning fork; different-sized containers, for example tins and mixing bowls; card and sticky tape to make an ear trumpet (a semicircle of card made into a cone and held in shape with tape).
Group activity: Photocopiable page 176, card, scissors, sticky tape, templates of circles or semicircles, rulers, pencils, paper clips.

PREPARATION

Put the resources for the Group activities out on the tables. Make up one card ear trumpet and have the resources for the Main teaching activity to hand.

Vocabulary

loud, quiet, volume

BACKGROUND

The reason that most instruments have some sort of 'box' or 'body' is that this part amplifies the sound: it makes it louder. The speakers on stereo systems need to be large for the same reason – they are amplifying small vibrations.

  The term 'volume' may be confusing, as it is also used in maths in relation to shape. If this becomes a problem, use the term 'loudness' instead.

INTRODUCTION

Review the ideas learned in previous lessons about vibration and pitch. Ask: *We've learned about changing the pitch, what else can we change about a sound?* (How loud it is.)

MAIN TEACHING ACTIVITY

Demonstrate the way sound can be amplified by striking a tuning fork and putting it onto a container. Ask: *Can you describe what is happening?* (The box is making the sound louder.)

Ask the children to predict what will happen to the sound when you put it over a small, medium and large container. Test out their predictions! Ask them to discuss, in pairs, an '-er' sentence about what they have observed. (The bigger the box, the louder the sound.) Discuss how the '-er' statements tend to have an opposite that is also true: 'The smaller the box, the quieter the sound'.

Show them a card cone 'ear trumpet'. Explain that you want them to investigate the question: 'What would happen to the sound if we changed the size of the ear trumpet?' Explain that they will investigate this in groups.

GROUP ACTIVITY

Ask each group to plan and record their investigation in note form according to the frame on photocopiable page 176. Circulate as the children are planning and carrying out their investigation, or focus support on children or groups who are lower attainers in investigative skills. Children may need help with how to make a sound that can be kept at the same volume: suggest quiet tapping with a pencil, or dropping a paper clip. Ask the children to record their results and to write what they found out in the form of an '-er' statement.

DIFFERENTIATION

Depending on the group, the investigation frame could be a prompt sheet for more independent recording, or it could be a worksheet-style frame to fill in with more or less support for the writing.

Some groups will need more adult intervention to support them in planning and carrying out their investigation, for example in deciding to keep the same distance away from the sound.

ASSESSMENT

Do the children relate the size of the vibrating part to the volume of the sound? Can they express their findings as a generalisation?

PLENARY

Ask the groups to report back their findings. Do all the groups agree? Were there any problems with the test?

OUTCOMES

● Can recognise that a large vibrating body makes a louder sound.
● Can make generalisations from the results of their own investigations.

LINKS

Music: sounds can be amplified.

LESSON 12

Objectives	● To apply knowledge and understanding of sound gained in previous lessons. ● To apply scientific understanding in a design and technology context.
Resources	A wide range of design and technology tools, junk materials, glue, tapes, paint. Or, set this activity as a homework project.
Main activity	Design and make a musical instrument from junk/reclaimed materials. It must make more than one sound.
Differentiation	Support children who are finding it difficult to raise ideas by suggesting possibilities.
Assessment	Does the instrument make more than one sound? Can the children explain how the sounds are made in terms of vibration? Can they explain variation in volume or pitch?
Plenary	Have a demonstration time in which children show and play their instruments. Ask them to explain how the sounds are made and the reason for their designs.
Outcome	● Can apply knowledge and understanding of sound in a design technology context.

LESSON 13

OBJECTIVES

● To know that sound can be reflected.
● To introduce 'echoes'.

RESOURCES

Group activities: 1. Skipping ropes (one per pair), secondary sources on echoes and echo location. **2.** 'Echo and Narcissus' from *Let's Learn at Home: Reading 8–9* by Sue Palmer (Scholastic.)
Plenary: A slinky.

PREPARATION

The Group activities are best carried out in the playground or hall as they need some space. If there is a good place to hear an echo within the school grounds or reasonable walking distance then take the children there to experience echoes.

Vocabulary

echo, reflect, wave

BACKGROUND

Sound can be reflected – it can bounce back from hard surfaces. This is what is happening when we hear an echo. It also explains why, when we shut a door, the sound seems to be kept in a room, even though we know that sound can travel through solid materials. Although it is not possible to demonstrate this directly, it can be modelled.

INTRODUCTION

Invite children to tell the rest of the class about places where they have heard an echo. Ask: *What did it sound like? What do you think an echo is?* Do the children know how to be your echo?

MAIN TEACHING ACTIVITY

Ask: *What do all those places that make good echoes have in common?* (A hard surface, usually large, often curved, like a cave or bridge.)

Explain that an echo is when sound bounces off a surface and comes back to us. Draw a parallel with what happens when light bounces off a mirror – it is reflected. Explain that because we can't actually see the sound travel we need to think of other similar things that we can see to help us understand it, and this is what they will be doing in the Group activities.

GROUP ACTIVITIES

1. Ask the children to work in pairs. Give each pair a skipping rope. Either tie one end of each rope to a fixed place, for example playground railings, or ask one child to hold the end as still as they can. The other child needs to make a wave run along the rope by giving it a gentle flick. Explain that if they shake the rope too hard they won't notice what is going on! By observing carefully, they should be able to see the wave bounce back. Ask: *Is the wave that comes back exactly the same as the wave that went out?* (It may be smaller, or less definite.) Ask: *In what way is that like an echo?* (The sound is distorted.)

2. Ask the children to read the echo myth 'Echo and Narcissus', in which the talkative nymph Echo annoys Hera and is condemned only to repeat the words of others. Ask them to perform part of it as a play, working in collaborative groups.

DIFFERENTIATION

Support children who have poorer observational skills by spending more time with them and targeting questions at them, for example: *Can you describe to me what you see?*
Some children may be extended by using secondary sources to explore echolocation.

ASSESSMENT

Can the children explain that an echo is the result of sound being reflected/bouncing back?

PLENARY

Gather the whole class around in a circle. Ask two children to sit opposite each other in the centre of the circle holding either end of a slinky. Ask one child to hold their end still and the other child to make a wave. Together observe what happens. Ask: *What happened to the wave when it got to the end?* (It bounced and came back.) Ask: *How does this help us understand an echo?* (In an echo, the sound bounces back.)

Ask: *Does anyone know how bats use echoes to help them?* Explain that bats have poor eyesight and hunt in the dark so they need another way of knowing where their prey is. They make a high-pitched noise, and if something is in the way there is an echo when the sound hits them that the bat can detect.

OUTCOMES

● Can recognise that sound can be reflected.
● Can explain an echo in terms of reflected sound.

LINKS

Literacy: myths, plays.
History: the Ancient Greeks.

LESSON 14

Objective	● To know that sound travels at a certain speed through air and that this is slower than the speed of light.
Resources	A thunderstorm! Take advantage of this whenever it occurs.
Main activity	Observe the flash of lightning and count aloud together until you hear the thunder. Ask: *Why don't the thunder and the lightning come at the same time?* Explain that although they are started at the same time, the light travels much faster than the thunder and so gets to us almost straight away. The thunder travels more slowly and so we can use it to work out how far away the storm is. Repeat, counting the time difference between the lightning and the thunder. If the time is getting shorter, then the storm is closer; if the time is getting longer then the storm is moving away. Ask: *What do you think is happening to the storm – is it coming closer or moving away?* Explain that for every second counted the thunder has travelled a distance of about a mile (1.6km) so that we can work out how far the thunder and lightning have travelled.
Differentiation	Some children will be familiar with this idea, so target questions at those for whom this is a new experience.
Assessment	Can the children state that in a thunderstorm we see the lightning before the thunder? Can they explain that this is because the sound takes a certain time to travel the distance to us.
Plenary	Ask: *In a thunderstorm, which comes first, the thunder or the lightning?* (The lightning comes first.) Ask: *What does this tell us about the speed of sound?* (It is slower than light.)
Outcomes	● Can recognise that sound travels slower than light. ● Can recognise that sound travels at a certain speed.

ASSESSMENT
LESSON 15

OBJECTIVE
● To assess children's understanding of light and sound.

RESOURCES
Assessment activities: 1. A copy of photocopiable page 178 for each child, writing materials.
2. Copy of photocopiable page 177 for each child, writing materials.

INTRODUCTION
These Assessment activities should be considered alongside the ongoing assessment opportunities indicated throughout the unit when making a judgement about the level the child is working at. If you are unsure what a child means by their response to a question, then discuss it with them afterwards.

ASSESSMENT ACTIVITY 1
Ask the children to draw a concept map on light and sound. Give them a copy of photocopiable page 178 and ask them to draw a line linking words if they think there is a relationship between them. They then need to write along the line explaining what the link is. One example is given. They can make more than one link between the same words.

Explain that there are no 'right' ways to make the links, but that it is their opportunity to show off as much as they can about what they have learned.

Children with poorer writing skills may make the links between words, and have help with scribing their ideas about the link along the line for them.

Looking for levels
The concept maps on photocopiable page 178 will allow you to make some judgements about the children's level of understanding. The least able children will offer few links, and those will be descriptive, for example 'You get a shadow in the sunlight', 'You see a reflection in the mirror'.

Expect most of the children to have most of the words linked to another, and these will show understanding of the unit of work, for example 'When light is blocked you get a shadow', 'When sound bounces back you get an echo', 'Light can be reflected by a mirror' (these indicate working at NC Level 3/Scottish Level C).

Level 4/Scottish Level C/D will be demonstrated if the explanations are more sophisticated, for example 'Light travels in straight lines, so when it is blocked there is a shadow'. There are also more complex links, for example 'Light and sound both travel', 'When light reflects, you get a reflection; when sound reflects, you get an echo'.

ASSESSMENT ACTIVITY 2

Give each child a copy of photocopiable page 179. You may want to read the questions to any children with poorer reading skills, or read each question to the whole class and explain what they need to do to answer them.

Looking for levels

For photocopiable page 179, most children will give simple explanations linking cause and effect, for example for question 1: 'The detective sees the reflection of the thief in the mirror.'; for question 2: 'The boy hears the sound because it travels to his ears.' The children will begin to make simple generalisations, for example 'Bigger instruments make lower sounds than small ones.' Some higher-attaining children may be able to provide more sophisticated explanations, for example for question 1: 'Light travels in straight lines so it reflects off the mirror into the detective's eyes.'; and for question 2: 'The vibration of the drum travels through the air and to the boy's ears.' Some children may only be working at Level 2/Scottish Level B. This will be indicated by answers that are descriptions, with little explanation, for example: 'The boy hears the sound with his ears.'

PLENARY

Ask the children to work in pairs for about 5 minutes to share their concept maps and decide on something they both learned during the unit. Ask the pairs to feed this back to the whole class. Discuss the answers to Assessment activity 2 with the children, reinforcing the use of explanations rather than descriptions.

Shadows

This is an acrostic poem for the word 'light':

Lifts the darkness
In the morning
Giving rainbows
Hope ahead
Travelling fast

Write an acrostic poem for the word 'shadow'. Try your ideas out on rough paper first.

S

H

A

D

O

W

Letting light through

Some children did an investigation to find out how much light can get through different materials. They presented their results in a bar chart.

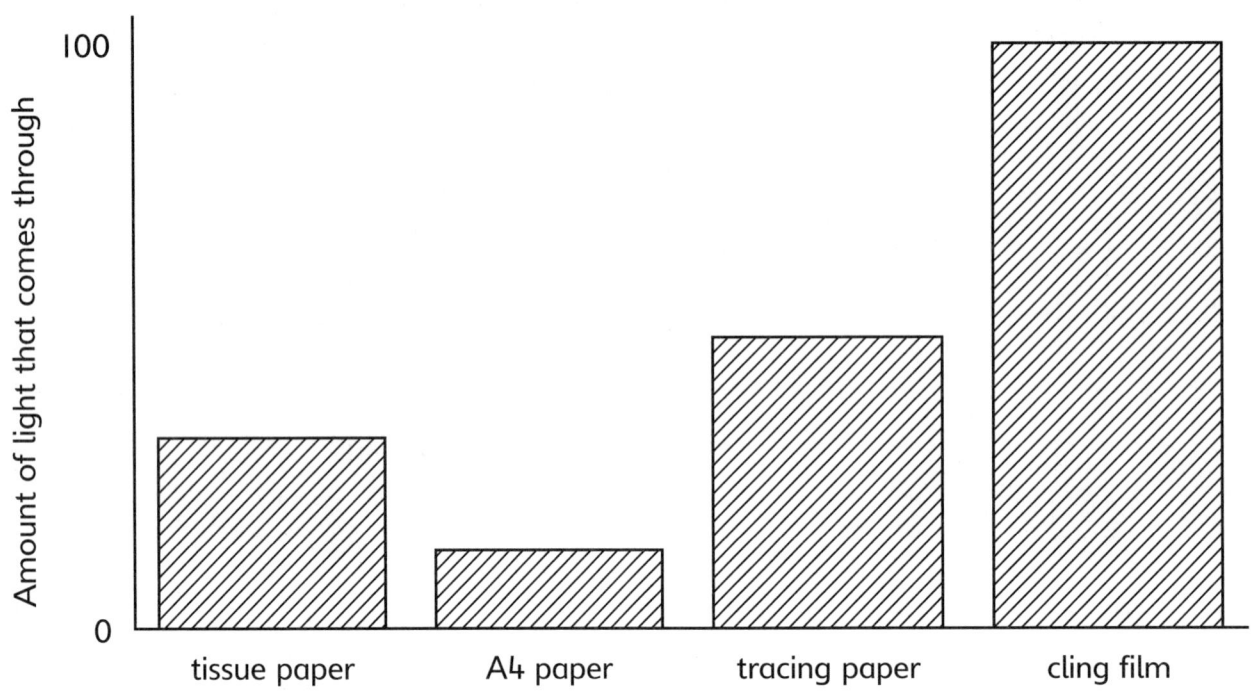

1. How many different materials did they try? _____

2. Which material let the most light through? _____

3. Which material let the least light through? _____

4. Tracing paper lets more light through than tissue paper. TRUE/FALSE

5. Clingfilm blocks more light than A4 paper.   TRUE/FALSE

6. Write the materials in order on this line.

lets least light   lets most light
through   through

Vibrations instruction cards

Guitar

Take it in turns to strum the guitar while the other children listen, look and feel. What do you notice?

fold

Ping pong balls and tuning fork

One person dangles the ping pong ball on the thread. Someone else strikes the tuning fork and touches the ping pong ball with it. Everyone looks, listens and thinks. Take turns. What is happening? Why?

Water and tuning fork

Take it in turns to strike the tuning fork and touch the water while everyone else watches carefully. What has this got to do with vibrations?

Drum and rice

Take it in turns to hit the drum while everyone else watches carefully. What happens to the drum skin? What happens to the rice?

Water and pebbles

Take it in turns to drop a small stone into the water while everyone watches carefully. Look and listen. What happens to the ripple? What has this got to do with sound?

Slinky spring

Two children sit cross-legged on the floor about two metres apart. Each of them holds one end of the slinky. Take it in turns to send ripples down the slinky. Everyone else watches carefully. What do you notice? Take turns watching and doing.

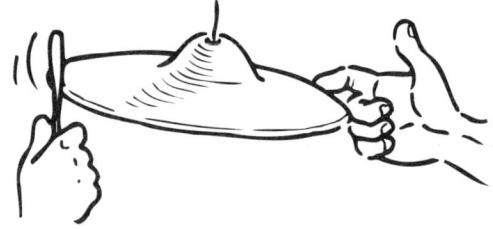

Cymbal and soft beater

One person hits the cymbal with the beater. Another person gently touches the edge of the cymbal. What does it feel like? Can you change the way the cymbal vibrates?

UNIT 7 **LIGHT & SOUND**

Our investigation 1

Our question: _____

_____

Our test: _____

_____

A drawing:

What we are going to change: _____

_____

What we are going to observe (or measure, if using data-logging

equipment): _____

_____

What we will keep the same: _____

_____

Name

Our investigation 2

What we predict will happen and why we think this: _____

_____

_____

_____

_____

Table of results:

What we found out (as an '-er' sentence): _____

_____

Name

Travelling and reflecting

echo

reflect

mirrors reflect light

mirror

sound

light

vibration

shadow

travel

Travelling and reflecting

1. Explain how the detective can secretly watch the diamond thief. You can draw on the picture to help explain.

2. a) How is the sound of the drum made?

_____

b) How could the sound be changed?

_____

c) How does the boy hear the sound?

3. a) The picture shows three chime bars. Which one would you expect to have the note with the lowest pitch? _____

a   b   c

b) Why did you choose that chime bar?

_____

_____

The Sun and stars

ORGANISATION (8 LESSONS)

	OBJECTIVES	MAIN ACTIVITY	GROUP ACTIVITIES	PLENARY	OUTCOMES
LESSON 1	● To elicit children's existing ideas about Earth and space. ● To stimulate question-raising.	Brainstorming 'things we know' and 'things we want to know' about Earth and space.	Modelling the Earth, Sun and Moon in Plasticine.	Considering how the questions raised could be answered.	● Have elicited children's existing ideas. ● Can raise questions.
LESSON 2	● To know that directions can be found using a compass. ● To be able to use a compass to find north, south, east, west, and midpoints between them, for example north east.	Explaining the four points of the compass and how to use a compass.	Using compasses to identify directions in the playground and recording features observed there.	Feedback of observations.	● Can use a compass to find the different directions on the ground.
LESSON 3	● To track the apparent movement of the Sun across the sky during the day. ● To relate this movement to the points of the compass. ● To carry out systematic observations over a period of time.	Recording the apparent movement of the Sun using a shadow stick.		Interpreting results, including discussing how it seems like the Sun is moving, but actually it is the Earth.	● Can recognise that the Sun appears to move across the sky during the day. ● Can explain that the Sun rises in the east, travels across the sky and sets in the west.
LESSON 4	● To know that the Sun's rays may be slanting at different angles. ● To investigate how shadows change when the angle of the Sun changes. ● To identify relevant variables.	Identifying variables for an investigation into the effect of changing the angle of the light source on the shadows produced.	Carrying out investigations as planned.	Discuss how the angle of the torch affects the length of the shadow and relate back to shadows in the playground.	● Can explain that the Sun's rays slant at different angles. ● Can recognise how shadows change when the angle of the light source changes. ● Can identify and control relevant variables.
LESSON 5	● To know that the way the Sun heats the Earth depends on the slant of the Sun's rays. ● To measure temperature.	Demonstration of how changing the angle of the light source affects how 'spread out' the spot of light is.	Measuring the temperature under the light source at different angles. Pictures to represent the seasons.	Discussion relating the angle of the Sun to the seasons of the year.	● Can recognise that the Sun's rays may slant at an angle and that this affects the temperature of the Earth. ● Can measure temperature.
LESSON 6	● To know that stars are sources of light.	Representing constellations by holes punched in black paper.		Discussion about what stars are like.	● Can recognise that stars are sources of light. ● Can explain that some stars are easier to see because they are bigger and brighter than others.
LESSON 7	● To know that groups of stars in the sky are known as constellations. ● To be able to identify some constellations.	Looking at pictures of constellations and naming them.		Discussing the real names and sharing 'better' names.	● Can explain what a constellation is. ● Can recognise some constellations.

	OBJECTIVES	ACTIVITY 1	ACTIVITY 2
ASSESSMENT 8	● To assess children's knowledge and understanding of the movement of the Sun and how this affects the light that reaches the Earth. ● To assess the children's knowledge of the nature of the Earth, Sun, Moon and stars.	Children use a torch representing the Sun to demonstrate their understanding of how the Sun shines on a Plasticine figure at different times of the day.	Test assessing children's understanding of the apparent movement of the Sun and their knowledge of the Sun, Moon and stars.

LESSON 1

OBJECTIVES
- To elicit children's existing ideas about Earth and space.
- To stimulate question-raising.

RESOURCES
Introduction: A glove puppet.
Group activity: Plasticine in various colours.
Main teaching activity: Flip chart and marker pens.

PREPARATION
Put the Plasticine out on tables for the Group activity. Have the resources for the Main teaching activity to hand.

Vocabulary

Earth, Moon, sky, Sun

BACKGROUND
This can be a difficult topic in that you are reliant on models and secondary sources. It also involves working in three dimensions, and these lessons try to give as many opportunities as possible for children to develop their spatial awareness. In this lesson, Plasticine modelling is useful to help children to communicate their ideas without struggling to make them into two-dimensional representations. The Group activities come before the Main teaching activity to facilitate this.

INTRODUCTION
Act out a discussion with the glove puppet in which the glove puppet says they were staring at the sky and thinking how soft it looked and what a good blanket it would make. Ask the puppet what it thinks the Sun is like and have the puppet answer that it looks like a big orange bouncy ball. Say to the children: *Our puppet thinks the Sun is a big orange ball.* Ask: *Do you agree with them?* Say: *Our puppet thinks the sky is a big blue blanket.* Ask: *Do you think the sky is like that? What do you think it is like?*

GROUP ACTIVITY
Ask the children to work in pairs or threes to make models in Plasticine of the Earth, the Sun and the Moon. Circulate and ask the children questions such as: *Why have you shown the Moon like that? What makes you think the Earth is that shape? Can you show me how they would be placed in space? Do you think the Earth is smaller or bigger than the Sun?*

MAIN TEACHING ACTIVITY
On the flip chart, make two columns and give them the following titles: 'Things we already know' and 'Things we want to find out'. Record the children's existing ideas, such as 'The Sun is a sphere'; 'The Sun shines', ensuring that different children contribute their ideas. Then ask them to think about things that they may want to find out or learn about during the topic, for example, 'Is the Sun hotter in the summer?', 'How far away are the stars?' Don't worry that you will not be able to answer all their questions through the topic – they are worth raising to stimulate thought and interest.

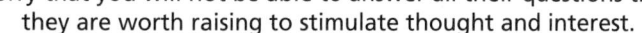

DIFFERENTIATION
Some children may use flat discs rather than spheres to represent the Earth, the Moon or the Sun. Ask them about this and begin to challenge their ideas by showing them a globe, or showing them how you would represent the moon as a sphere. If children seem confident about their models, probe their understanding further by asking them to arrange the models to show how they relate to each other. Ask questions, such as: *Do you think the Sun and the Moon are the same distance from Earth?*

ASSESSMENT
From observing and discussing the children's models, what are their existing ideas about the Earth and the Sun? Do any of them hold ideas that need to be challenged? Are they able to raise questions about the topic?

PLENARY

Ask: *How do you think we might be able to answer our questions?* (By tests; observing the Sun and sky; reading books; using CD-ROMs; asking people.) Remind the children that it is not safe to look directly at the Sun and they must not do so in their investigating.

OUTCOMES

● Have elicited children's existing ideas.
● Can raise questions.

LINKS

Unit 7 Light and sound: the Sun is a source of light.
Literacy: myths, legends, creation stories about the Sun.

LESSON 2

OBJECTIVES

● To know that directions can be found using a compass.
● To be able to use a compass to find north, south, east, west, and midpoints between them, for example north east.

RESOURCES

Main teaching activity: A globe compass, compass points drawn up on a sheet of sugar paper.
Group activities: 1. A compass for each group, a copy of photocopiable page 190 for each child. **2.** Photocopiable page 191.

PREPARATION

Draw the compass points as on photocopiable page 190 onto a sheet of sugar paper, but with only 'north' written on. Copy photocopiable page 190 for each child. Have the class sitting in a circle.

> **Vocabulary**
> compass, east, north, point, south, west

BACKGROUND

This activity is a preparation for the subsequent lesson on the path of the Sun, and is also useful background for the work on star constellations. Remember that the intermediate points of the compass are referred to using the North Pole or South Pole first, for example, it is south-east, not east-south.

INTRODUCTION

Show the class a globe. Point to the North Pole and South Pole, asking: *Can you tell me the names of these points?* Find the UK. Say: *We could travel north or south, but we could also travel this way* (point east), *or this way* (point west). Ask: *Does anyone know the names of these directions?* Ask: *Why do we have names for directions? How does it help us?* Establish that it provides a way of communicating information about position. Explain that this will help them in their topic about Earth and that they will be learning how to find different directions.

MAIN TEACHING ACTIVITY

Reveal the sugar paper drawing of compass directions. Ask the children to identify the four points of the compass, writing them on the paper as you go. They may know mnemonics such as 'Never Eat Shredded Wheat' that help them to remember the points. Explain that they will be using a real compass to find out the different directions in the playground. Pass around compasses and ask the children to try turning them around so that the needle lines up with the N for north. Explain that the needle will always point to north because the North Pole is a bit like a magnet and pulls the needle towards it. Together, point to the direction of north. Put the sugar paper in the middle of the circle and turn it, asking the children to tell you when to stop so that the paper 'north' is pointing to the real north. Ask children who are sitting at the south of the circle to put their hands up. Repeat this with the east and west. Explain that when they go outside they will need to use the compass to find out which direction is north, and work out the other directions from that.

GROUP ACTIVITIES

1. In the playground, give each group a 'base' by marking a place with a hoop. Each group uses the compass to identify north. On photocopiable page 190 they can write down some features that they see in that direction. They then work out the other points and record what they can see looking in those directions.

2. Give pairs of children a copy of photocopiable page 191. Ask them to work with a partner and take turns to decide on a starting place and a destination. They give their partner directions using 'north', 'south, 'east' or 'west' for them to follow to reach the destination. For example, a child could choose a journey from the fish and chip shop to the bank and could say 'Start at the fish and chip shop. Walk south until you reach the newsagent, then go east. You will find the bank on the south side of the road'.

DIFFERENTIATION

Some children can record using drawing rather than writing. It may be necessary to limit the task by asking children only to record north and south. Other children can have the task extended by learning about the midpoints, for example south east.

ASSESSMENT

Can the children use the compass to identify the direction of north? Can they use the compass to work out the direction of the other compass points?

PLENARY

Bring the children together. Ask them to point to north, south, east, and west as they have identified them and to share what they have recorded as features in that direction.

OUTCOME

● Can use a compass to find the different directions on the ground.

LINKS

Geography: map work.

LESSON 3

Objectives	● To track the apparent movement of the Sun across the sky during the day. ● To relate this movement to the points of the compass. ● To carry out systematic observations over a period of time.
Resources	A sunny area (check that it does not become shaded later in the day) for each group; a stick mounted in a container of sand; compass; large sheet of paper (possibly several sheets of sugar paper taped together), felt-tipped pens.
Main activity	This activity develops observations made in Year 3/Primary 4 by asking children to consider the direction of the apparent movement of the Sun, building in progression. Ask the children if the Sun stays the same all day. (It appears to move across the sky.) In the morning, each group records the shadow cast by the stick. Discuss with the class what would be appropriate time intervals to come back and check the shadow. Draw around the shadow at intervals throughout the day. Use the compass to mark the direction the shadow is pointing in. Remember the Sun will be coming from the opposite direction to the way the shadow is pointing.
Differentiation	Have mixed groups so that the children can support each other.
Assessment	Can the children describe the apparent movement of the Sun across the sky? Can the children recognise the different parts of the sky the Sun passes through during the day?

Plenary	Bring the children together with their records. Ask them: *Which way was the shadow pointing first thing this morning? So which way does that mean the Sun was shining from? What happened to the shadow during the day?* (It moved around.) *Which direction did it move? Where was the shadow pointing at the end of the day? What does that tell us about where the Sun is at the end of the day? If we could stay at school and record where the shadow was going next, where do you predict it would go? Can you tell me which compass direction the Sun rises and which it sets from?*
	    Explain that actually, it is not the Sun that is moving; it is the Earth, but it seems like the Sun is moving.
	    Ask: *Was it just the direction of the shadow that changed or did anything else change?* (The length of the shadow.)

Outcomes	● Can recognise that the Sun appears to move across the sky during the day. ● Can explain that the Sun rises in the east, travels across the sky and sets in the west.

LESSON 4

OBJECTIVES
● To know that the Sun's rays may be slanting at different angles.
● To investigate how shadows change when the angle of the Sun changes.
● To identify relevant variables.

RESOURCES

Main teaching activity: A large matchbox, a small matchbox, two different torches, a ruler, a felt-tipped pen, a large sheet of white/pale coloured paper.
Group activities: 1. A domino or matchbox, torch, paper, and a ruler for each group; a copy of photocopiable page 192 and writing materials for each child. **2.** Photocopiable page 193.

PREPARATION

Put the resources for the Group activities out on the tables. Have the resources for the Main teaching activity to hand.

Vocabulary

angle, light, shadow, torch

BACKGROUND

This work links with the children's understanding of light gained in Unit 7. They need to have previous experience of shadows and understand that a shadow is formed when light is blocked. In this lesson, the focus is on how the length of the shadow changes as the angle of the light source changes. This can then be related back to the shadows that the children have seen cast by the sun, and used to provide evidence that the angle of the Sun with respect to the Earth must be changing. This, in combination with Lesson 5, will begin to give children some insight into seasonal change.

   The lesson also aims to help children identify the variables that will need to be controlled to carry out a fair test.

INTRODUCTION

Stand the matchboxes on a large sheet of paper and shine the torch at the large one so that a shadow of the box is formed on the paper. Ask the children to describe what is happening.

MAIN TEACHING ACTIVITY

Ask the children to brainstorm all the different things that could be changed about the situation. Demonstrate some examples to start them off, such as use a different torch, use a smaller matchbox. Record their ideas on a flip chart. Make sure that the list includes changing the position of the torch and clarify different aspects of the torch position that could be changed, for example distance away, position around the box, angle.

   Now ask the children what things could be measured or recorded about the shadow for example it's direction, width, length, shape. Record these in a separate list. Explain that in this investigation you want them to explore the changes of the length of the shadow. Ask: *How could we measure the length of the shadow?* (Use a ruler; use squared paper; draw around it, then measure it.)

   Return to the list of things that could be changed. Explain that you want the children to focus on the angle of the torch, because this will help them to understand more about the Sun. Without saying anything, shine the torch on the large matchbox and mark the length of the shadow on the paper with the felt-tipped pen. Then say: *Now I'm going to try putting the torch at a different angle*, and do so, but shine it onto the small matchbox. Ask: *Which angle made the shadow longer, the first or the second?* One of the children may well suggest that it is not a fair comparison because of the change in size of the matchbox. If not, you will need to 'realise' it yourself. Explain that it must be the same matchbox, or we won't know if the shadow is different because the angle of the torch is different, or if it's to do with the matchbox.

   Repeat this process using the same matchbox, but changing to a different torch, and then holding the torch exaggeratedly close and far away. Discuss the need to keep everything the same except the one thing you are investigating. Refer back to the list and go through it item by item, identifying that each needs to be kept the same, except the angle of the torch. Explain that this is what we mean by a 'fair test'.

GROUP ACTIVITIES

1. Give each child a copy of photocopiable page 192, explaining how you want them to record their investigation on the sheet. The children carry out the investigation.
2. Give the children a copy of photocopiable page 193. Ask them to look carefully at the graph and then answer the questions.

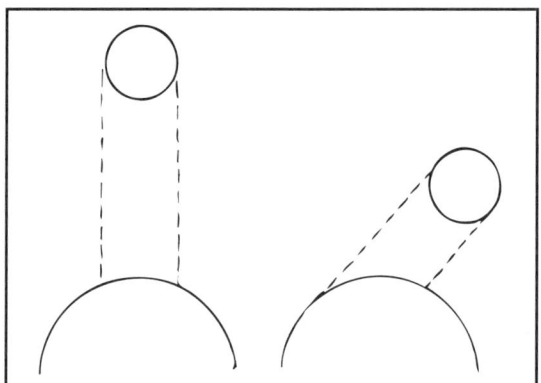

DIFFERENTIATION

Those children who are more mathematically able could record the area of the shadow, rather than the length by using squared paper. Ask the higher attainers in maths: *Would it be a good idea to record the shadow length in millimetres?* (No, it wouldn't be appropriate, because it is not possible to be very accurate about the angle of the torch, so very accurate measurement of the shadow length wouldn't be very meaningful.) Lower attainers in maths will need adult or peer support with the measurement or, if they are not ready to use standard units, could cut strips of coloured paper to the length of the shadow and so represent it visually.

ASSESSMENT

Are the children aware of the need to control the different variables and do they try to do so in their investigation? Do they recognise that the shadow changes in length with the angle of the torch? Can they relate this knowledge to what happens to shadows cast by the Sun?

PLENARY

Ask the groups to report back on what they have found. Ask: *Does changing the angle of the torch affect the length of the shadow?* (Yes.) *In what way?* (When the torch is low/flat, the shadow is long and when the torch gets higher/more angled the shadow is shorter.) Ask the groups to demonstrate their findings to the class.

Ask: *Do shadows stay the same length when we are out in the Sun?* (No.) The children may have observed this in previous years in science. Look back at some of the recordings made in Lesson 3 and note that the shadows changed length as well as direction. Ask: *What does this tell us about the angle of the Sun?* (It must be changing.) Say: *So we know two things about the Sun.* Write these on the board: 'The Sun seems to move across the sky, and it changes its angle.'

OUTCOMES

● Can explain that the Sun's rays slant at different angles.
● Can recognise how shadows change when the angle of the light source changes.
● Can identify and control relevant variables.

LINKS

Unit 7 Light and sound: Lessons 2 and 3.

LESSON 5

OBJECTIVES

● To know that the way the Sun heats the Earth depends on the slant of the Sun's rays.
● To measure temperature.

RESOURCES

Main teaching activity: An 'angle-poise' lamp, a sheet of white card, a model person (such as Lego or Plasticine), a thermometer, an electronic temperature sensor or data-logging equipment with temperature sensor.
Group activities: 1 and 2. Writing materials, coloured pencils, photographs and books showing different seasons.

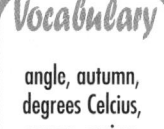

Vocabulary

angle, autumn, degrees Celcius, season, spring, summer, temperature, winter

PREPARATION

If the room has blinds or curtains, it is helpful to close them for the Main teaching activity.

BACKGROUND

The Sun shines on the Earth at different angles. This is the case at different times of the day, but the angle of the Sun also varies through the year, being higher in the sky in the summer and lower in the winter. When the Sun is high in the sky, the light hits the ground straight-on, and so the heat is 'concentrated' in one place, but if the Sun is lower and the light hits the ground at an angle, it is spread over a larger surface area and so each part of the ground is heated less. (See diagram top left.)

INTRODUCTION

Ask the children what they have learned about light and the Sun so far. (The Sun seems to move across the sky, it changes angles – which we know because of the way the shadows change position and length.) Explain that the children are going to find out more about the effect of the angle of the Sun.

MAIN TEACHING ACTIVITY

Shine the lamp on the white card from directly overhead. Explain that this is like the Sun in the summer. Ask: *What does the spot of light look like?* (Round and bright.) Now move the lamp so it is shining at an angle. Explain that this is more like the Sun in the autumn. Ask: *What does the spot of light look like now?* (Stretched out and not as bright.)

Repeat this with the model figure standing in the spot of light. Ask: *I wonder what it would feel like to this person?* (Bright and hot/Not as bright, not as warm.)

Ask: *We can see that it is not as bright when it is at an angle; how can we tell if it is not as hot?* (Measure the temperature.) Explain that each group will have the opportunity to come and measure the temperature for themselves.

GROUP ACTIVITIES

1. One group at a time will, with support, measure and record the temperature with the light directly above and at a low angle. The difference is not huge, so the two angles need to be exaggerated as much as possible. Work with the groups, ensuring that they are waiting for the thermometer/sensor to adjust and are able to read the scale and record the units (degrees Celcius).

2. Other groups work independently on drawings to represent the different seasons of the year. They could either work as a group to produce one large picture of their season, or each child could produce a drawing to show their own representation of the seasons. The books and photographs will stimulate ideas for a discussion in the Plenary session.

DIFFERENTIATION

Some children may need more guidance with the drawing and they can be given a paper circle folded into quarters on which to show their ideas about the seasons.

Some children could calculate the mathematical difference between the temperatures. Some groups may try a third lamp position and record the temperature.

ASSESSMENT

Can the children state that the light coming at a low angle produces less heat than that coming from directly above? Can they relate this to their ideas about the seasons?

PLENARY

Ask: *What did we find out about the effect of the angle of the light?* (It is hotter when the torch is directly above.) *Is it generally hotter in summer or winter?* Use the pictures from Group activity 2 to stimulate discussion about the sunshine in different seasons. *Can someone come and show me with the lamp how they think the Sun is shining in the summer/winter?* Invite a child to use the lamp to demonstrate. *Can you explain why you think that?*

The pictures could be displayed alongside the following poem:

The spring Sun is young,
The summer Sun is bold,
The autumn Sun is quiet,
The winter Sun is old.

OUTCOMES

● Can recognise that the Sun's rays may slant at an angle and that this affects the temperature of the Earth.
● Can measure temperature.

LINKS

Geography: seasons.
Unit 4 Materials: measuring temperature.
Unit 7 Light and sound: Lessons 2 and 3.

LESSON 6

Objective	● To know that stars are sources of light.
Resources	A room that can be blacked-out with blinds or curtains; black card, torches, Plasticine; tools for making holes (bradawls), sharp pencils, knitting needles.
Main activity	Discuss the children's experiences of seeing stars in the night sky: *Do they always seem the same? Can you always see the same number of stars?* Recite the rhyme 'Twinkle, twinkle, little star'. Ask: *What do you think a star is?* Listen to the children's ideas. Explain that stars are like the Sun: they are balls of fire and give out light, but as they are further away they look smaller. Ask the children to make some different-sized holes in their pieces of black card, showing them how to make a hole safely by pushing the bradawl through the card into the Plasticine. Working in small groups, the children can shine their torches through the cards and experiment with moving nearer and further from each other to explore how that changes what they can see. Ask: *Are all the 'stars' as easy to see? What makes some easier to see than others?* (The brightness of the torch, the size of the hole.)
Differentiation	Work in mixed groups so that children can support each other.
Assessment	Do the children realise that stars are sources of light? Are they aware that stars vary in size and brightness?
Plenary	Ask a group at a time to stand together, shining torches through their cards to give the effect of a patch of night sky. Ask: *What can you tell me about stars?* (They are like the Sun, they give out light, they are balls of fire, some are brighter than others, they are different sizes.)
Outcomes	● Can recognise that stars are sources of light. ● Can explain that some stars are easier to see because they are bigger and brighter than others.

LESSON 7

Objectives	● To know that groups of stars in the sky are known as constellations. ● To be able to identify some constellations.
Resources	Copies of photocopiable page 194 cut up into individual cards; books and CD-ROMs with information about constellations including The Plough, Great Dog, Orion, Leo, Cassiopeia, and Gemini.
Main activity	Ask the children what they can say now about stars. Explain that when we look at the night sky we can see groups of stars. These are arranged in patterns and that in the ancient past, people have imagined that these look a bit like a person or an animal and have given them special names. Give out books with the named constellations in and a set of cards to each group. Explain that the lines have been drawn between the stars to help make it easier to recognise the 'pictures' like a dot-to-dot pattern. Challenge the children to name each constellation. Ask: *What do the constellations look like to you? Can you draw new, twenty-first century shapes around the constellations and rename them for the new millennium?*
Differentiation	Extend children who are interested by asking them to research different constellations using the secondary sources provided. Use mixed groups for peer support in the matching activity.
Assessment	Can the children explain what is meant by a constellation? Have they successfully identified the constellations?
Plenary	Check that the constellations have been correctly named and share the names the children have devised. Suggest the children take a copy of page 194 home with them and look at the night sky with their parents for homework. (Note they will be able to see all the constellations at all times of the year.)
Outcomes	● Can explain what a constellation is. ● Can recognise some constellations.

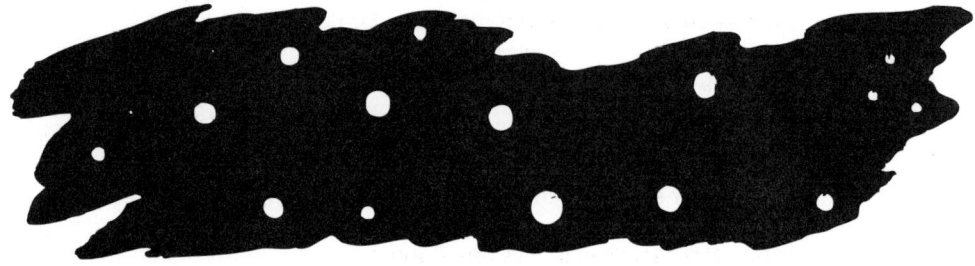

ASSESSMENT

LESSON 8

OBJECTIVES

● To assess children's knowledge and understanding of the movement of the Sun and how this affects the light that reaches the Earth.
● To assess the children's knowledge of the nature of the Earth, the Sun, Moon and stars.

RESOURCES

Assessment activities: 1. Plasticine, a torch for each child. **2.** A copy of photocopiable page 195 for each child, writing materials.

INTRODUCTION

These Assessment activities should be considered alongside the ongoing assessment opportunities indicated throughout the unit when making a judgement about the level the child is working at. If you are unsure what a child means by their response to a question, then discuss it with them afterwards.

ASSESSMENT ACTIVITY 1

Work with a group of up to six children so that you can observe and note their responses. Ask them to quickly make a simple figure from Plasticine. Ask them to shine the torch on the figure so that it makes a shadow. Ask them to make the shadow longer and shorter. Note whether the children do this by trial and improvement or looking at their neighbour, or if they are able to alter the angle of the torch confidently to produce the desired result. Ask: *How is the shadow being changed? Can you explain why this is happening?*

Ask the children to show you how the light from the Sun would shine on the figure at midday, early in the morning and late in the evening. It is a good idea to ask each individual child to show you a different time of day. Ask: *How do our shadows change during the day? Can you explain why this happens?*

Ask: *Where do you think the Sun is at night?* Are the children aware that the Sun is shining on the other side of the globe, or do they have other ideas?

Looking for levels

If the children can describe that the apparent position of the Sun changes, and this changes the length of the shadow, with a simple explanation then they are working at NC Level 3/Scottish Level C. Higher attaining children will give a more detailed account of how the length of the shadow changes with the movement of the Sun across the sky, with some explanation of the change in angle of the light (NC Level 4/Scottish Level C/D). Lower attaining children will only describe the changes in the shadow, but not offer an explanation.

ASSESSMENT ACTIVITY 2

Give each child a copy of photocopiable page 195. Ask them to answer the questions. You may want to sit with a group with poorer reading skills and read the questions to them, or even read each question to the whole class, explaining what kind of answer is required. It is a good idea to go through the questions with the children as soon as possible to discuss any incorrect answers. The children could mark their answers with a different coloured pencil.

Answers

1. There are two elements to this question: on the illustration has the child shown the movement of the Sun from one side to the other, and have they shown the change in the height of the Sun?

2. In the UK, it is colder in the summer than in the winter: false
The Moon is the shape of a sphere (a ball): true
Stars are further away from Earth than the Sun: true
A group of stars is called a constellation: true
The Sun is closer to Earth than the Moon: false
The stars are all smaller than the Sun: false.

4. The constellation is The Plough, which is part of The Great Bear/Ursa Major.

Looking for levels

The majority of the class will get most of the questions on photocopiable page 195 right, showing that they are working at Level 3/Scottish Level C. Children who get a significant number of wrong answers may be working at a lower level, and this will need to be checked by referring to their work during the unit.

PLENARY

Go through the answers to Assessment activity 2 with the children, discussing any that have caused difficulty. Ask the children to tell you what they found most interesting in the unit. Return to the list of questions raised in Lesson 1. Ask if they still have any questions they would like to find out the answers to about the topic and briefly discuss how they might follow this up for themselves.

The points of the compass

Draw what you can see in each compass direction.

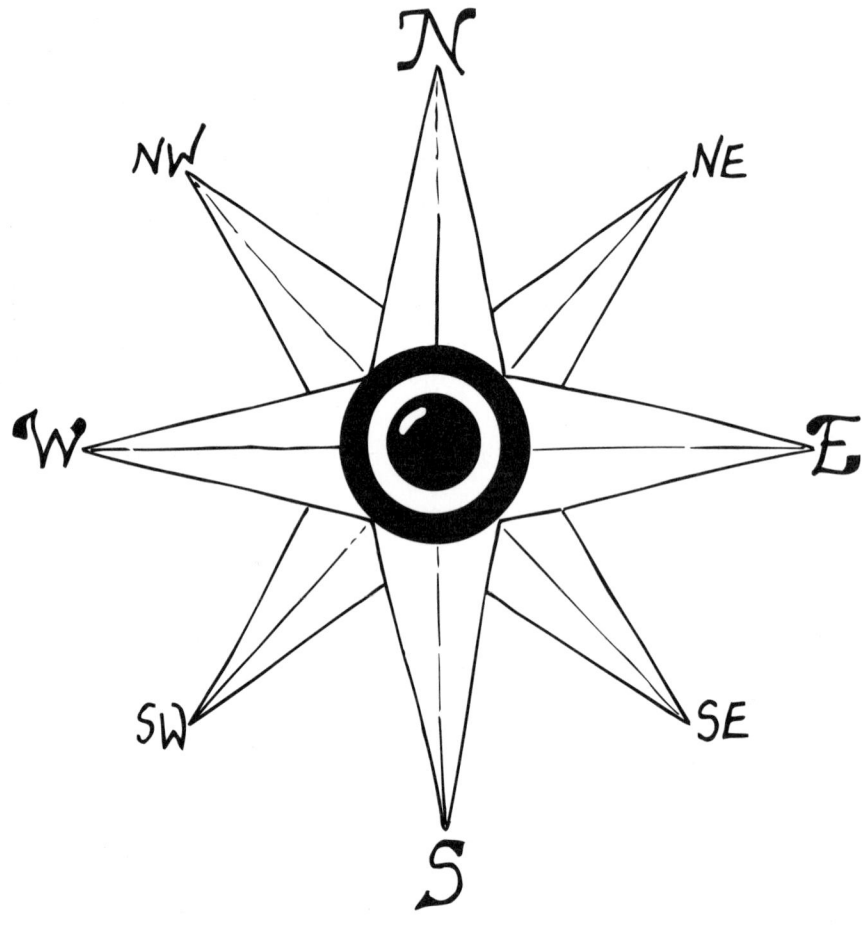

Giving directions

Work with a partner. Take it in turns to choose a starting place and a destination. Tell your partner where you want them to start and tell them where to go using 'north', 'south', 'east' and 'west'. For example, you could choose a journey from the fish and chip shop to the bank and you could say 'Start at the fish and chip shop. Walk south until you reach the newsagent, then go east. You will find the bank on the south side of the road.'

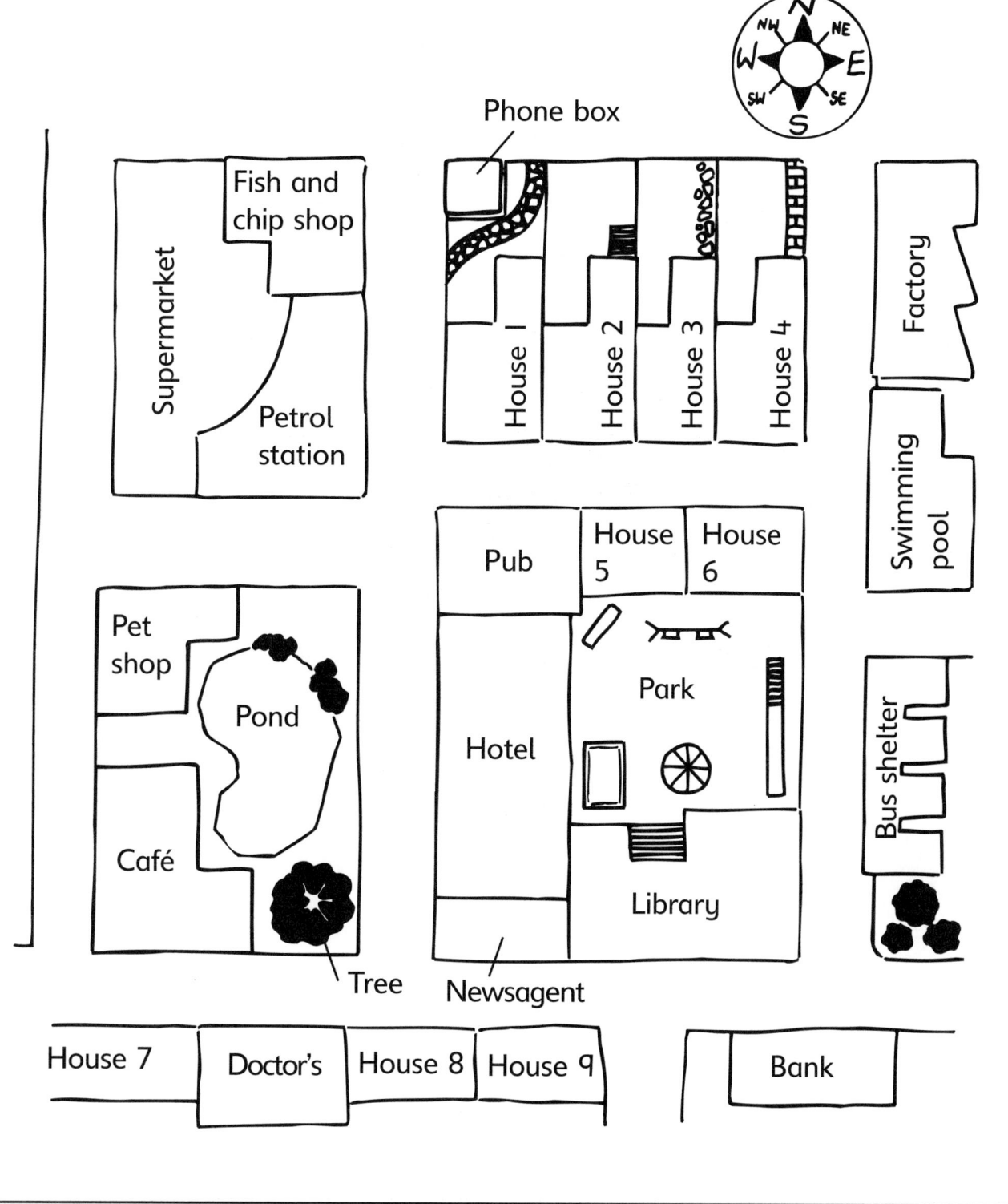

Shadows and angles

Our question: What happens to the length of the shadow when we change the angle of the torch?

What we changed: _____

_____

What we kept the same: _____

_____

_____

Our table of results

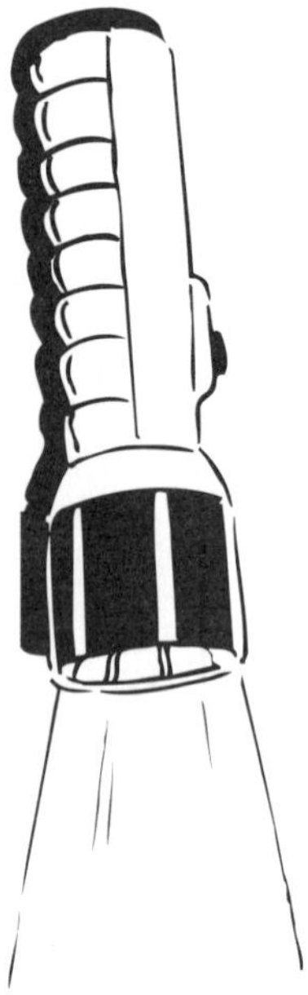

Angle of torch (drawing)	Length of shadow (cm)

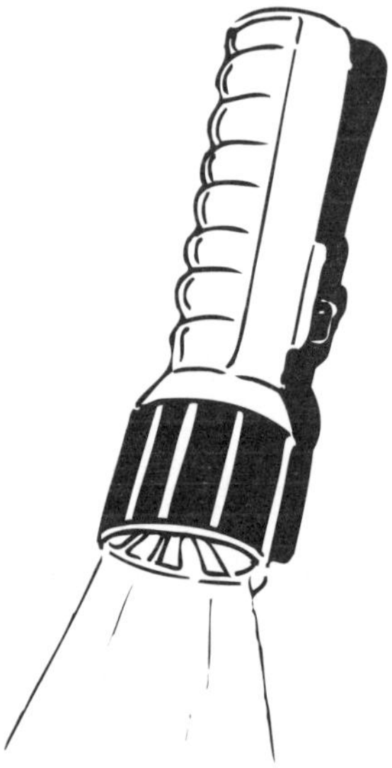

We found out that when the torch _____

_____

then the shadow gets _____

_____.

Name

Measuring shadows

These children measured a shadow
at different times of day.

**Length of
shadow** (cm)

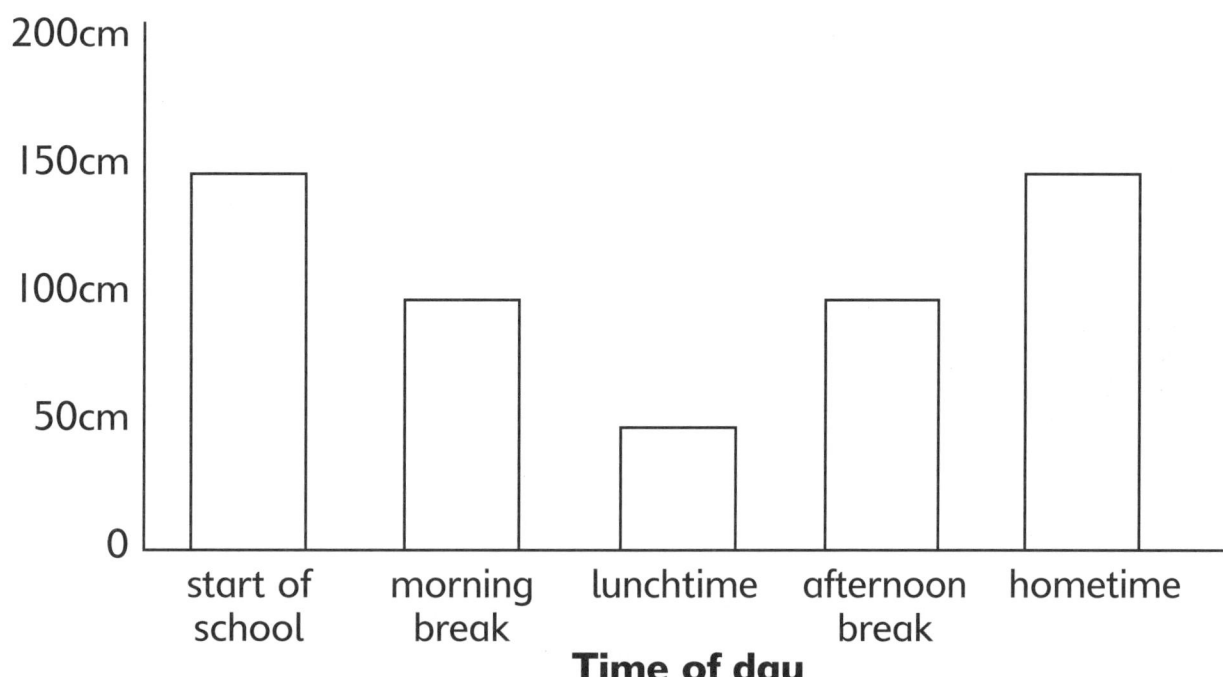

1. How many times did the children go and measure the shadow? _____

2. When was the shadow the shortest? _____

3. How long was the shadow at morning break? _____

4. How long was the shadow at the start of school? _____

5. Estimate how long the shadow was at breakfast time. _____

6. Describe what happened to the length of the shadow. _____

_____

_____

Name

Star patterns

The Sun and stars

1. The Sun seems to move during the day.

On the picture, draw where the Sun seems to be at different times of the day.

East   West

2. Tick (✔) the correct box for each sentence.

	TRUE	FALSE
In the UK, it is colder in the summer than in the winter.		
The Moon is the shape of a sphere (a ball).		
Stars are further away from Earth than the Sun.		
A group of stars is called a constellation.		
The Sun is closer to Earth than the Moon.		
The stars are all smaller than the Sun.		

3. Label this compass with the correct points. North has been put in already.

4. What is the name of this constellation?

National Curriculum in England

LINKS TO QCA SCIENCE SCHEME OF WORK

SC1 SCIENTIFIC ENQUIRY

1 Ideas and evidence in science
a that science is about thinking creatively to try to explain how living and non-living things work, and to establish links between causes and effects
b that it is important to test ideas using evidence from observation and measurement

2 Investigative skills – Planning
a ask questions that can be investigated scientifically and decide how to find answers
b consider what sources of information, including first-hand experience and a range of other sources, they will use to answer questions
c think about what might happen or try things out when deciding what to do, what kind of evidence to collect, and what equipment and materials to use
d make a fair test or comparison by changing one factor and observing or measuring the effect while keeping other factors the same

Investigative skills – Obtaining and presenting evidence
e use simple equipment and materials appropriately and take action to control risks
f make systematic observations and measurements, including the use of ICT for data-logging
g check observations and measurements by repeating them where appropriate
h use a wide range of methods, including diagrams, drawings, tables, bar charts, line graphs and ICT, to communicate data in an appropriate and systematic manner

Investigative skills – Considering evidence and evaluating
i make comparisons and identify simple patterns or associations in their own observations and measurements or other data
j use observations, measurements or other data to draw conclusions
k decide whether these conclusions agree with any prediction made and/or whether they enable further predictions to be made
l use their scientific knowledge and understanding to explain observations, measurements or other data or conclusions
m review their work and the work of others and describe its significance and limitations

SC2 LIFE PROCESSES AND LIVING THINGS

1 Life processes
a that the life processes common to humans and other animals include nutrition, movement, growth and reproduction
b that the life processes common to plants include growth, nutrition and reproduction
c to make links between life processes in familiar animals and plants and the environments in which they are found

2 Humans and other animals – Nutrition
a about the functions and care of teeth
b about the need for food for activity and growth, and about the importance of an adequate and varied diet for health

Humans and other animals – Circulation
c that the heart acts as a pump to circulate the blood through vessels around the body, including through the lungs
d about the effect of exercise and rest on pulse rate

Humans and other animals – Movement
e that humans and some other animals have skeletons and muscles to support and protect their bodies and to help them to move

Humans and other animals – Growth and reproduction
f about the main stages of the human life cycle

Humans and other animals – Health
g about the effects on the human body of tobacco, alcohol and other drugs, and how these relate to their personal health
h about the importance of exercise for good health

3 Green plants – Growth and nutrition
a the effect of light, air, water and temperature on plant growth
b the role of the leaf in producing new material for growth
c that the root anchors the plant, and that water and minerals are taken in through the root and transported through the stem to other parts of the plant

Green plants – Reproduction
d about the parts of the flower and their role in the life cycle of flowering plants, including pollination, seed formation, seed dispersal and germination

4 Variation and classification
a to make and use keys
b how locally occurring animals and plants can be identified and assigned to groups

c that the variety of plants and animals makes it important to identify them and assign them to groups

5 Living things in their environment
a about ways in which living things and the environment need protection

Living things in their environment – Adaptation
b about the different plants and animals found in different habitats
c how animals and plants in two different habitats are suited to their environment

Living things in their environment – Feeding relationships
d to use food chains to show feeding relationships in a habitat
e about how nearly all food chains start with a green plant

Living things in their environment – Micro-organisms
f that micro-organisms are living organisms that are often too small to be seen, and that they may be beneficial or harmful

SC3 MATERIALS & THEIR PROPERTIES

1 Grouping and classifying
a to compare everyday materials and objects on the basis of their material properties, including hardness, strength, flexibility and magnetic behaviour, and to relate these properties to everyday uses of the materials
b that some materials are better thermal insulators than others
c that some materials are better electrical conductors than others
d to describe and group rocks and soils on the basis of their characteristics, including appearance, texture and permeability
e to recognise differences between solids, liquids and gases, in terms of ease of flow and maintenance of shape and volume

2 Changing materials
a to describe changes that occur when materials are mixed
b to describe changes that occur when materials are heated or cooled
c that temperature is a measure of how hot or cold things are
d about reversible changes, including dissolving, melting, boiling, condensing, freezing and evaporating
e the part played by evaporation and condensation in the water cycle
f that non-reversible changes result in the formation of new materials that may be useful
g that burning materials results in the formation of new materials and that this change is not usually reversible

3 Separating mixtures of materials
a how to separate solid particles of different sizes
b that some solids dissolve in water to give solutions but some do not
c how to separate insoluble solids from liquids by filtering
d how to recover dissolved solids by evaporating the liquid from the solution
e to use knowledge of solids, liquids and gases to decide how mixtures might be separated

Lessons where curriculum content is the main objective are listed below. Lessons where content is included but is not the main focus are shown below in brackets.

Unit 1: Ourselves	Unit 2: Animals & Plants	Unit 3: The environment	Unit 4: Materials	Unit 5: Electricity	Unit 6: Forces & motion	Unit 7: Light & sound	Unit 8: Earth & beyond
How I move	Different sorts of skeletons	Habitats and food chains	Warm liquids, cool solids	Switches and conduction	Friction	Travelling and reflecting	The Sun and stars
UNIT 4A	UNIT 4A	UNIT 4B	UNIT 4C, 4D	UNIT 4F	UNIT 4E	–	–
2	2	(5), 14	4	1	4	1, 7, 10, 11, 13	1
3, 4	6, (8)	15	3	4	1	1, 6, 11	2, 3
3		3	4, 14	1	1	2, 11	
			12, 13	3		11	2
		5, 14	12	4, 7	5, 6, 13	2, 3, 5, 11	3, 4
		5, 7	6, 15	4, 8, 9	5, 6, 8, 9, 11	4	4, 5
5	2, 6	4, 14	2, 6, 10, 12, 16	1, (2)	3, 6, 8	2, 6	2, 6
3, 4		3	(2)		3, 6	4	3, 5
		7	10, 15		3, 6	8, 11	
4, 6	1, (3)	3, 4, 7, 8, 9, 10, 11, 12	1, 2, 5, 9, 11	5, 8, (10)	1, (2), 6, 9, 12	4, 6	
1, 2, 7	2, 3, 4, 5, 7, 8	1, 2, 11, 12, 13	5, 8		3, 6, 9, 10, 11	4, 7, 8, 9, 10, 11, 14	3, 4
1, 3, 4, 9	3, 6	6, 7, 8, 14	4		3, 6, 9	4	2, 4
		5	3, 15		5, 6	3, 5	4
8	2, 4, (7)	6, 13, (15), (16), (17)	4, 7, 14, 17	6	4, 7, 9, 11, 13	4, (12), 15	1, 5, 6, 7
	(5), (8)	6, 7			8, 9		5
(1)							
(1)							
1							
(8)							
1, 2, 3, 6, 7, 8, 9	2, 3, 4, 6, 7, (8)						
(3), (4)							
	(5)						
	5, 8, 9						
	1, (2), (3), 4, 5, (6), (7), (9)	1					
	1, 4						
		(15), (16)					
		2, (3), 4, 5, 6, (8), 17					
		(2), (3), 4, 5, 6, (7)					
		9, 10, 11, 12, 13, 17					
		(9), (10), 11, 12, 13					
			1				
			4, 5, 6, 7, 18				
			8, 9, 10, 11				
			14				
			12, 13, 18				
			2, 3				
			12, 13, 18				
			14, 18				
			15				
			16, 17, 18				

SC4 Physical processes overleaf

National Curriculum in England (cont)

LINKS TO QCA SCIENCE SCHEME OF WORK

SC4 PHYSICAL PROCESSES		
	1 Electricity – Simple circuits	
	a	to construct circuits, incorporating a battery or power supply and a range of switches, to make electrical devices work
	b	how changing the number or type of components in a series circuit can make bulbs brighter or dimmer
	c	how to represent series circuits by drawings and conventional symbols; how to construct series circuits on the basis of drawings and diagrams using conventional symbols
	2 Forces and motion – Types of force	
	a	about the forces of attraction and repulsion between magnets, and about the forces of attraction between magnets and magnetic materials
	b	that objects are pulled downwards because of the gravitational attraction between them and the Earth
	c	about friction, including air resistance, as a force that slows moving objects and may prevent objects from starting to move are pushed or pulled
	d	that when objects are pushed or pulled an opposing pull or push can be felt
	e	how to measure forces and identify the direction in which they act
	3 Light and sound – Everyday effects of light	
	a	that light travels from a source
	b	that light cannot pass through some materials, and how this leads to the formation of shadows
	c	that light is reflected from surfaces
	Light and sound – Seeing	
	d	that we see things only when light from them enters our eyes
	Light and sound – Vibration and sound	
	e	that sounds are made when objects vibrate but that vibrations are not always directly visible
	f	how to change the pitch and loudness of sounds produced by some vibrating objects
	g	that vibrations from sound sources require a medium through which to travel to the ear
	4 The Earth and beyond – The Sun, Earth and Moon	
	a	that the Sun, Earth and Moon are approximately spherical
	The Earth and beyond – Periodic changes	
	b	how the position of the Sun appears to change during the day, and how shadows change as this happens
	c	how day and night are related to the spin of the Earth on its own axis
	d	that the Earth orbits the Sun once each year, and that the Moon takes approximately 28 days to orbit the Earth

National Curriculum in Wales

SCIENTIFIC ENQUIRY		
	1 The nature of science	
	the link between ideas and information in science	
	1	to apply their ideas and knowledge and understanding of science when thinking about and investigating phenomena in the world around them
	2	to consider information obtained from their own work and also, on some occasions, from other sources
	3	that scientific ideas can be tested by means of information gathered from observation and measurement
	2 Communication in science	
	presenting scientific information	
	1	to report their work clearly in speech and writing using relevant scientific vocabulary
	2	to use a range of methods, including diagrams, drawings, graphs, tables and charts, to record and present information in an appropriate and systematic manner
	3	to use ICT to select and present a range of relevant information, when this is appropriate
	4	to use standard measures and units handling scientific information
	5	to search for and access relevant scientific information, using ICT to do so on some occasions
	6	to recognise that it is useful to present and consider scientific information in an appropriate form, making use of ICT to do so when appropriate
	planning an investigation	
	1	to turn ideas suggested to them, and their own ideas, into a form that can be investigated
	2	that asking questions, and using their knowledge and understanding of the context to anticipate what may happen, can be useful when planning what to do
	3	to decide what information should be collected
	4	that in situations where the factors can be identified and controlled, a fair test may be carried out
	5	to consider what equipment or other resources to use
	6	to recognise the hazards and risks to themselves and others obtaining information
	7	to use equipment or other resources correctly, taking action to control risks
	8	to make careful observations and measurements and record them appropriately
	9	to check observations and measurements by repeating them, when this is appropriate
	10	to use ICT equipment and software to monitor changes
	considering information	
	11	to make comparisons and to identify and describe trends or patterns in data
	12	to use the results of their investigations to draw conclusions
	13	to try to relate the outcomes of their investigation or their conclusions to their scientific knowledge and understanding
	14	to review their work and suggest how their data could be improved

LIFE PROCESSES AND LIVING THINGS		
	1 Life processes	
	1	that there are life processes, including nutrition, movement, growth and reproduction, common to animals, including humans
	2	that there are life processes, including growth, nutrition and reproduction, common to plants
	2 Humans and other animals	
	nutrition	
	1	how the teeth break up food into smaller pieces and the importance of dental care
	2	that the body needs different foods for activity and for growth
	3	that an adequate and varied diet is needed to keep healthy
	circulation	
	4	that the heart acts as a pump
	5	how blood circulates in the body through arteries and veins
	6	that the pulse gives a measure of the heart beat rate
	7	the effect of exercise and rest on pulse rate
	movement	
	8	that humans and some other animals have skeletons and muscles to support and protect their bodies and to help them to move
	growth and reproduction	
	9	the main stages of the human life cycle

Lessons where curriculum content is the main objective are listed below. Lessons where content is included but is not the main focus are shown below in brackets.

Unit 1: Ourselves How I move	Unit 2: Animals & Plants Different sorts of skeletons	Unit 3: The environment Habitats and food chains	Unit 4: Materials Warm liquids, cool solids	Unit 5: Electricity Switches and conduction	Unit 6: Forces & motion Friction	Unit 7: Light & sound Travelling and reflecting	Unit 8: Earth & beyond The Sun and stars
UNIT 4A	UNIT 4A	UNIT 4B	UNIT 4C, 4D	UNIT 4F	UNIT 4E	–	–
				1, (2), (3), 4, 5, 6, 7			
				(10), 11			
				8, 9			
				1, 11			
					1		2
					10, 11, 12, 13		
					4, 5, 6, 7, 8, 9, 11, 13		
					1, 2		
					1, 3, 13		
					1, 2, 15		6, 7, 8
					3, (4), 5, 15		
					6, 15		
					7, 8, 12, (13), 14		
					9, 10, 11, 12, 15		
					14, 15		
							(1), 8
							(1), (2), 3, 4, 5, 8
							(1)
							(1)

Unit 1: Ourselves How I move	Unit 2: Animals & Plants Different sorts of skeletons	Unit 3: The environment Habitats and food chains	Unit 4: Materials Warm liquids, cool solids	Unit 5: Electricity Switches and conduction	Unit 6: Forces & motion Friction	Unit 7: Light & sound Travelling and reflecting	Unit 8: Earth & beyond The Sun and stars
1	7	1, 14	1	1	1, 8	1, 7	1
4	1, 3	9, 10, 15	15		1, 8	3, 13	2
3, 4	1	5	12	4	5, 6, 8	2	2
	(1), 3	2, 16	2, 13, 16	2		13	3, 6, 7
4, (5), 6	5, 6	6, 11, 12, 13	4, 7, 9	1, (10)	1, (2), 4, 12	1, 2	3
4	(5)	9, 10, 11, 13, 15	10		6, 9	4	3
			2, 3		5, 6, 8, 9		5
	3	3, 9, 10, 11	13	3			
	(5)	3, 6	8		6, 11	4	5
3, 4		5		8, 9	5, 11, 13		
4			15		5	3	
(3), 4	(2)		15		8		
		5, 7	15	8, 9	8, 9, 11		4
3	7	7	2, 3, 6		3	4, 8, 9, 12	2
(4)	7	4		1	3, 6, 8	4, 8, 9, 12	2
5		4	2, 3, 6		3, 8	4, 8, 9, 12	2, 6
3	2, 4		5, 10	4	3, 5, 8, 9	4	3
4, (7)		7	3	4	5, 8	4	4
		3				4	5
1, 2, 8	8	14, (16)	3, 5, 8, 11, 12		5, 10	3, 5, 6, 8, 9, 14	3, 5, 8
3, 9		8	5		8, 9	4, 5, 8	3, 4
4		4, 8	8, 14, 17	5	7, 9	6, 10, 11, 12, 15	1
3, 4		4	15	6, 7	8		
(1)							
(1)							
(1)							
(8)							
(8)							
1, 2, 3, 4, 5, 6, 7, 8, 9	2, 3, 6, 7						
3, 4							

Life processes and living things continued overleaf

National Curriculum in Wales (cont)

LIFE PROCESSES AND LIVING THINGS (cont)		**health**	
		10	that tobacco, alcohol and other drugs can have harmful effects
	3	**Green plants as organisms**	
		growth and nutrition	
		1	to investigate the effect on the growth of plants of changing their conditions
		2	that plants need light to produce food for growth, and the importance of the leaf in this process
		3	that the root anchors the plant, and that water and nutrients are taken in through the root and transported through the stem to other parts of the plant
		reproduction	
		4	the main stages in the life cycle of flowering plants including pollination, seed production, seed dispersal and germination
		5	about the process of pollination in flowering plants
		6	how pollen and seeds can be transported
	4	**Living things in their environment**	
		adaptation	
		1	to find out about the variety of plants and animals found in different habitats including the local area
		2	how animals and plants in two different habitats are suited to their environment
		feeding relationships	
		3	that food chains show feeding relationships in an ecosystem
		4	that nearly all food chains start with a green plant variation
		5	how locally occurring animals and plants can be identified and assigned to groups, by making and using keys

MATERIALS & THEIR PROPERTIES	**1**	**Grouping and classifying materials**	
		1	to compare everyday materials, on the basis of their properties, including hardness, strength, flexibility and magnetic behaviour, and to relate these properties to everyday uses of the materials
		2	that some materials are better thermal insulators/conductors than others
		3	that some materials are better electrical conductors/insulators than others
		4	to describe and group rocks on the basis of appearance and texture, and soils on the basis of particle size and permeability
		5	to recognise differences between solids, liquids and gases, in terms of their properties.
	2	**Changing materials**	
		1	to explore changes in materials and recognise those that can be reversed and those that cannot
		2	that dissolving, melting, condensing, freezing and evaporating are changes that can be reversed
		3	that irreversible changes result in a new material being produced, which may be useful
		4	that the changes that occur when most materials are burned are not reversible, and result in a new material being produced
		5	that mixing materials can cause them to change
		6	that heating or cooling materials can cause them to change
		7	that temperature is a measure of how hot or cold things are
		8	the part played by evaporation and condensation in the water cycle
	3	**Separating mixtures of materials**	
		1	that solid particles of different sizes can be separated by sieving
		2	that some solids are soluble in water and will dissolve to give solutions but some will not, and that this provides a means of separating different solids
		3	that insoluble solids can be separated from liquids by filtering
		4	that solids that have dissolved can be recovered by evaporating the liquid from the solution

PHYSICAL PROCESSES	**1**	**Electricity**	
		simple circuits	
		1	that a complete conducting circuit, including a battery or power supply, is needed for a current to flow to make electrical devices work
		2	to investigate how switches can be used to control electrical devices in simple series and parallel arrangements
		3	that the brightness of bulbs and the rotation of motors can be controlled by altering the current
		4	ways of varying the current in a circuit, including changing the power supply, and changing the length of conductor in a circuit
		5	how to represent simple circuits by drawings and diagrams, and how to construct such circuits on the basis of drawings and diagrams
	2	**Forces and motion**	
		behaviour of forces	
		1	to measure forces between objects and find out how the forces change in size
		2	that forces act in particular directions
		3	that forces con make things speed up, slow down, or change direction
		types of force	
		4	that there are forces of attraction and repulsion between magnets, and forces of attraction between magnets and some materials
		5	that the weight of an object is the force of the Earth on the object and is measured in newtons
		6	about friction, including air resistance, as a force between surfaces which slows moving objects and may prevent them from starting to move
		7	that objects that are stretched or compressed exert a force on whatever is changing their shape
		8	that the change in shape of a spring is used in force meters for measuring forces
	3	**Light and sound**	
		everyday effects of light	
		1	that light travels from a source
		2	that we see light sources because light from them travels to and enters our eyes
		3	we see objects because light falling on them is reflected
		4	that most of the light falling on shiny surfaces and mirrors is reflected
		5	that light cannot pass through some materials, and that this leads to the formation of shadows
		vibration and sound	
		6	that sounds are made when objects vibrate but that vibrations are not always directly visible
		7	that the pitch and loudness of sounds produced by some vibrating objects can be changed
		8	that vibrations from sound sources can travel through a variety of materials
	4	**The Earth and beyond**	
		the Sun, Moon and planets	
		1	that the Sun, Earth and Moon are approximately spherical
		2	the relative positions of the Sun, Earth and other planets in the solar system
		periodic changes	
		3	how the position of the Sun appears to change during the day, and how shadows change as this happens
		4	that the Earth spins around its own axis, and how day and night are related to this spin
		5	that the Earth curbits the Sun once each year, and that the Moon takes approximately 28 days to orbit the Earth

Lessons where curriculum content is the main objective are listed below. Lessons where content is included but is not the main focus are shown below in brackets.

Unit 1: Ourselves How I move	Unit 2: Animals & Plants Different sorts of skeletons	Unit 3: The environment Habitats and food chains	Unit 4: Materials Warm liquids, cool solids	Unit 5: Electricity Switches and conduction	Unit 6: Forces & motion Friction	Unit 7: Light & sound Travelling and reflecting	Unit 8: Earth & beyond The Sun and stars
		2, (3), 4, 5, 6, 15, 16					
		(3), 4, 5, 6, 7, 8, 14, 15, 16					
		(9), 10, 11, 12, 13, 17					
		11, 15, (17)					
	(1), 4, 5, 8, 9	(1)					
			1				
			4, 5, 6, 7, 18				
			8, 9, 10, 11				
			12, 13, 18				
			12, 13, 18				
			12, 13, 18				
			2, 3				
			14, 18				
			15				
			16, 17, 18				
				1, 2, (3), (4), (5), (10), (11)			
				6, 7			
				8, 9			
				8, 9			
				1, 11			
					1		2, 8
					3, 10, (12), 13		
					4, 5, 6, 7, 8, 9, 11, 13		
					(1), (2), 3		
					(1), (2), 3, (13)		
						1, 2, 15	6, 7
						2, 15	
						6, 15	
						6, 15	
						3, 4, 5, 15	
						7, 8, 12, (13), 15	
						9, 10, 11, 12, 15	
						12, 14, 15	
							(1), 8
							(1), (3)
							(1), (2), 3, 4, 5, 8
							(1)
							(1)

The Northern Ireland Curriculum

INVESTIGATING AND MAKING IN SCIENCE AND TECHNOLOGY		Pupils should be encouraged to adopt safe practices when undertaking science and technology activities. They should be made aware of potential hazards and the appropriate actions necessary to avoid risks.

Planning

a recognise a fair test

b suggest ideas which can be investigated and make predictions

c choose appropriate materials and components when planning what to make

d suggest how to carry out a fair test

e plan what they are going to make and talk about the materials and components they could use

f design a fair test

Carrying out and making

a reinforce measuring skills using non-standard measures and progress to using standard measures

b develop manipulative skills using a range of materials and tools

c record what they have done or observed using appropriate methods

d make decisions about what, when and how to measure

e carry out a fair test

f make observations and measurements, taking account of the need for care and accuracy

g develop competence in the safe use of appropriate tools and techniques to cut, shape and join materials

h record findings choosing appropriate methods

i construct working models which incorporate an energy source and which can be controlled

j carry out a fair test that they have designed and record results systematically in tables

Interpreting and evaluating

a present their findings using appropriate methods

b relate what happened to what they predicted

c talk about what they have made in terms of materials, colour, size or shape and make suggestions for improvement

d choose appropriate methods to present results and make a record of their conclusions

e use results to draw conclusions or make comparisons

f evaluate what they have made, in terms of appearance and fitness for purpose, and suggest improvements

g use results to identify patterns

h evaluate a model that they have made bearing in mind their original intentions

KNOWLEDGE AND UNDERSTANDING OF SCIENCE AND TECHNOLOGY

Living things

Ourselves

a find out about themselves, including how they grow, move and use their senses

b identify major organs, including brain, heart, lungs, stomach, liver, bladder, small and large intestines, kidneys, and place these organs on an outline of the human body

c learn about factors that contribute to good health including diet, exercise, hygiene and develop an awareness of the safe use of medicines and the harmful effects of tobacco, alcohol and other substances

d develop an awareness of puberty-related changes, through discussion with the teacher or other professionals, for example, discuss with the teacher the changes that occur in their bodies during puberty

e investigate how basic life processes including circulation, simple respiration and digestion relate in order to maintain healthy bodies

f understand that humans have skeletons and muscles to support their bodies and help them move

Animals and plants

a find out about other animals, including how they grow, feed, move and use their senses

b observe similarities and differences among animals and among plants

c discuss the use of colour in the natural environment

d find out ways in which animal and plant behaviour is influenced by seasonal changes

e investigate a local habitat, including the relationship between the animals and plants found there, and develop skills in classifying animals and plants by observing external features

f find out about the main stages in the life cycle of some animals including a butterfly and a frog

g investigate the conditions necessary for the growth of familiar plants including light, heat and water

h learn about the life cycle of a flowering plant including how pollen is taken from the stamen into the stigma, fertilised in the ovule and a seed produced which is dispersed in a variety of ways

i order living things in a simple food chain and understand the dependency of one on the other

Materials

Properties

a investigate similarities and differences in materials and objects and sort them according to their properties

b find out about the origins of materials and learn that some are natural and others are manufactured

c investigate the properties of materials and how these relate to their uses

d investigate the distinctive properties of solids, liquids and gases as exemplified by water

Change

a investigate which everyday substances dissolve in water

b know that when materials are changed this may be desirable or undesirable

c investigate the changes of state brought about by heating and cooling everyday substances

d relate changes of state to the water cycle

e understand that when new materials are formed, change is permanent

f investigate how rusting can be controlled

Environment

a find out how human activities create a variety of waste products

b find out that some materials decay naturally while others do not

c understand that some waste materials can be recycled and that this can be of benefit to the environment

Physical Processes

Forces and energy

a find out about the range of energy sources used in school and at home

b find out the sources of energy in a variety of models and machines

c investigate how forces can affect the movement and shape of objects

d investigate the effect of friction on the movement of objects

e understand the differences between renewable and non-renewable energy resources and the need for fuel economy

Electricity

a know about the safe use of mains electricity and its associated dangers

b construct simple circuits using components, such as switches, bulbs and batteries

c investigate materials as to whether they are insulators or conductors

d investigate the effects of varying current in a circuit to make bulbs brighter or dimmer

Sound

a investigate how sounds are produced when objects vibrate

b investigate that sound travels through a variety of materials

Light

a explore how light passes through some materials and not others

b find out that when light travelling from a source does not pass through materials, shadows are formed

c investigate the reflection of light from mirrors and other shiny surfaces

EMU and cultural heritage Pupils should have opportunities to develop an understanding of themselves and others by exploring similarities and differences between themselves and other children, and developing a sense of their own individuality. They should appreciate the environment around them, the need to

Lessons where curriculum content is the main objective are listed below. Lessons where content is included but is not the main focus are shown below in brackets.

SCIENCE KS2

Unit 1: Ourselves How I move	Unit 2: Animals & Plants Different sorts of skeletons	Unit 3: The environment Habitats and food chains	Unit 4: Materials Warm liquids, cool solids	Unit 5: Electricity Switches and conduction	Unit 6: Forces & motion Friction	Unit 7: Light & sound Travelling and reflecting	Unit 8: Earth & beyond The Sun and stars
			15	9	5, 6, 8, 9, 11	4, 11	4, 5
3, 4			4, 12, (13)	1	4, 5, 6, 8, 9, 11	3, 5, 7	
		14		6, 7		11	6
		5, 7	15	9	5, 6, 8, 9, 11	4, 11	4
(5)				6, 7		11, 12	2, 6
		5, 7	15	9	5, 6, 8, 9, 11, 13	4, 11	4, 5
3, 4			2, 3, 6	8, 9	3, 4	3, 4	5
5				6, 7		11, 12	6
3, 4	4	2, 3, 4			3	8, 9, 10	
3, 4					3		
		5, 7	15	9	5, 6, 8, 9, 11	11	4, 5
	7	3	5, 8, 10, 11		3	2, 11	2, 3
2						12	
	3	5, 7, 14				11	2, 3
				6, 7			
			15	9	5, 6, 8, 9, 11	11	4, 5
1, 4	1, 6	9, 10, 11, 12, 13	1, (9)	2, 3, (5)	1, (2), 12	1, 4	3, 5, 7
4		7, 8	4, 12		5, 6, 8, 9, 11	3, 5, 9	3, 5
				6, 7			6
4		6	4, 7, (9)		5, 6, 8, 9, 11		
3, 4, 9	2	5, (15), (16)		4	7, 10, 13	6, 15	
	(5), (8)	1	(14)		8, 9	12	6
			(16), (17)	8, 9	5, 6, 8, 9, 11	9, 10, 11, 14	(1), 4, 5
5, (7)	(5), (8)			6, 7, (10)		12, (13)	6
(3), (4)							
1, 6							
(8)							
(1)							
1, 2, 3, 4, 5, 6, 7, 8, 9							
	2, 3, 6, 7	(1)					
		14					
	1, 4, 5, 8, 9	1, 2, 3, 4, 5, 6, 7 8, 17					
		(8)					
		9, 10, 11, 12, 13, 17					
			1, 4, 5, 6, 7, 18				
			(1)				
			8, 9, 10, 11, (14), (18)				
			15, (16), (17)				
			2, 3, 12, 13, 18				
		15, 16					
		(15), (16)					
		15, 16					
					1, 2, 3, 10, 11, 12		
					4, 5, 6, 7, 8, 9		
				2, 3			
				1, (10), 11			
				4, 5, (6), (7), 11			
				8, 9			
						8, (9), (10), (11)	
						(13)	
						4, 5	(1)
						(2), 3	(1), 3, 4, 8
						6	

take care of it and how human activities can upset the natural environment. They should consider how some toys and devices work and know that the technology which drives them has been developed over a period of time.

PROGRAMME OF STUDY

ENVIRONMENTAL STUDIES 5–14 SCIENCE

	LEVEL	
SKILLS IN SCIENCE: INVESTIGATING		**Preparing for tasks**
		Understanding the task and planning a practical activity. Predicting. Undertaking fair testing
	B	• plan simple approaches by asking questions and making suggestions
		• make suggestions about what might happen
		• recognise when a test or comparison is unfair
	C	• suggest a question for exploration and decide how they might find an answer
		• make reasoned predictions about a possible outcome
		• suggest some ways of making a test fair
	D	• identify two or three questions to investigate
		• provide reasons for planning decisions
		• include fair testing in planning by changing one factor
		• show awareness of the significance of variables
		Carrying out tasks
		Observing and measuring. Recording findings in a variety of ways.
	B	• use simple equipment and techniques to make measurements
		• record findings in a range of ways
	C	• select and use appropriate measurement devices or make appropriate observations
		• record findings in a greater range of ways
	D	• make an appropriate series of accurate measurements
		• select an appropriate way of recording findings
		Reviewing and reporting on tasks
		Reporting and presenting. Interpreting and evaluating results and processes.
	B	• make a short report of an investigation
		• answer questions on the meaning of the findings
		• recognise simple relationships and draw conclusions
	C	• make a short report of an investigation, communicating key points clearly
		• explain what happened, drawing on their scientific knowledge
		• make links to original predictions
	D	• make an organised report of an investigation using appropriate illustrations
		• provide explanations related to scientific knowledge
		• draw conclusions consistent with the findings
		• identify limitations of the approach used
EARTH AND SPACE		**Earth and space**
		Developing an understanding of the position of the Earth in the Solar System and the Universe, and the effects of movement and that of the Moon.
	B	• associate the seasons with differences in observed temperature
		• describe how day and night are related to the spin of the Earth
	C	• describe the solar system in terms of the Earth, sun and planets
		• link the temperature of the planets to their relative positions in the atmospheres
	D	• relate the movement of planets around the Sun to gravitational forces
		• give some examples of the approaches taken to space exploration
		Materials from Earth
		Developing an understanding of the materials available on our planet, and the links between properties and uses.
	B	• make observations of differences in the properties of common materials
		• relate uses of everyday materials to properties
		• explain why water conservation is important
	C	• describe the differences between solids, liquids and gases
		• give some everyday uses of solids, liquids and gases
	D	• describe the internal structure of the Earth
		• describe the processes that led to the formation of the three main types of rock
		• give examples of useful materials that we obtain from the Earth's crust
		• describe how soils are formed
		• name the gases of the atmosphere and describe some of their uses
		Changing materials
		Developing an understanding of the ways in which materials can be changed.
	B	• describe how everyday materials can be changed by heating or cooling
		• give examples of everyday materials that dissolve in water
		• give examples of common causes of water pollution
	C	• describe changes when materials are mixed
		• describe how solids of different sizes can be separated
		• distinguish between soluble and insoluble materials
		• describe in simple terms the changes that occur when water is heated or cooled
	D	• describe what happens when materials are burned
		• explain how evaporation and filtration can be used in the separation of solids from liquids
		• describe the effect of burning fossil fuels
ENERGY AND FORCES		**Properties and uses of energy**
		Developing an understanding of energy through the study of the properties and uses of heat, light, sound and electricity.
	B	• identify the sun as the main source of heat and light
		• link light and sound to seeing and hearing
	C	• link light to shadow formation
		• give examples of light being reflected from surfaces
		• link sound to sources of vibration
		• construct simple battery-operated circuits, identifying the main components
		• classify materials as electrical conductors or insulators and describe how these are related to the safe use of electricity
	D	• distinguish between heat and temperature
		• describe in simple terms how lenses work
		• give examples of simple applications of lenses
		• use the terms 'pitch' and 'volume' to describe sound
		• construct a series circuit following diagrams using conventional symbols
		• describe the effect of changing the number of components in a series ciruit

Lessons where curriculum content is the main objective are listed below. Lessons where content is included but is not the main focus are shown below in brackets.

Unit 1: Ourselves How I move	Unit 2: Animals & Plants Different sorts of skeletons	Unit 3: The environment Habitats and food chains	Unit 4: Materials Warm liquids, cool solids	Unit 5: Electricity Switches and conduction	Unit 6: Forces & motion Friction	Unit 7: Light & sound Travelling and reflecting	Unit 8: Earth & beyond The Sun and stars
3, 5			16		1, 8		
7			16	1, 4	1, 5, 6	11	
			4, 5, 6, 17	4	5, 16	4	
		5	16	6, 8	1, 8		
		5, 7	12	9	1, 9	3, 5	
		7	4, 5, 6	4	8	11	4, 5
			3		11		
3			5		5, 6	4	
		7	4, 15	4	5, 6, 11		4, 5
		7	5, 6		11		4, 5
4		3, (4)	2, 3, 10		3, 5, 6, 8	4	3, 5
1	2	3, 4	4	4	1, 8	1	
			3, 10			4	5
		7				4	
4			3			4	
4		7	5		5, 6	9	1, 3
2, 9	1, 3, 4, 5, 6	4	1, 4, 16	4, 6, 8	1	4, 11	4
			17	4, 6, 8	5, 8		
4			14	4, 8	5, 8	4, 9	
6	7, 8	7	3	8	6, 12	9, 11	
		7	3, 14, 17	6, 8	6	4	
		5		1, 9	1, 9	3, 5	
	7, 8	6, 8			9	1	
			16	9	9		1
4		7	15	9	1, 5, 6, 12	3	
4		7, 8	15	9	9	11	
							(5)
							1, 3, 4, 8
							3, (6), (8)
							(5)
			1, 4, 5, 6			4	
			4, 7			(4)	
			8, 9, 10, 11				
			(8)				
			12, 13				
			15				
			15				
			14				
			15				
			12, 13				
			16, 17, 18				
						1	
						1, 2, 7, 11, 12, 14	
						1, 4, 5, 15	3, 4, 8
						2, 6, 15	
						7, 8, 11, 12, 13, 14, 15	
				1, 4, 10, 11			
				4, 5, (6), (7), (11)			
			2, 3, 18				5
						9, 10, 11, 12, 15	
				(1), (11)			
				8, (11)			

Energy and forces continued overleaf

National Guidelines for Scotland

ENERGY AND FORCES

LEVEL	
	Conversion and transfer of energy
	Developing an understanding of energy conversion in practical everyday contexts.
B	• give examples of being 'energetic'
	• link the intake of food to the movement of their body
C	• give examples of energy being converted from one form to another
	• describe the energy conversions in the components of an electrical circuit
D	• give some examples of energy conversions involved in the generation of electricity
	• describe how electrical energy is distributed to our homes
	• name some energy resources
	Forces and their effects
	Developing an understanding of forces and how they can explain familiar phenomena and practices.
B	• describe the effect that a push and pull can have on the direction, speed or shape of an object
	• give examples of magnets in everyday use
	• describe the interaction of magnets in terms of the forces of attraction and repulsion
C	• give some examples of friction
	• explain friction in simple terms
	• describe air resistance in terms of friction
D	• give examples of streamlining and explain how this lowers resistance
	• describe the relationship between the Earth's gravity and the weight of an objective

LIVING THINGS AND THE PROCESSES OF LIFE

LEVEL	
	Variety and characteristic features
	Developing an understanding of the characteristic features of the main groups of plants and animals including humans and micro-organisms.
	The principles of genetics are also considered.
B	• give some of the more obvious distinguishing features of the major invertebrate groups
	• name some common members of the invertebrate groups
C	• give some of the more obvious distinguishing features of the five vertebrate groups
	• name some of the common members of vertebrate groups
	• name some of the common animals and plants using simple keys
D	• give the main distinguishing features of the major groups of flowering and non-flowering plants
	The processes of life
	Developing an understanding of growth and development and life cycles, including cells and cell processes. The main organs of the human body and their functions are also considered.
B	• give examples of how the senses are used to detect information
	• recognise the stages of the human life cycle
	• recognise stages in the life cycles of familiar plants and animals
	• identify the main parts of flowering plants
C	• name the life processes common to human s and other animals
	• identify the main organs of the human body
	• describe the broad functions of the organs of the human body
	• describe the broad functions of the main parts of flowering plants
D	• describe the role of lungs in breathing
	• outline the process of digestion
	• describe the main changes that occur in puberty
	• describe the main stages in human reproduction
	• describe the main stages in flowering-plant reproduction
	Interaction of living things with their environment
	Developing an understanding of the interdependance of living things with the environment. The conservation and care of living things are also considered.
B	• give examples of feeding relationships found in the local environment
	• construct simple food chains
C	• give examples of living things that are very rare or extinct
	• explain how living things and the environment can be protected and give examples
D	• describe examples of human impact on the environment that have brought about beneficial change, and examples that have detrimental effects
	• give examples of how plants and animals are suited to their environment
	• explain how responses to changes in the environment might increase the chances of survival

	Developing informed attitudes: pupils should be encouraged to develop an awareness of, and positive attitudes, to:
	A commitment to learning
	• the need to develop informed and reasoned opinions on the impact of science in relation to social, environmental moral and ethical issues
	• working independently and with others to find solutions to scientific problems
	Respect and care for self and others
	• taking responsibility for their own health and safety
	• participating in the safe and responsible care of living things and the environment
	• the development of responsible attitudes that take account of different beliefs and values
	Social and environmental responsibility
	• thinking through the various consequences for living things and the environment of different choices, decisions and courses of action
	• the importance of the interrelationships between living things and their enviroment
	• participating in the conservation of natural resources and the sustainable use of the Earth's resources
	• the need for conservation of scarce energy resources and endangered species at local and global level

Lessons where curriculum content is the main objective are listed below. Lessons where content is included but is not the main focus are shown below in brackets.

Unit 1: Ourselves How I move	Unit 2: Animals & Plants Different sorts of skeletons	Unit 3: The environment Habitats and food chains	Unit 4: Materials Warm liquids, cool solids	Unit 5: Electricity Switches and conduction	Unit 6: Forces & motion Friction	Unit 7: Light & sound Travelling and reflecting	Unit 8: Earth & beyond The Sun and stars
				3, 8, 9			
				9			
				(1), 2, 3			
				2			
				3			6, (7)
					1, 2, (3), 13		
					(1)		2
					1, 7		
					4, (5), (6), (13)		
					4, (5), (6), (13)		
					9, 11, (12), (13)		
					8, 11, 12, 13		
					10, 11, 12		
	1, 4, 7, 8, 9						
	1, 4, 7, 8, 9						
	1, 4, 8, 9						
	1, 4, (5), 8, 9						
	5, 7, 8, 9						
(3), (4)							
	(1)						
(1), 2, 3, 4, (8)	2, 3, 6	1, 7, 8					
		(7), 8, 9					
		9, 10, 11, 12, 13, (14), 17					
		(15)					
		15					
		5, 7, 8					
		16					
				2			
	7	(2), (4), (5)					

Series topic map

Year/Primary	YR/P1	Y1/P2	Y2/P3	Y3/P4	Y4/P5	Y5/P6	Y6/P7
Unit 1: Ourselves	This is me!	Me and my body	Keeping healthy	Teeth and food	How I move	Growing up healthy	New beginnings
Unit 2: Animals & plants	Looking at animals and plants	Growing and caring	Growing up	The needs of plants and animals	Different sorts of skeletons	Life cycles	Variation
Unit 3: The environment	Out and about	Environments and living things	Life in habitats	How the environment affects living things	Habitats and food chains	Water and the environment	The living world
Unit 4: Materials	Exploring materials	Properties of materials	Materials and change	Natural & manufactured materials	Warm liquids, cool solids	Gases, solids and liquids	Reversible and non-reversible changes
Unit 5: Electricity	Making things work	Using and misusing electricity	Making circuits	Electricity and communication	Switches and conduction	Making and using electricity	Changing circuits
Unit 6: Forces & motion	Pushing and pulling	Introducing forces	Making things move	Magnets and springs	Friction	Exploring forces and their effects	Forces and action
Unit 7: Light & sound	Looking and listening	Sources of light and sound	Properties and uses	Sources and effects	Travelling and reflecting	Bending light and changing sound	Light and sound around us
Unit 8: Earth & beyond	Up in the sky	Stargazing	The Sun and the seasons	The Sun and shadows	The Sun and stars	Sun, Moon and Earth	The Solar System